The Civilization of the American Indian Series

THE MESCALERO APACHES

THE
MESCALERO
APACHES

by C. L. SONNICHSEN

University of Oklahoma Press : Norman

By C. L. Sonnichsen

Billy King's Tombstone (Caldwell, Idaho, The Caxton Printers, Ltd., 1942)

Roy Bean (New York, The Macmillan Co., 1943; New York, The Devin-Adair Co., 1958)

Cowboys and Cattle Kings (Norman, University of Oklahoma Press, 1950)

I'll Die Before I'll Run (New York, Harper & Brothers, 1951)

Alias Billy the Kid (Albuquerque, N. M., University of New Mexico Press, 1955)

Ten Texas Feuds (Albuquerque, N. M., University of New Mexico Press, 1957)

The Mescalero Apaches (Norman, University of Oklahoma Press, 1958)

Library of Congress Catalog Card Number: 58–11610

FOR CAROL

CONTENTS

ILLUSTRATIONS

MAPS

THE MESCALERO APACHES

Chapter I

AFTER FOUR CENTURIES
An Introduction

ONLY A LITTLE over one hundred years ago the United States took possession of New Mexico and immediately became involved in Indian trouble. In theory the country belonged to the people of Spanish blood who had been holding the upland sheep pastures and the narrow fields beside the rivers for two and one-half centuries. But it was an enormous and an untamed land—far too big for the handful of Mexicans to occupy—and the Apaches and Navajos regarded it as their own particular and private preserve. It was their home, and they were ready to fight for it.

Actually, much of it seemed hardly worth fighting for. Miles of burning desert intervened between wooded mountain ranges and fertile valleys. To the east, beyond the Pecos, the endless, inhospitable plains began. To the west, the mountain wilderness of the Black Range, the Mimbres, and the Mogollon challenged the courage and endurance of the few hardy souls who ventured there. The Great River of the North flowed down the middle, and the tides of commerce and settlement mostly followed its banks. In 1846 it was hard to imagine that any significant portion of the country would ever be useful to civilized

3

people. Nevertheless, the Americans claimed it, as the Spaniards had before them, and spent many lives and much treasure trying to make their title good.

West of the river they had the Gila Apaches and the Navajos to contend with. Eastward the Jicarilla and Mescalero subdivisions of the Apache people shared the country. The Jicarillas ranged north and east of Santa Fé; the Mescaleros branched out fanwise from the Sierra Blanca in the southeast—into the Texas Panhandle, south to the Big Bend country of Texas, and on into Mexico, where, with their cousins the Lipans, they had raided the ranches and villages for centuries.

There were Mescalero bands in the Sierra Blanca, the Guadalupes, and the Davis Mountains. They were people of the mountains, but they were equally at home in the parched desert wastes by which they were surrounded. They moved about freely, wintering on the Río Grande or farther south, ranging the buffalo plains in the summer, always following the sun and the food supply. They owned nothing and everything. They did as they pleased and bowed to no man. Their women were chaste. Their leaders kept their promises. They were mighty warriors who depended on success in raiding for wealth and honor. To their families they were kind and gentle, but they could be unbelievably cruel to their enemies—fierce and revengeful when they felt that they had been betrayed.

It became the mission of the white invaders to convince this free and proud people that the country did not belong to them after all—to assure them, in effect, that the Maker of All had turned his face from his red children and that the white man had a divine right to whatever he could lay his hands on. It was now the duty of the Indian to submit, no matter what cruelties and injustices were visited upon him.

The Indian could not understand or accept any such point

of view. He felt no inferiority; he saw no reason why he should allow himself to be pushed around. Yet the white man was always giving him the short end of the stick. When some squatter abused a native, that was unfortunate. If the native retaliated upon the squatter, that was armed rebellion.

"When three or four bad white men stop and rob one stage, maybe kill somebody," one old Indian put it, "you send one sheriff to catch three, four bad men; same way when some bad white men steal some cattle or some horses, you send one sheriff; but when three, four bad Injun stop one stage, kill somebody, steal some men's horse or cow, you try catch three, four bad Injun? No! All white men say, 'Injun broke out, Injun on warpath,' and then come soldier for to kill everybody."[1]

It need not have been that way. Primitive as the red men were, they held no grudges at the start. They were not unfriendly toward the Spaniards until the Spaniards betrayed them.[2] There is evidence to show that they were friendly toward the Americans until the Americans betrayed them in their turn. Once the cycle of murder and revenge was started, the situation went from bad to worse; but it might all have been unnecessary with a better beginning. And time and again as the years went on, good men tried to help their Indian friends toward self-respect and independence, only to see them slip backward under the pressure of starvation, coercion, or outrages by white men more savage than they.

The main trouble was lack of comprehension. The Indians, not knowing about politics, expediency, and instructions from Washington, could not understand how a white man could say

[1] Laurence F. Schmeckebier, *The Office of Indian Affairs, Its History, Activities, and Organization*, 82 (quoting Howe, *Life and Labors of Bishop Hare*).

[2] Herbert E. Bolton, *Spanish Exploration in the Southwest 1542–1706*, 253, "Letter of Oñate": "We were not disturbed by them, although we were in their land, nor did any Indian become impertinent."

5

one thing on Sunday and reverse himself on Monday. Likewise, it seemed to them that any and all white men were accountable for the misdeeds of one.

The "White Eyes," as the Apaches called the Americans, saw a creature with a complexion different from their own, a set of customs which seemed barbarous to them, and a language which they could not understand. "Heathens and savages," they said, "standing in the way of progress. They must be restrained or removed, and they have no right to resent what we do to them because they are inferior." And they had the idea, too, that what one Indian did, all Indians were accountable for.

The gulf between the two races was widened and deepened because they were so completely opposite in their system of values. The Americans were punctual, acquisitive, and laborious. The Indians cared little for time, personal property, or work. The white man thought the Indian was lazy. The Indian thought the white man ran himself to death. Cadete, the great Mescalero chief, explained his views on these matters to Captain John C. Cremony when the tribe was rotting at Bosque Redondo in the sixties:

> You desire our children to learn from books, and say, that because you have done so, you are able to build all those big houses, and sail over the sea, and talk with each other at any distance, and do many wonderful things; now, let me tell you what we think. You begin when you are little to work hard, and work until you are men in order to begin fresh work. You say that you work hard in order to learn how to work well. After you get to be men, then you say, the labor of life commences; then too, you build big houses, big ships, big towns, and everything else in proportion. Then, after you have got them all, you die and leave them behind. Now, we call that slavery. You are slaves from the time you begin to talk until you die; but we are free as air. We never work, but the Mexicans and others work for us. Our wants are few and easily supplied. The river, the wood and

6

plain yield all that we require, and we will not be slaves; nor will we send our children to your schools, where they only learn to become like yourselves.[3]

Cremony had nothing to say in reply. "It was so utterly impossible to make them comprehend the other side of this specious argument," he adds, "that it was not attempted."

Impossible as it was to reconcile the Apache and white points of view, there would have been less difficulty if the white man had known his own mind. Whenever the administration changed in Washington, whenever a new agent appeared on the reservation, the game had to be played by a new set of rules. The military insisted that the red men must be "civilized," which meant that they must stop being Indians and become second-class white men. One Indian commissioner would recommend that all the tribes should be herded together as far from the settlements as possible with the army standing guard. The next man in office would be convinced that the only solution was to give every brave 160 acres of land and turn him loose.

There was never any stable attitude. A consistent policy was beyond the reach of the official imagination. All that anybody appeared to be sure of was that the Indian was a hopeless creature who seemed, fortunately, to be eliminating himself as fast as a declining birth rate could arrange it. Meanwhile, he must be forced to become something different from what he was, whether he liked it or not.

---

[3] Cremony, "The Apache Race," *Overland Monthly,* Vol. I (September, 1868), 207; William A. Keleher, *Turmoil in New Mexico,* 52: "A vast majority of the Apaches and Comanches live chiefly by depredation; they look upon the cultivators of the soil with contempt, as inferior beings, the product of whose labor legitimately belongs to power—the strongest arm; and believe that labor, except in war and love, and in the chase, is degradation; and the man who has not stolen a horse or scalped an enemy is not worthy of association with these lords of the woods." (James S. Calhoun to the Commissioner of Indian Affairs, Oct. 1, 1849.)

The Indian did not like it. He was satisfied with himself just as he was. In fact, he felt superior to the government official —often a soft and helpless one—who was telling him what to do. He saw no point in trying to remodel himself according to the white man's suggestions, especially when the white man seemed unable to inform him what he was supposed to be like when the remodeling was finished. Was he supposed to be a pensioner, a farmer, or a corpse? Some officials wanted him to be one of these things, some another; and a few seemed to feel that he should be all three at once.

The Indian reacted as any human creature would. He rebelled when he was angry; he submitted when he had to. For the first forty years of Indian-American contact in the Southwest he starved and fought. For the next forty years he mostly just starved. Every year his numbers diminished and his hopelessness grew greater. The traditional pattern of his life was ended forever. The game was gone; his old life of raiding and warfare was forbidden. Yet there was no place for him in white society even if he had been prepared to take it. It seemed that there was no way out.

Then, after World War I, things commenced to change. A new spirit of helpfulness began to stir among the whites. More intelligence and sympathy were applied in the consideration of the aborigine and his problems. Education, sanitation, and better management altered the picture. In 1928 for the first time since the Americans came, the birth rate of the Indians caught up with the death rate. In 1934 the Indian Reorganization Bill gave the race new life and hope.

But, as usual, the white man was unable to do the thing reasonably. Now the pendulum swung to the other extreme and the "Indianists" took charge. Indian religion suddenly became nobly spiritual. Indian life and customs seemed admirable, es-

8

pecially to people who had never been on a reservation. Indian arts and crafts embodied all beauty and originality. The market was soon glutted with junk manufactured by Indians who had long since lost any need to follow their ancestral crafts and had therefore forgotten them. At the same time anthropologists, psychologists, journalists, and collectors of folklore pursued the tribesmen into their tipis and, in the name of science, pumped information out of them which even a white man would have preferred to keep to himself.

How the Indian stood up to this new form of persecution is a real modern miracle. But he was hardened by eighty years of paleface capriciousness and eccentricity; he endured, and still endures, the assault by kindness just as he once withstood more lethal weapons.

He knew it would not last—and it didn't! By 1950 the forces of opposition were organized. The Indian was costing too much money. He was taking too much time in becoming civilized. Why should he be getting so much attention, anyway? It was time, as one writer put it, to "give the Indian back to the country"—in other words to turn him out, ready or not, to make his own way in the World he Never Made. The Indian Bureau itself proclaimed that its sole object was to go out of business as soon as possible—to liquidate its wardship and take one bureau out of the bureaucracy.

A thoughtful Indian could only shake his head and wonder, "What next?"

Meanwhile most of the tribes live in poverty far below the white average. Education is available only in small quantities to most of them. Integration and acceptance in white communities continue to be painfully slow. There is still much to be done before the Indian is self-sufficient.

The two things most needed are now, as always, understanding and a shoulder to the wheel. Even a little comprehension of what an Indian is, what he comes from, and where he wants to go would help the situation.

So here is the story of a group of First Americans—the Mescalero subdivision of the Eastern Apaches, a people with a long history which epitomizes what the white man has done to the Indian, and vice versa—a group which has refused to be defeated by ignorance and lethargy, which has held to a reasonable proportion of its traditional culture but has taken much of what the white man has to give; a tribe of relatively poor Indians who are making progress in working out an Indian destiny in a white man's world. Their story is the story of the red man in America, sad in places, hopeful in others—a long road traveled and a longer one still to go; a road which can be easier if the white brother shows any symptoms of knowing and understanding what it means and has meant to be an Indian.

Chapter II

THE DESERT BREED

The Apaches and Their Way of Life

AN OLD-TIME APACHE doesn't talk much. To strangers, especially white strangers, his remarks are few and to the point. His dark, immobile face doesn't tell a great deal, either. Not a muscle twitches, though his black eyes may be watchful and suspicious. A white man who has had little to do with Indians might consider him sullen or stupid. He is neither, but he does have extraordinarily good reasons for keeping his mouth shut.

His reticence is the wariness of one who walks among potential foes. During the last four hundred years and more, there has scarcely been a day when somebody was not scheming to run him out of his native country and take his living away from him. Always he has had to struggle for his existence, whether the enemy was a hostile Indian or an official in Washington. His ancestors lived with danger. He is not out of danger himself. Why should he be trustful and confiding?

Peril and distress brought him to the American Southwest. His forebears straggled down from the Arctic regions centuries ago with other offshoots of the great Athapascan family.[1] They

---

[1] For the Athapascans, see Frank Boas, *Handbook of American Indian Languages*, Part I, 91–92; Clark Wissler, *The American Indian*, 404.

had to move on or die. Two hundred—three hundred—perhaps five hundred years before the arrival of Europeans, the Apaches and their cousins the Navajos, under pressure from fiercer or more numerous tribes, took refuge in the harsh country where they live today.[2] As time drifted by, they adapted themselves so successfully to their new environment that the cactus and the horned toad and the rattlesnake were not more at home in it than they.

The Spaniards called it *Apachería*. It was an enormous expanse of sandy plains and rocky mountains reaching from California to Texas, and from Colorado into Old Mexico. Most of it was wasteland—practically a desert—where only the hardiest of God's creatures were at home.

Here and there in the endless reaches of the dry country the green mountain ranges rose up—pine clad, watered by spring-fed streams, hospitable to deer and elk, enriched with fruits and berries. The Apaches loved the mountain valleys and stayed in them during the summers. But the highland winters were cold, and a brush shelter or a skin tipi was no place to live in zero weather. The desert down below was warm, if otherwise discouraging. Therefore the Apache became a migrant, at home anywhere, an Arab of the New World, especially adept at making the most of the scanty resources of a land of little rain. The desert was his mother, and he was the desert's child.

The school he learned in was a hard one. The plants and

[2] For theories about the first migration and later relationships of the Apaches see Charles Amsden, "Navajo Origins," *New Mexico Historical Review*, Vol. VII (July, 1932), 197; Edward Twitchell Hall, Jr., "Recent Clues to Athapascan Pre-History in the Southwest," *American Anthropologist*, Vol. XLVI (January–March, 1944), 98–105; John P. Harrington, "Southern Peripheral Athapaskawan Origins, Divisions, and Migrations," *Smithsonian Miscellaneous Collections*, Vol. C, 502–32; Frederick Webb Hodge, "The Early Navajo and Apache," *American Anthropologist*, Vol. VIII (July, 1895), 232–40. (The *New Mexico Historical Review* is hereafter designated as *N.M.H.R.*) Dolores A. Gunnerson concludes tentatively that the Apaches reached Texas–New Mexico about 1525 (*El Palacio*, Vol. LXIII [November–December, 1956]), 346–65.

animals he lived with were armed with spines and thorns, fangs and claws. Everything lived on something else, and every existence had to be bought with another. Kindness and pity were luxuries which the desert could not afford.

As a result, the Apache developed into one of the toughest human organisms the world has ever seen. His powers of endurance, his ability to live off the country, his skill in eluding pursuers and surprising his foes—these things have become legendary, yet the prosaic pages of history testify to the truth of the legends.

"To the natural acuteness of all his kind, the country of his nativity adds a finish peculiarly his own," says one chronicler. "His whole existence a hardship, a struggle with a nature from whose gaunt fist only the most persistent and skillful wrenching can wring bare life, the Apache was whetted to a ferocity of edge, an endurance of temper, which were impossible in a more endurable country. He earned the eye of the kite, the ear of the cat, the cunning of the fox, the ferocious courage and tirelessness of the gray wolf. Over the crags of his arid ranges he could travel farther in a day than the world's champion on a cinder track, and keep it up for more days. . . . In a word, the Apache would wear out in physical endurance the most enduring of his white foes. Hunger he could stand twice as long, and thirst four times as long, as the best of them."[3]

The early-day Apache was seldom large or heavy. His height was perhaps a little under that of the average white man and his frame was usually wiry. He was built for speed and endurance, with good lung capacity and tough muscles. His head seemed large because of the shock of straight black hair, which he sometimes braided but usually left hanging loose with

[3] Charles F. Lummis, "The Apache Warrior," *The Land of Poco Tiempo,* 118–19.

13

a headband to keep it out of his eyes. He was proud of this copious gift of hair, and there were ceremonies for children which were intended to insure a good and permanent growth.

His face was broad and round and rather flat. Its color varied from a light tan to a rich chocolate. In some cases his eyelids drooped over his eyes, giving them a hooded effect. By white standards there were not many handsome Indian men, but they had power, and their great men had dignity.

The young women were oftentimes pleasing to look at, though they were apt to shrivel up into animated bags of bones in later life. Childbearing, hard physical work, and the stresses of a precarious existence aged them early.

Traditionally the Mescaleros dressed in buckskins; for ceremonial occasions they still do. The women wore skirts and jumpers. The men appeared in shirt and breechclout—the latter a long strip of material hung over a belt fore and aft—plus high moccasins which could be pulled up to the knee or folded down. They clung to this ancestral costume as long as they possibly could. In fact, the United States government was not able to get the Mescalero men into trousers until 1898, and even then it took force and persistence to do it. Now all of them dress like white people in rural areas, except on state occasions when a few of them may put on special costumes.

Their homes were poor and primitive—usually brush shelters or wickiups, made by fastening leafy branches over an oven-shaped framework. Contact with Plains Indians in buffalo-hunting times made the tipi a part of their equipment also, and they used it extensively in the early days. When buffalo hides were no longer obtainable, they used the white man's canvas to cover these structures, sometimes switching to army-type wall tents when it was too much trouble to set up housekeeping in traditional style.

14

In the days when they could move around as they pleased, these shelters were adequate, if not luxurious. It was possible to go south to get warm,[4] and the desert sun was hot anywhere in the daytime. There was no trouble about housing until the white man came with his notions of staying in one place. The Apaches suffered severely when they had to endure the bitter weather of their mountain reservation with only a thickness of canvas and one blanket between them and the winter sky.

The problem of sanitation was handled better, also, in the days of free movement. Instead of keeping his place cleaned up, an Apache simply moved his family to a new camp site every now and then. He had to move anyway, looking for game or following the fruit and berry crops or hiding from enemy raiders. In this way he avoided sickness and infection, and at the same time gave himself more time to do the things that interested him.

Under a system like this, the Apache naturally never got around to the invention of the privy, but the old men say they would walk two miles from camp to find a suitable place for a bowel movement. Complaints about the filthiness of Indian encampments are seldom encountered before the natives were herded together in restricted areas and forbidden to leave.

Since the Mescaleros followed a hunting-gathering-raiding pattern in their economy, they had to be a foot-loose people, and after the Spaniards provided them (unwillingly) with horses, they enlarged their range hundreds of miles in all directions. They hunted the buffalo annually as long as there were buffalo to hunt—a whole band riding out fourteen or fifteen days into the Comanche country and bringing back a supply of hides, sinew, tallow, and jerked meat. War parties journeyed far into

---

[4] Lieutenant Whiting reported in 1849: "Their winter towns are extensively upon its banks [the Río Grande]; their spring and summer retreats are found in the mountains which extend from the Presidio to Santa Fe." (*Report of the Secretary of War for 1849*, 289.)

Texas and Mexico in search of spoils and glory. Even within the elastic boundaries of their own special country, the tribe moved constantly in order to keep up with the food supply. New hunting grounds had to be located. Fruits and berries, nuts and seeds had to be gathered when they were ready. In good years the women were frantically busy trying to harvest everything as it ripened. In bad years they were even busier trying not to miss whatever there was.

The mountains provided most of their living, and they looked upon them as their real home. The largest band, the nucleus of the present-day Mescaleros, haunted the slopes of the Sierra Blanca, whose highest peak soared twelve thousand feet into the sky out of its green cloak of pine and cedar. They camped also in the Sacramentos, a southward extension of their own range. Other Mescalero offshoots were just as devoted to favorite spots in the Guadalupes on the New Mexico–Texas line and in the Davis Mountains in the Big Bend of the Río Grande. All the Mescaleros were related, intermarried, and very much at home throughout this mountain area, but the Sierra Blanca band alone has survived in its original homeland.

"When the earth had been made, Killer of Enemies put us down right here in the vicinity of White Mountain," say the modern Mescaleros. " 'That which lies on this mountain will be the land of the Mescalero,' he said. Killer of Enemies put us down right here. We are still here. Still poverty-stricken, we live just so. But then God created us that way. He created us without anything. We still go on in that way."[5]

The Mescaleros did much of their traveling in order to get at the mescal, which was their staple food and the source of their name. *Mescalero* means "mescal maker."

[5] Harry Hoijer, *Chiricahua and Mescalero Texts*, 188 (Fred Pelman, informant).

The mescal is a big desert plant, an agave with thick, fleshy green leaves, each of which ends in a murderous, flesh-tearing spike. It grows in the foothills and on the lower mountain slopes where the sun, soil, and altitude are just right. Of the several varieties of this plant, the Mescaleros used at least two, and sometimes threw in a sotol for good measure.[6]

At the proper season—usually in May or June, when the massive red flower stalks began to push upward in the mescal patches—the Apache women would arm themselves with hatchets and four-foot piñon sticks flattened and sharpened at one end, and sally forth. In very early times, when raiding war parties might be encountered, some of the men might go along to provide protection, but it was their job to range far afield hunting and scouting, and they did not show up in camp much. In later times a mescal party would consist of twenty or thirty people, including a few men and all the big boys the women could induce to come along. The bigger the boys, the harder it was to persuade them.[7]

The mescal is rather finicky about where it grows. Sometimes it was necessary to travel many miles to find a good supply, and the party might be out two or three weeks. And it was dawn-to-dark labor for those Indian women every day. They were furious workers at such a job.

Once they had located a mescal field not too far from water and a supply of wood, the action started. First, the big leaves were cut off as close to the heart as possible. Then the Apache woman would use her piñon stick like a chisel to cut the roots, hammering on the end with her hatchet. When she finished, she

[6] John G. Bourke, "The Folk Foods of the Río Grande," *Journal of American Folklore*, Vol. VIII, 41–71; Edward F. Castetter, Willis H. Bell, and Alvin R. Grove, *The Early Utilization and Distribution of Agave in the American Southwest;* Ross Calvin, *Sky Determines*, 229. (The *Journal of American Folklore* is hereafter designated as *J.A.F.*)

[7] Paul Blazer, Sept. 8, 1955.

had an ivory-white bulb sometimes two or three feet in circumference all ready to cook.

It was a hard way to make a living, but the worst was still to come. The cooking pit had to be dug in the dry, rocky soil, and it had to be big enough and deep enough to hold a ton or so of the bulbs. If an old pit was handy, the women cleaned it out; otherwise, they dug a new one somewhere between four and fifteen feet long and close to four feet deep. The bottom they covered with stones.

When everything was ready, they built a fire on top of the stones in the pit and kept it going from sunrise to noon—longer if necessary. Then the raw mescal was put in and covered with a thick layer of grass. On top of that they piled dirt and rocks to keep in the heat and steam. A number of detached leaves were allowed to protrude above the cover to be used for later testing.

In this crude but efficient pressure cooker the steaming went on all day and all night, or until the test leaves came out of the cooking pit done. Then the mescal feast began, and everybody had a sticky, happy time eating the syrupy mess which the cooking had produced. What was not eaten was spread into thin sheets, dried on a flat rock, and taken home for storage. It would keep practically forever and played an important part in the economy of the tribe. They carried it as a sort of hardtack or C-ration when they were on the move, and sometimes they used it for barter when they had any to spare. It was about the only thing they had which could be used for trading purposes.

Mescal is no longer plentiful on the reservation, but it is still made for the great feast in July, when everybody comes in for the girls' puberty ceremony and the general celebration that follows. The Apache women serve it in two forms in the big cooking shelter beside the dance ground near the ceremonial

18

tipi. Dried mescal is laid out on a table in sheets about two feet long—a mass of fibrous material with some hard, dry, reddish pulp clinging to it. To eat it, you cut off a piece with a knife and chew for dear life. Mescal in this form has a molasses-like flavor which tastes good even to a white man, but the fibers are so tough that one mouthful is usually enough for even an earnest experimenter.

From the dried mescal the Mescaleros also make a sort of pudding which looks a little like melted strawberry ice cream with excelsior in it. It has an acrid flavor which can be tolerated, but after consumption it sometimes produces a "second taste" which causes feelings of regret.

In recent years, as fences have gone up and ways of living have changed, mescal in any form has grown scarcer. In 1954, Mrs. Willie Magoosh went out with a party to Hop Lee's ranch just west of the Sacramentos. They took the agency wood truck and got permission to go back into the hills, where they dug up about thirty heads. It was necessary to bring the raw material to the agency for cooking, since there was no wood handy on the Lee ranch. It was a big undertaking, and seemed hardly worth the effort. Mrs. Magoosh hasn't been out since, though a few others have gone.[8]

The mescal plant could furnish drink as well as food, though the Mescaleros did not often put it to such use.[9] In Mexico, however, mescal is still fermented with impressive results, — the product being a colorless, fiery, volcanic potion which is supposed to give more action with fewer aftereffects than any of the many other Mexican intoxicants. Many an old time American along the border today would rather have a bottle of *mezcal* than a quart of Scotch.

[8] Mrs. Willie Magoosh, Feb. 5, 1955.
[9] Reverend J. J. Methuen describes a "mescal revelry" in *Andele*, 17.

19

The Mescalero Apaches

The Apaches had another concoction called *tulpai* or *tis-win*,[10] made from fermented corn sprouts, which they preferred to use when they could get it. At one time the American Indian agents would issue only ground corn to the Mescaleros because the whole corn too often fell into the hands of the old women who kept the *tiswin* business going.

The mescal plant had many other uses. Thread and fabric could be made from its fiber. Sandals and bags could be whipped together from its raw materials in short order by any competent Indian housewife. It was a storehouse of good and desirable things.

Not that the Mescaleros depended on it exclusively! There was hardly a plant or an animal in the whole country which they did not have a use for, and it is a humbling and an illuminating thing for a white man who has become aware of such matters to take ten steps across the desert and notice the unobtrusive growths whose names he barely knows which would keep him alive if he only knew what to do with them.

Almost everything was usable, and much of it was edible. They ate yucca flowers and fruits, the fruit of various kinds of cactus, mesquite beans, screw beans (or *tornillos*), wild potatoes, acorns, juniper berries, sumac berries, cattail and tumbleweed roots, even the inner bark of the yellow pine. The use of pine bark was a specialty of the Jicarilla Apaches, and the scarred trunks of venerable trees on the reservation today are reminders of a period when Washington thought—mistakenly, it turned out—that the two groups could live comfortably together.

They made bread out of sunflower seeds, jam out of sumac berries, greens out of a number of leafy weeds, chewing gum

---

[10] Professor David M. Schneider of the University of California says *tulpai* is the Mescalero word, and *tiswin* "is a word used by the whites and is shunned by the Apaches for that reason." (Schneider to Sonnichsen, Sept. 28, 1957.)

Life in the old days. A grandmother gives her grandson a scalp treatment.

Mescalero country. Looking westward down Dog Canyon to the White Sands.

out of milkweed sap and pine gum. It seemed that there was nothing animal or vegetable which they could not put to use.[11] Even the rattlesnake was not safe during a time of hunger. Some tribal groups refused to eat fish, and a subdivision of the Mescaleros rejected jack rabbit, but those were about the only things they wouldn't touch.[12] As one old Apache remarked to a curious white man, "There is food everywhere if one only knows how to find it."[13]

Picture to yourself a meal of cottontail-rabbit stew with sunflower-seed bread, some dried mescal boiled for the occasion and kneaded up with ground walnuts or juniper berries (they sometimes use peanuts now), boiled yucca flowers as a vegetable, pigweed greens, chokecherry jelly, and some dried grapes for dessert. It sounds nourishing and even appetizing—and all of it free and readily available!

The trouble was that nature was not always generous. Frost and hail, fire and drought were frequent visitors. Game could be scarce or nonexistent. As time went on and the country filled up, it seemed that there was less and less to eat. When the Americans came, with their rules about reservations and bound- → *white* aries, life became next to impossible for the Apaches. They could stay on the reservation and starve, or leave the reservation and be shot at. Many of them decided that it was better to dodge bullets and eat occasionally.

When the good times came and there was peace and food, the Apaches were a happy people. Those of us who have heard

[11] Edward F. Castetter and Morris Edward Opler, *The Ethnobotany of the Chiricahua and Mescalero Apaches*, 4: "Well over 100 plants were used by the Mescaleros."

[12] Washington Matthews, "Ichthyophobia," *J.A.F.*, Vol. XI (April–June, 1898), 105–12; Castetter and Opler, *op. cit.*, say that the Mescaleros had no fish taboo, but many Mescaleros would not eat jack rabbit.

[13] Ralph Hedrick Ogle, *Federal Control of the Western Apaches 1848–86*, New Mexico Historical Society *Publications in History*, Vol. IX, 17–18.

so much of their ruthlessness and cruelty, cunning and treachery, will find it difficult to believe that at home these terrible destroyers were kind to their children, full of fun, and faithful to a complicated code of conduct which made practically every act of daily life a matter of religious significance. Yet the white men who have known them best say that this was true of the Mescaleros before "civilization" engulfed them entirely.

One white leader of Apache scouts seventy-five years ago thought his men were the jolliest fellows he had ever known, behaving in camp like a bunch of "frolicsome schoolboys" on a holiday.[14]

"It makes me sad to think of the mescal trains that used to come in after two weeks or more in camp," says Paul Blazer, who grew up on the reservation. "They would pack their horses and drive them in, strung out for half a mile or more, and you could hear them coming a long way off. They talked and sang and didn't keep their voices down. They were a pretty happy people in those days, much happier than white people. Not now!"[15]

They had a social system which worked very well for them. The tribe was a loosely knit organization of independent bands, each under its own leader. In periods of emergency or danger these leaders met as a tribal council and elected one of their number to act as principal chief, but in ordinary times nobody cherished his right to independent action more fiercely than a Mescalero. They were all "pure democrats, each warrior being his own master, and submitting only to the temporary control of a chief elected for the occasion."[16]

This fact caused much grief and misunderstanding after the Americans arrived. Time and again army officers or civilian

White ←

[14] A. G. Tassin, "Reminiscences of Indian Scouting," *Overland Monthly,* Vol. XIV (August, 1889), 155.
[15] September 7, 1955.
[16] John C. Cremony, *Life Among the Apaches,* 21–22.

officials would negotiate an agreement of some kind with an Apache leader, expecting him to act for all his people, not realizing that he could speak only for his own band and only for such of them as chose to go along. Indians who had made no promises and ratified no agreements could never understand why they should be punished for violating treaties which had been made without their knowledge and consent.

They had trouble also in understanding why the Americans were so horrified over their way of making a living and winning prestige. Raiding was their business, and, like Falstaff, they considered it no sin to labor in their vocation. They trained for war as an athlete trains for a race. They educated their boys with the idea of making them sly and successful thieves. It seemed to them that it was a warrior's privilege and duty to levy tribute on lesser peoples. How else could he be known as a great warrior? Mexicans existed to provide the Apaches with the things they needed—just as the white man's cow existed to provide him with milk.

All outsiders, including the White Eyes, were enemies. One's own people were to be treated honorably, but everybody else could be deceived and preyed on without scruple—a point of view not unknown among other races, including the white.

Nor did the Apache think that great personal risk and vainglorious exhibitions of courage were necessary or desirable in going about his business. Like any professional soldier the world over, he took the realistic view that the most successful operator was the one who gained the greatest possible benefit with the least damage to himself. The admiration of the women and the praise of his fellow warriors went to the man who brought in the plunder—not to the dead hero who was not smart enough to get away.

As a fighting man the Apache brave felt that it was beneath

23

him to engage in physical toil—just as the Prussian officer of the old regime could not engage in humble tasks. To care for and use one's weapons was all that society could expect, and all that society did expect. Indians left it to their women to take care of everything else.

The women were content with this arrangement, for in their own sphere they had things their own way.[17] The mother was the focus of family life. When a girl married, her husband came to live in her community, with her sisters and their husbands. Her mother was likely to be near by—not too close, for there was a mother-in-law-avoidance taboo which made it impossible for a man to look at or be with his wife's mother. Supposedly this rule cut down on the number of family squabbles. It also gave an aggressive grandmother a great deal of power and influence, since she could make trouble for an unsatisfactory son-in-law. The women had shrill, happy times working together about their camp arrangements, and nobody suffered from having to carry the whole burden herself.

The Apache women tried to teach their children to live right, and usually the young ones were obedient and respectful. "Do not use a bad word which you wouldn't like to be used to you. Do not feel that you are anyone's enemy. In playing with children, remember this: do not take anything from another child. Don't steal from your own friends. Don't be unkind to your playmates. If you are kind now, when you become a man, you will love your fellow men"—so spoke the Indian mother.

"When you go to another camp, don't stand at the door. Go right in and sit down like a grown person," she would say—and then would instruct her child not to hang around at meal time waiting for an invitation to eat.[18]

[17] Regina Flannery, "The Position of Women Among the Mescalero Apache," *Primitive Man*, Vol. V (April–July, 1932), 26–32; Robert N. Bellah, *Apache Kinship Systems*, 129 ff.

24

The boys underwent rigorous training since they were preparing for the life of a warrior. They had to listen when a grownup wanted to show them how to finish an arrow or tell them a story which would be good for them to hear. They had to go through severe physical conditioning and memorize the words that were for use only on the warpath.[19]

The girls learned what they would need to know when they became women and were taught to behave themselves circumspectly. White observers gave grudging approval to the success of the Apache training program for girls. "In virtue and modesty," one of them reported in 1887, "the Eastern Apaches compare favorably with the best of the Indians."[20]

In July the girls had their own special day, when the ones who were ready for marriage went through a complicated four-day ceremony to prepare them for what was ahead.[21] The sacred tipi was raised, facing the east. The girls appeared in beautifully beaded buckskins and the medicine men prayed for long life and happiness for them.

> He is holding up his hand painted with the rays of the sun.
> The sun, the sun has come down,
> It has come down to the earth,
> It has come to her.
> He will paint her with red clay,
> Long life! Its power is good.
> He will paint her with white clay,
> Long life! Its power is good.[22]

[18] Opler, An Apache Life Way, 27.
[19] Opler and Hoijer, "The Raid and Warpath Language of the Chiricahua Apache," American Anthropologist, Vol. XLII (October–December, 1940), 617–34.
[20] Frederick Schwatka, "Among the Apaches," Century Magazine, Vol. XXXIV (May, 1887), 49.
[21] Dan Nicholas, "Mescalero Puberty Ceremony," El Palacio, Vol. XLVI (September, 1939), 193–204; Ann Pence Davis, "Apache Debs," New Mexico, Vol. XV (April, 1937), 10–11; Opler, "Sacred Clowns," El Palacio, Vol. XLIV (March, 1938), 75–79.
[22] Hoijer, op. cit., 48.

The drums and the songs, the sacred yellow pollen on her cheeks and forehead, the gifts and congratulations of her friends and relatives, the feasting and good fellowship—all made the puberty ceremony a happy and a solemn occasion for a Mescalero girl. It made her think seriously of her responsibilities and of her obligations to the power that gives and takes away. The high-pitched wailing songs touched her with a glimpse of the beauty of the world in which she lived:

> *The sunbeams stream forward, dawn boys, with shimmering shoes of yellow.*
> *On top of the sunbeams that stream toward us they are dancing.*
> *At the east the rainbow moves forward, dawn maidens, with shimmering yellow shoes and shirts of yellow, dance over us.*
> *Beautifully over us it is dawning.*[23]

All this was part of a mythology which explained everything that had happened since before people came up out of the ground. The old medicine men told it and chanted it. It was reflected in a thousand acts and attitudes as the people went about the business of life.

In the beginning there was Yusn, the Creator of All, whom nobody knew very much about. Closer to the soul of the Apache was White Painted Woman, whose children were taken away by a terrible giant, until finally she bore Child of Water. It was he who destroyed the destroyer and all the other monsters who would not allow people to live on the earth.[24] Under the protec-

[23] Margot Astrov, *The Winged Serpent*, 216 (quoting P. E. Goddard, *Gotal: A Mescalero Apache Ceremony*, 392).

[24] Hoijer, *op. cit.*, 5–13; Bourke, "Notes on Apache Mythology," *J.A.F.*, Vol. III (April–June, 1890), 209–12; Opler, "The Role of Creative Shamanism," *J.A.F.*, Vol. LIX (July–September, 1946), 268–81; Opler, "The Slaying of the Monsters," *El Palacio*, Vol. LIII (August, September, 1946), 242–58; Opler, "Three Types of Variation," *Language, Culture, and Personality*.

tion of these two beneficent deities, mother and son, the Apaches lived their lives.

> White Painted Woman, do not push toward us all of that which is evil on earth. White Painted Woman, all of us were created from you. Because this is so, you have brought to us the earth pollen which lies in the space between the earth and the sky. There is nothing wrong with it. We are still living in it.[25]

Even closer to the people were the Mountain Spirits, who lived inside the sacred mountains and sometimes revealed themselves to those in need or distress. At the great ceremonials, men of the tribe in masks and costumes impersonated them, performing the dance taught to tribal ancestors generations before by the Spirits themselves. It was bad luck, perhaps death, to recognize a friend beneath the mask. It was necessary to keep one's mind on the meaning of the dance and on the words of the songs:

> *Big Blue Mountain Spirit,*
> *The home made of blue clouds,*
> *The cross made of the blue mirage,*
> *There, you have begun to live,*
> *There, is the life of goodness,*
> *I am grateful for that made of goodness there.*[26]

For practical instruction, boys and girls alike listened to the tales of the Coyote cycle which the grandfathers told around the campfire in winter and at other times when a precept, reinforced by an example, was needed. Coyote was the personification of antisocial habits—a trickster and a low fellow who got into difficulties and made himself a laughingstock because he

[25] Hoijer, *op. cit.*, 58.
[26] *Ibid*, 69–70.

did not behave as a decent Indian should. He did manage to get fire away from the flies, who were its first keepers, and bring it to men, but he nearly burned everything up doing it.[27] Modern Mescaleros still talk about "doing a little coyote" when they are describing a sneaky trick.

There was beauty and poetry in such a religion, and its many ceremonials fed the soul of an Apache as fully as more sophisticated rites lift up the hearts of other races. It gave meaning to his life on this earth and told him of a better place where he would be with his fathers after death—a country beneath the ground where everyone lived according to the old Indian ways and where there was no more sickness or pain or hunger.[28] He felt that it was good to have faith in these things, and when he had occasion to compare the fruits of his creed with those of the white man's, he had reason to prefer his own.

Dark and sinister pages existed in his unwritten Bible, of course. He was terribly afraid of ghosts and of the dead. He had to be eternally careful of what he did and said, lest bad luck should follow. The medicine men had had some knowledge of herbs and medicinal plants, but they probably killed as many as they cured—some undoubtedly scared to death by their hocus-pocus, and others damaged fatally by overvigorous massage of a sick man's abdomen.

Like a modern scientist, the Mescalero knew that there was power in every atom of nature. It could be tapped and channeled, for good or bad. One who used it for bad purposes was a witch, and a primitive Apache was deathly afraid of witchcraft. He spent much time and energy making sure that he was not liable to harm from secret spells. On the other hand, he could

[27] *Ibid.*, 17; Asa Daklugie, "Coyote and the Flies," *New Mexico Folklore Record*, Vol. X (1955–56), 12–13.

[28] Opler, "Reaction to Death," *Southwestern Journal of Anthropology*, Vol. II (Winter, 1946), 460–61.

tap the power in nature for his own and others' good if he had the right revelation and could acquire a ceremony from another Indian or from some supernatural power.[29]

The old-time Mescalero was a very busy and a very religious man. Unhappily, his Christian brothers never learned much about his beliefs and observances in the days when understanding was most needed. Since 1930 much information has been gathered by anthropologists, linguists, and historians, but it is hard for ordinary people to get at, and ignorance of Indian ways and beliefs is as universal as it was one hundred years ago. This ignorance is a constant irritation to people who know the natives well.

"I hate to hear people talk about those Apaches as savages," says Paul Blazer, remembering the old days on the reservation. "They were men and women just like us. An Indian is supposed to be a savage because when he wants to relieve himself, he goes behind a bush. Some white men don't even go behind a bush. And if an Indian is a savage, a lot of white men are savages too. Look at General Garland. He was a savage. Teddy Roosevelt was a savage. Some of the Mescaleros *were* savages—like Muchacho Negro, and a few more. But they were no worse than the white men who 'hit them in the rear with a saddle.' They used to come into the store where I worked. I would give them a smoke and they would sit around and tell me stories—folk tales. There was poetry and beauty in them. That was when I began to see that they were folks just like us."[30]

The old-style Indians that Paul Blazer knew in his boyhood

---

[29] *Ibid.*, 454–65; Bourke, "The Medicine-Men of the Apache," *B. A. E. Ninth Annual Report, 1887–88,* 451 ff.; Opler, "The Concept of Supernatural Power among the Chiricahua and Mescalero Apaches," *American Anthropologist,* Vol. XXXVII (January–March, 1935), 65–70; Opler, "Notes on Chiricahua Apache Culture," *Primitive Man,* Vol. XX (January, April, 1947), 1–14.

[30] September 7, 1955.

are almost all gone now. Their descendants have taken mighty strides in the direction of a better life, but something has been displaced in the process. Much of the good in the old culture has been lost. Much of the new has been only half-assimilated. The Mescalero is caught in the wheels of transition. He lives in a house like a white man, but he doesn't always take care of it, and sometimes he goes back to a brush shelter in the summer. He keeps some of his traditional beliefs, but they do not mean as much to him as they did to his fathers.

The puberty ceremony, the only religious festival which he still observes, shows what is happening. It is becoming increasingly commercialized. The first three days are still more or less private and sacred, but the fourth day, arranged to fall on or near the Fourth of July, is strictly for tourists. Visitors jam the bleachers at the rodeo ground and eat hamburgers around the dance plaza, staring uncomprehendingly at the Mountain Gods when the dance begins, poking at Indian babies, and taking pictures of everything. The Mescaleros forgive them for their bad manners as they pocket their money, and seemingly do not regret the decay of their most sacred ceremonial.

Only occasionally will some old Mescalero say a good word for the ways which his people followed in the days before the white men came with their guns and their Bibles to destroy the Indian world:

"You who are white people, then, do not realize that, even though these ancient people knew nothing, they taught their children in a good way inside their wretched camps. . . . Though their camps were everywhere poor, they inside of them spoke by means of good words and good thoughts."[31]

[31] Hoijer, *op. cit.,* 47.

Chapter III

CRUCIBLE OF COURAGE

Apache Against Spaniard

THE FIRST EUROPEAN to see the Eastern Apaches was Don Francisco Vásquez de Coronado, who was on his way to Kansas to look for the mythical Gran Quivira. Pedro de Castañeda, his historiographer, was favorably impressed. The tribesmen were a poor scrambling lot who followed the buffalo for a living. They had only their legs to carry them. Their only domestic animal was the dog, which they used to carry or drag their burdens. They lived in buffalo-hide tents, ate buffalo meat either jerked or raw, and drank buffalo blood. Life was not easy for them, but Castañeda remarked approvingly, "They are a kind people and not cruel. They are faithful friends."[1]

Coronado called them *Querechos*, a Pueblo word meaning "Buffalo Eaters."[2] Explorers who came along later described them as *Indios Vaqueros*—"Cowboy Indians"—because they lived on the cows or buffalo. Oñate the Colonizer, who came

[1] George Parker Winship, *The Journey of Francisco Vázquez de Coronado, 1540–42*, 60.

[2] Hodge, *Handbook of Indians North of Mexico*, I, 63. It is usually assumed that Coronado's *Querechos* were Apaches, but Hodge in "Early Navajo and Apache," *loc. cit.*, asks if the *Querechos* were not really Texas Tonkawas. Cf. *Handbook*, II, 338; Alfred Barnaby Thomas, *After Coronado*, 5; Adolph F. A. Bandelier, *Final Report*, I, 178–80.

31

in 1598, was the first to call them Apaches. There has been much argument since about what the word means, but the theory that pleases most people holds that the suffering Zuñi lumped their nomadic neighbors under a title which means "The Enemy."[3] It was certainly an apt designation, for as time went on, their hand was against every man, and every man's hand was against them.

In 1541, the Apache tribes were already well established in the region and were scattered about much more widely than in more recent times. The ancestors of the Western Apaches had found their permanent home in the wilderness beyond the Río Grande, but the Eastern Apaches, including some of the forebears of the Mescaleros, were camping out on the buffalo plains, some of them living as far north as Kansas. They were broken up into a hodgepodge of tribal subdivisions which still frustrate the researches of historians and anthropologists.

There were Carlanas, Palomas, Jicarillas, Faraones, Lipanes, Natagés, Apaches del Perillo, and Mescaleros, to mention the names most frequently heard in Spanish times. Some of these bands were named for their favorite haunts, some for their chiefs, some for their habits and customs. They migrated, combined, split off, and subdivided. They were given one name by this explorer and another by that. The Jicarillas, Lipans, and Mescaleros managed to hang on to their names and hand them down to posterity. The rest have disappeared, we do not know how or where.[4]

[3] Bolton, *Spanish Exploration,* 253; Donald E. Worcester, "The Beginning of the Apache Menace in the Southwest," *N.M.H.R.,* Vol. XVI (January, 1941), 1 ff. Harrington says the Spaniards got the word "Apache" from the Yavapai. Hodge in "Early Navajo and Apache," *loc. cit.,* 232 n., says the word is of Yuman origin, probably from *e-patch,* a name for "man."

[4] For discussion of early tribal subdivisions and habitats, see Bolton, *Athanase de Mézières,* I, 24; Thomas, *After Coronado,* 3; Hodge, *Handbook,* I, 64; Bandelier, *Final Report,* I, 180–81; Thomas, *Teodoro de Croix,* 40; Thomas,

The Navajos had forgotten long ago that the Apaches were their cousins, and even fought their kinsmen from time to time. Among themselves, however, the Apaches kept up a fairly close connection. The Spaniards spoke of the "Apache Nation" as if it were a political unit. Later on the Americans adopted the view that all Apaches were in league with each other.[5] It was certainly true that, although one band sometimes disagreed with another, these people knew that blood was thicker than water—a fact which the Spaniards found out at no small cost.

When the invaders first appeared, the Buffalo Eaters were more curious than hostile. They might conceivably have learned to tolerate, if not to love, the bearded men-at-arms. But the Spaniards mishandled their opportunities from the start.

There was Gaspar Castaño de Sosa, for instance, who came to New Mexico on an unauthorized scouting expedition in 1590. A party of *Indios Vaqueros* decided to raid his camp. In the melee which followed, one friendly Indian was killed and some stock was driven off. Captain Cristóbal went in pursuit, caught up with the raiders, killed some, and captured four. Of the captives one was hanged and the others were kept "to serve as interpreters."[6]

No doubt Castaño felt that severe measures were needed, but he should have known that such retaliation was not the way to make friends among savages in a new land.

The Apaches were wary of Spaniards after that, and they had good reason to be. The conquerors looked on the wild tribes as their legitimate prey, to be seized and sent to do hard labor

The Plains Indians and New Mexico, 7; W. E. Dunn, "Apache Relations in Texas," *The Quarterly of the Texas State Historical Association,* Vol. XIV (January, 1911), 266.

[5] Padre Andrés Cavo, *Supplemento,* 79: ". . . *pero llamese como quieran, es constante que la Apachería es una misma nación."*

[6] Worcester, *loc. cit.,* 3–4.

wherever a slave was needed. Traffic in human flesh was forbidden by law, but this meant nothing to some of the Spanish governors, who were completely unscrupulous in their attempts to secure this sort of raw material and make money from it.

The good fathers who wanted to save the Apaches' souls were often horrified at what they had to watch. Fray Alonso de Benavides told about one case in his Memorial to King Philip IV of Spain, written in 1630. He had almost accomplished the conversion of an Apache chief, who had listened to instruction "with much devotion" and was nearly ready to be baptized, when a party of slave hunters fell upon the band. An enemy Indian chief was the leader, but the Spanish governor had organized the expedition. There was a battle in which many Apaches were slain, the converted chief among them. In his last moments he held out his rosary to the leader of the slave hunters, begging him by the Mother of God not to kill him, but his entreaties were wasted.

When the party returned to Santa Fé, they found that word of their cruelty had preceded them. There was such an uproar that the governor hardly dared accept the spoils which he had been waiting for, "and wished to hang him whom he himself had sent." His cupidity, however, was well recognized, "the which caused all this province to rise in rebellion, although (God be blessed) we are reclaiming it anew, and the Indians already know who is at fault, and that God ought to be adored above everything."[7]

It was such episodes which turned red man against white in the first place. The Spaniards complained that "these people do not keep their word."[8] The Indians resented being hauled

[7] Fray Alonso Benavides, *Memorial* (trans. by Mrs. Edward Ayer), 57. Forrestal's translation, 55–56, differs slightly.
[8] Adolph F. A. and Fanny R. Bandelier, *Historical Documents*, III, 108 (petition of Father Juan de Prada).

away into captivity and retaliated by making slaves out of any Mexicans they could catch, especially young ones.

white

Three hundred years later the Americans took note of this now venerable custom of mutual depredation between Mexican and Apache. Captain John Pope commented:

> In this habit they are closely imitated, or have been set the example, by the people of New Mexico, and it is very doubtful whether a settlement can be found in the valley of the Río Grande not possessed of Indian slaves. These poor creatures are bought and sold like horses or mules, and it seems rather too much to expect that the Indians shall deliver up the Mexican prisoners in their possession to the authorities which countenance openly the sale and slavery of numbers of their tribe. So far as three years experience in the country has enabled me to judge, it has seemed to me that the amount of robbery is about equal between the lower classes of New Mexicans and the Indians, whose herds of stock are frequently together, and that protection from plunder, which we are expending so much money to secure the former, could with equal justice be extended to the Indian.
>
> It is difficult to say upon which side plundering predominates, although all depredations committed by the Indians, tenfold exaggerated, are duly laid before the authorities.[9]

white

Indians Slaves too

The bad blood which existed almost from the beginning between the Spaniards and the Eastern Apaches boiled up continually on the outskirts of settlement. The contact point between the two races was the line of mission villages—Abó, Cuarac, Chilili, Taxique, and Jumanos—extending in a north-south line along the foothills of the Manzano Range east of Albuquerque. This was the extreme edge of *Apacheria*, the bloody

[9] Pope, *Report of Exploration of a Route for the Pacific Railroad*, 19. The problem of slavery was a serious one until after the American Civil War. See Cremony, *Life Among the Apaches*, 313; *Report of the Commissioner of Indian Affairs for 1850*, 104–105; *Condition of the Indian Tribes* (1867), 326 ff. (testimony of Judge Kirby Benedict).

35

fringe of Christendom. The Piros and Tompiros, Tanos and Tiguas, who cared for the apple orchards and bean fields in these pueblos, were peaceful farmers—easy pickings for the hungry Apaches after the troubles started. The prayers of the fathers who cared for their souls and the efforts of the soldiers who were sent to protect their bodies were not enough to save them from plunder and death.

What kept hostilities within bounds for a time was the possibility of commerce between the Spaniards and the Apaches. A trading post was set up at Pecos and another at Jumanos, southernmost of the eastern pueblos, which probably rose on the Mesa de los Jumanos where the great ghostly ruin called the Gran Quivira now stands.[10] At these points brisk bartering went on, when the Mescaleros and Jicarillas brought in buffalo hides and meat to trade for cotton cloth, maize, and whatever foodstuffs and ornaments were available. Both sides gained by the exchange, and as a result an uneasy peace was kept until the middle seventeenth century—a peace continually broken by raids, ambushes, massacres, and reprisals.

The pueblo of Jumanos was closest to the home country of the Sierra Blanca Mescaleros, and it suffered most. Time and again the Mescaleros raided the place and kept ahead of their pursuers until they got back to their mountain refuge. A typical mission report (1639–42) tells how Captain Juan Domínguez de Mendoza made an expedition to the "*Syerra Blanca a dar Gerra a los enemigos comun de Nuestra Santa Fé catolyca de Nassyon Apaches por aver profanado y robado el Santo Templo de Jumanas, sacando de su poder Beynte y syete mujeres y Nynos, que tenian cautybos con todo lo demas que se abyan llebado, y*

---

[10] George Kubler, "Gran Quivira and Jumanos," *N.M.H.R.*, Vol. XIV (October, 1939), 418–21; Joseph H. Toulouse, Jr., History of the Salinas Province (MS in the Library of Gran Quivira National Monument).

The standard housing unit. An Apache brush shelter.

The Mescaleros were a sturdy people. They loved their children.

*dejandolos byen castygados, dyo la Buelta, abyendo ganado
mucho Reputassyon con Amygos, y enemigos.*"[11]

In this instance the pursuers got their women and children
back from the enemy "with everything else they had taken
away," but such success was unusual. And although the Indians
were for once "well punished," they never stopped trying for
more loot and more captives. From year to year the situation
worsened. Only by constant vigilance and continual counter-
raids could the Spaniards maintain themselves in New Mexico
at all. The Apaches stole their horses at every opportunity, and
soon had mounts while the conquerors were practically afoot.[12]
In 1638, the commissary general of the Franciscans, Father Juan
de Prada, reported that the main business of everybody in Santa Fé was fighting the "barbarous and ferocious heathen." The
feud lasted as long as Spanish blood ruled in New Mexico, and
for forty years after the Americans moved in. Through all those
bitter years, from 1630 to 1886, Father Benavides' summary of
Apache nature held good: "It is a nation so bellicose that it has
been the crucible for the courage of the Spaniards."[13]

The Apache could be as subtle as he was fierce, and was
willing to make alliances and treaties with the mission Indians
if he could poison them against their masters. The fifth-column
activities of the wild tribes were as real a menace as their sudden attacks, and perhaps did as much damage. Whenever a
Christianized Indian grew disgruntled over something, his first
thought was to flee to the Apaches, "believing," as Father de
Prada said, "they enjoy greater happiness with them since they
live according to their whims and in complete freedom."[14]

[11] France V. Scholes and H. P. Mera, "Some Aspects of the Jumano Problem," *Contributions to American Ethnology and History*, Vol. VI, No. 34, p. 280.
[12] Francis Harris, "Where Did the Plains Indians Get Their Horses?"
American Anthropologist, Vol. XL (January–March, 1937), 112–17.
[13] Worcester, *loc. cit.*; Benavides, *op. cit.*, 41.
[14] Bandelier and Bandelier, *op. cit.*, III, 111.

Whatever they could do to contribute to their own ruin, the Spaniards did. They effectively urged matters along by dividing themselves into two fiercely contending factions—civil authorities on one side and religious dignitaries on the other—which quarreled and insulted each other over the question of authority. The governor and his henchmen considered themselves the supreme power. The religious leaders, backed by the terrible force of the Inquisition, were grimly determined to hold the reins themselves. In the time of Don Bernardo López de Mendizábal, who was governor from 1659 to 1661, the feud became open and scandalous.

The eastern pueblos were battle grounds between the factions, and there the charges and countercharges flew thick and fast. Mendizábal's lieutenant, Nicolás de Aguilar, *Capitán a Guerra* and *Alcalde Mayor*, accused the friars of making slaves of the Indians, of misconduct with the native women, and of enriching themselves at the expense of their poor charges.[15] The priests got even by making some accusations of their own. Aguilar, they said, encouraged the converts to neglect their Christian duties and to resume the performance of the Catzinas, the most unholy and shocking of their heathen ceremonials.[16] The Indians stood by in amazement, and probably in disgust, as the great men wrangled.

In June, 1660, the people of Jumanos planned, as they had for the past thirty years, to celebrate the feast of their patron saint, San Buenaventura. It was customary for people from the other pueblos to be invited in to help with the celebration, and a particular invitation was sent to the *guardián* at Cuarac, ten leagues away, to bring some of his parishioners. Twenty of them

[15] Scholes, "Troublous Times," Ch. 3, *N.M.H.R.*, Vol. XII (October, 1937), 193–97.
[16] Bandelier and Bandelier, *op. cit.*, III, 132–34.

—singers and sacristans—brought their adornments and came with happy faces up the path to the top of the mesa.

Aguilar met them, backed by half a dozen soldiers, and they did not sing the mass for Father Diego de Santander that day. The soldiers tied them up and gave them fifty lashes apiece. They were so shaken by this treatment, said Father Nicolás de Freitas, when he testified concerning these matters in the City of Mexico in 1661, that "the poor things have not since dared to take part in any sung mass, wherefore the divine service has been much impeded."[17]

Mendizábal even forbade the Indians to work on the great new church which was being erected to the glory of God and San Buenaventura, but this was more than the tribesmen could take. They "continued at great risk in the construction of the edifice, for they had no church."[18]

God did not allow his enemies to continue long in power. In April, 1662, Aguilar was arrested by the Inquisition. Four months later Mendizábal himself was taken into custody, and shortly afterward both of them disappeared into the secret prisons in Mexico City, never to trouble New Mexico any more. But the seed they had planted grew and flourished. The Christian Indians began to slip back into the old heathenish ways. The Apaches rejoiced and grew bolder.

Sometime between 1653 and 1656, the wild warriors descended on the community of Jumanos in a howling raid and hustled off into captivity more than twenty women and children. A punitive expedition followed and took revenge, but the Apaches could play that game, too. They came back again and again.

In the forest country farther north they lay in wait for

17 *Ibid.*, III, 135–60.
18 *Ibid.*, III, 144.

wood-gathering parties, and the story was told and believed (Aguilar himself told it) that each captive was tied near a great fire, after which the Apaches danced around him, "cutting off parts of his body, which they cook and eat until they entirely consume him, cutting him to pieces alive."[19]

The whole country was overrun. The highway from the Río Grande settlements to the Salt Lakes region was closed. "No road is safe," wrote one missionary father; "everyone travels at the risk of his life, for the heathen traverse them all being courageous and brave and they hurl themselves at danger like a people who know no God nor that there is any hell."[20]

Famine inevitably followed. In 1661, food was so short that both Indians and Spaniards consumed their crops before they were ripe, and ate up every green thing they could find, though some of the plants and herbs were "of a very injurious character." Father Juan Bernal reported in 1669 that no grain had been harvested for three years. "In the past year, 1668, a great many Indians perished of hunger, lying dead along the roads, in the ravines, and in their huts. There were pueblos (as instance Humanas) where more than four hundred and fifty died of hunger. The same calamity still prevails for, because of lack of money, there is not a *fanega* of corn or of wheat in the whole kingdom, so that for two years the food of Spaniards, men and women alike, has been the hides of cattle which they had in their houses. To make them edible they toast them, and then eat them. And the greatest misfortune of all is that they can no longer find a bit of leather to eat, for their herds are dying."[21]

A great sickness followed the great hunger. The disease—it

[19] *Ibid.*, III, 161.
[20] *Ibid.*, III, 271–72; Worcester, *loc. cit.*, 13.
[21] Bandelier and Bandelier, *op. cit.*, III, 272.

was probably smallpox, which had raged in the Indian towns before—carried off many of the Indians who had survived the famine.

And then in 1672 the final blow fell. The Apaches descended for the last time. Father Francisco de Ayeta told about it: "In the year 1672, the hostile Apaches who were then at peace rebelled and rose up, and the said province was totally sacked and robbed by their attacks and outrages, especially of all the cattle and sheep, of which it had previously been very productive."[22]

It was the absolute end. Men could not work in the fields. Hunting parties were cut off. The raiders crept up to the edge of the pueblo at night, and in the morning new widows mourned in the narrow street. The great church at Jumanos was nearing completion, but work had to be stopped before the roof beams were laid. Word came that the place must be abandoned and the inhabitants moved to some place away from the frontier. The fathers gathered up their holy vessels and vestments; the Indians loaded themselves with what they could carry; and one day the whole unfortunate community took the trail down the mesa for the last time—five hundred families in all. After that Jumanos, or Quivira, was at the mercy of the centuries, for its children never returned.

Within eight years the whole Spanish enterprise had crashed in ruins. The Indians, hungry, afraid, and disillusioned by the long feuds among the invaders, decided to get rid of them. The schemers and plotters were egged on by the Apaches, who welcomed renegades, stirred up the lukewarm, and whetted their knives for what was to follow. The red storm broke on August 10, 1680, not quite according to plan, but close enough.

[22] *Ibid.*, III, 302.

Of the three thousand white men in New Mexico, one-third were slaughtered, and many loyal Indians met death also.[23]

The tide of conquest and conversion ebbed southward down the Río Grande as far as El Paso, where the refugees made new towns with the old names at Ysleta, Socorro, and San Lorenzo. Their descendants still live in those little towns and until recently remembered and cherished their heritage, although they have become almost completely Mexicanized. As independent tribal units, they disappeared from the face of the earth, except for one group of Tiguas at Ysleta. Those who were left behind in New Mexico soon vanished, likewise. One group of Jumanos probably joined the Wichitas far to the east on the Red River, and Professor Bolton has uncovered evidence to show that others merged with their old enemies, the Mescaleros.[24]

It was the day of triumph for the Eastern Apaches. They had undermined the Spaniards, had seduced the Pueblo Indians to their side, and had made a reconquest impossible without a full-scale military expedition. Flushed with success, they followed their victims down the Río Grande and began to let blood in the new settlements.

In January, 1682, they carried off two hundred horses belonging to *Maestro de Campo* Alonso García of El Paso. Governor Cruzate sent an expedition in pursuit with better than usual success. The soldiers killed some Indians, captured twenty-two, and gave the rest a bad scare.[25] After that lesson the Mescaleros were harder to catch, but just as dangerous. In 1694 they struck El Paso again, and again the soldiers went in pursuit, this

[23] Charles Wilson Hackett, *Revolt of the Pueblo Indians of New Mexico*, I, *xxvii, cxx,* 161.

[24] Bolton, "The Jumanos Indians in Texas," *Texas State Historical Association Quarterly*, Vol. XV (July, 1911), 66 ff.

[25] Annie E. Hughes, *The Beginnings of Spanish Settlement in the El Paso District*, 335.

time without success. Captain Madrid "visited all the places where they were accustomed to place their rancherías," but found not a single one.[26]

Within a dozen years the Spaniards were back in New Mexico, but they had no rest from the Apaches, who seemed to be everywhere. They haunted the road from Chihuahua to Santa Fé, coming across the crest of the San Andres or slipping through what is now Mockingbird Gap to lie in wait for the caravans. Just above the future site of Las Cruces the *Camino Real* cut across a bend of the river and entered on a ninety-mile stretch of waterless desert—a short cut which saved distance but cost many lives, since the raiders could lurk in the mountains and pounce on their victims without warning. So many travelers were killed that this particular stretch was known as the *Jornada del Muerto*—the "Day's Journey of the Dead Man."

From Santa Fé to Chihuahua they raided and burned and killed. The settlements at El Paso del Norte, reaching for twenty miles down the river from the *presidio* and church where Juárez now stands, were always tender spots, and for two hundred years the inhabitants lived there in dread of the midnight pillager and the attack at dawn. An old folk song survives from those times which begins, "*Ay vienen los Indios por el chaparral*"— "Here come the Indians through the underbrush." It is a quiet little song, but there was a time when its quietness was the calm of desperation.

From the Mescalero point of view these were fine times. But the good days never lasted very long for them, and great trouble was at hand. About the year 1700, the advance guard of a strange Indian people, as tough as the Apaches themselves, appeared in the high plains country east of the Pecos. They were the Comanches, late-comers from the north. Almost immediate-

[26] *Ibid.*, 238.

43

ly they began to exert severe pressure on the Eastern Apaches.[27]

It was a new thing for the Mescaleros and their kin to lose battles to a merciless and triumphant foe and to be forced from their homes and hunting grounds. But that is what happened to them. There are vague reports of an Indian Waterloo, fought some time between 1720 and 1723, when the Comanches defeated the Lipans and their Apache allies in a nine-day battle somewhere east of the Pecos.[28] In the years that followed, the defeated bands were driven farther and farther south. Some of them crossed the Río Grande, and for almost a century their history is part of the history of Mexico. These exiles, with some Mescalero bands included, lived as best they could in the barren desert and mountain country of Coahuila, where their presence created terrific problems. They raided and robbed in their new home as they had in the old. The Spaniards constantly tried to find new men and methods for controlling them, and were constantly frustrated.

Many, perhaps most, of the ancestors of the present-day Mescaleros stayed on in their home country in spite of the Comanche menace. Some of them may have crossed the Río Grande and joined the Gila Apaches. Scattered bands skulked furtively about in the Sacramentos, in the Guadalupes, and on the slopes of the Sierra Blanca. One group is known to have gone to earth in the Organ mountains for a while. We can be certain of just one thing—for a long time they found the climate of their old home extremely unhealthy, and Mescaleros of one variety or another were raiding and camping in the vicinity of Saltillo and Monclova, a thousand miles away, by 1735.[29]

Those were bad and bloody times. The Spaniards in north-

[27] Ernest Wallace and E. Adamson Hoebel, *The Comanches*, 8.
[28] Bolton, *Athanase de Mézières*, I, 25; Thomas, *Forgotten Frontiers*, 60.
[29] W. E. Dunn, *loc. cit.*, 4n.

eastern Mexico made forays against the immigrant Apaches which seem to have been no more than slave-hunting expedi-tions.[30] The Apaches retaliated in the way they best understood —with torch and knife. There were lulls and intervals when both sides caught a few hard-drawn breaths—as, for instance, after the Mescalero leader Cabellos Colorados was captured in 1737 and sent to Mexico City, never to be heard from again. He must have been a mighty chieftain, since it took his people some time to recover from his loss, but we know nothing more about him—not even why an Apache chief should have been called Red Hair.[31]

Matters could hardly have been worse for the Mescaleros, Jicarillas, and other tribal groups who stayed in the north. The Apaches of the plains had been driven out of their hunting grounds in Kansas and northern Texas by the all-conquering Comanches. Gradually they concentrated in the Pecos country, mingling with the Apaches already on the ground. The farther they retreated, the farther the foemen followed. In 1724, the Comanches mounted a mass attack on the Jicarillas, carrying off half the women and children and killing all but a handful of the men.[32] Hungry and desperate, the Eastern Apaches stepped up their inroads on the Spanish settlements, and the result was the almost complete depopulation of the eastern frontier north-ward from Albuquerque in the 1740's.[33]

The infection spread. In Chihuahua, war was officially de-clared against the Apaches in 1748,[34] and there were few times during the next half-century when both sides were not cam-paigning or getting ready to campaign. In the uneasy lulls be-

[30] *Ibid.*, 241 ff.
[31] *Ibid.*, 241.
[32] Thomas, *Forgotten Frontiers*, 58.
[33] Thomas, *The Plains Indians and New Mexico*, 16.
[34] Thomas, *Forgotten Frontiers*, 5.

tween hostilities the Apaches were described as maintaining a "perfidious peace."[35]

Year by year the Spaniards came closer to desperation; their resources and their will to resist dwindled under the constant abrasion of Indian raids and forays. By the middle 1760's the whole Spanish enterprise in New Mexico, Texas, and the northern states of Mexico was threatened with collapse. Poor administration, lack of money, and antiquated methods of making war had opened the door to the red menace. Now something drastic had to be done before it was too late.

The heavy wheels of official machinery began slowly to turn. First a Royal Commission made a thorough survey of conditions. This took two years—from 1766 to 1768. A report was presented to a *Junta de Guerra* in 1769. Three years later, in 1772, the Spanish government produced a royally approved plan to promote stability in the region.[36] In 1775 the great campaign began.

During the nine years of preparation the garrisons on the frontier held the line as best they could, carrying the war to the enemy in spasmodic attacks. One group of Mescaleros, concentrated in the Organ Mountains near where Las Cruces, New Mexico, now stands, were especially troublesome. Their favorite trick was to come to El Paso to negotiate a peace and steal a few horses on their way back to the tribe. Time and again they were pursued, and just as regularly the soldiers were turned back by the "craggedness" of their mountain refuge. Don Pedro José de la Fuente led a successful expedition against them in July of 1766. In 1769, they beat off an attack by Captain Lope de Cuéllar.

Farther south, General Hugo O'Conór had better luck. He

---

[35] Thomas, *The Plains Indians and New Mexico*, 37 (this was in 1763).
[36] Thomas, *Teodoro de Croix*, 16.

46

went after the Mexican division of the tribe in the arid wastes of the Bolsón de Mapimí in 1773, broke them up, and drove them northward beyond the Río Grande. The fortunes of war inclined one way today, another tomorrow, but the Apaches showed little sign of weakening and the Spaniards were in difficulties most of the time. It was a problem even to keep a mount of horses on hand for the cavalrymen, and new supplies had to be sent in periodically to replace the ones the savages had stolen.[37]

And even when matters were going moderately well, the Spaniards always seemed to do the wrong thing. In the sixties, for instance, when the great survey of frontier conditions was going on, it was discovered that peacefully inclined Apaches had been coming to El Paso and had been admitted by the commandant, Captain Don Pedro del Barrio. Barrio lost his post for this some time later. His successor, Don Antonio Darioca, received orders to arrest any Indians he found in the pueblo. He was not able to lay his hands on many of them, but he seized a few women, who "ended their days miserably in the wool mills of Ensenillas."[38] The Indians understandably wanted revenge for that. In 1774, they killed ten men and raided Darioca's horse herd.

The next year it was the turn of the Spaniards at last, as the greatest Indian campaign of the century was put in motion. Over two thousand men were mustered in southern New Mexico, and the whole force, following a well-laid plan, moved into the Apache country in a vast, three-pronged pincers movement.[39]

[37] Thomas, *Forgotten Frontiers*, 5–9; James M. Daniel, "Diary of Pedro José de la Fuente," *Southwestern Historical Quarterly*, Vol. LX (October, 1956), 260–81. (The *Southwestern Historical Quarterly* is hereafter designated as *S.H.Q.*)

[38] Thomas, "Antonio de Bonilla," *New Spain and the Anglo-American West*, I, 198–99.

[39] Thomas, *Forgotten Frontiers*, 11–12.

The old records give the barest outline of this campaign, omitting all the details we should like to know about, but some of the statistics are interesting. According to the Spaniards, the Apaches were defeated in fifteen engagements—losing 138 dead, 104 captives, and 1,966 animals.[40]

Such a victory was the best possible evidence of expert management, and for the next fifty years the victors made good use of the tricks they learned in that campaign of extermination. In the words of Felipe de Neve, who followed up the triumph in later excursions, the proper method was "to proceed silently at night without fires; to hide during the day and to send out spies to hunt trails; to investigate every noise and finally to surprise the foe."[41]

One year later, in 1776, a successful follow-up campaign was set in motion. The troops drove the Mescaleros out of the Organ Mountains to the Sacramentos, to the Pecos, and even to the Colorado River in Texas. There a band of Comanches did the Spaniards' dirty work for them, wiping out three hundred Apache families.[42]

This was enough for the Mescaleros who escaped. On December 14, 1777, an Indian emissary came to El Paso, offering to make peace for all his people in the Sierra Blanca, Sacramento, and Organ Mountains. He said that his tribe was having more trouble than the Spaniards knew, for the Comanches had taken over their camping places and were pushing them "right into the houses of the Spaniards." The Spaniards had only to look around them to realize that this was true. One Apache band was squatting just out of gunshot of the village of San Elizario, twenty miles from El Paso; another had gone to earth at the Hueco Tanks thirty miles east.

[40] *Ibid.*, 11.
[41] *Ibid.*, 63–64.
[42] Thomas, *Teodoro de Croix*, 17.

The commandant at the El Paso presidio undoubtedly gave the Mescalero messenger a noncommittal answer. Negotiations were out of place at the moment, for the Spanish government was about to take further measures which would alter the whole complexion of life in the Indian country. After ten years of preparation, His Majesty's officers were ready to reorganize the whole cumbersome structure of frontier administration. In 1776, the land of the Comanche and the Apache was separated from the rest of Mexico and organized as the Commandancy-General of the Interior Provinces of New Spain. It was to be separate and independent—no part of the Vice-Royalty; a distinguished gentleman named Teodoro de Croix was named commanding general.[43]

De Croix's idea was to overhaul the military system completely—abandoning useless posts, setting up others at better locations, organizing light-armed troops and militia units, making the rich citizens contribute to their own defense, and stabling a few good horses instead of herding large numbers for the Indians to run off. It was his thought also that diplomacy might be as useful as firearms in dealing with the red man.

He was able to do one thing which had never been done before: he promoted a split between the Mescaleros and the Lipans which resulted in fighting between the tribes. Caught between the Comanches and the Mescaleros, the Lipans begged for peace. The Mescaleros in Chihuahua followed suit and were allowed to settle down at the abandoned pueblo of San Francisco, where they tried out the attractions of sedentary life, and were disappointed.[44]

De Croix might well have accomplished much more if he had been allowed to continue his operations, but he was sent off

43 *Ibid.*
44 *Ibid.*, 37–62, 92, 96, 125, 129.

to become viceroy of Peru. The cause of Indian management suffered by his removal, but there were other good men on the border. From 1779 to 1783 the driving energy of Juan de Ugalde (for whom Uvalde, Texas, is named) resulted in four successful campaigns against the southern Mescaleros and allied bands of Plains Apaches. The moment the pressure against them was relaxed, however, the tribesmen initiated furious campaigns of retaliation. When Ugalde retired temporarily to Mexico City, one Mescalero war party raided almost as far as Guadalajara and the capital itself, wiping out the towns of Sabana Grande and Gruñidora.[45]

Ugalde was recalled to the frontier to defeat his old enemy, the formidable Mescalero chief *Zapato Tuerto*. Eventually, in 1787, the Spaniards put diplomacy to work and made an alliance with the Comanches in the hope of eliminating the Mescaleros once and for all. They felt that it was necessary to get on one side or the other of the Indian fence, but they may have been mistaken in their choice of allies. Al B. Nelson, who recounts what is known of these long-forgotten troubles, thinks they backed the wrong party. There would have been less difficulty in the long run if they had helped the Apaches in their feud with the Comanches. As it turned out, they had both tribes to fight.[46]

In 1790, Ugalde won a final great victory over both the Comanches and the Apaches on the plains of Texas;[47] but farther west, in Sonora and Chihuahua, there was no let-up of tension until the commanders added to the force of their arms a system of free rations.

[45] Thomas, *Forgotten Frontiers*, 5–9; Al B. Nelson, "Campaigning in the Big Bend," *S.H.Q.*, Vol. XLII (September, 1939), 200–27.

[46] Nelson, "Juan de Ugalde and Picax-Ande Ins-Tinsle," *S.H.Q.*, Vol. XLII (April, 1940), 438–64.

[47] Hubert Howe Bancroft, *History of the North-American States and Texas*, I, 669.

This was part of a new approach to the problem conceived by Bernardo de Gálvez when he took charge of the *Provincias Internas* in 1786. He thought he could weaken the Indians by keeping them at peace, debauching them with liquor, and providing them with inferior firearms which would not stand up against the better equipment of the soldiers.[48]

"I do not believe that the Apaches will submit voluntarily," he declared in the instructions he issued to his subordinates for dealing with the wild tribes, "(God alone could work this miracle) but we may contribute to the means of attracting the different factions of this tribe, making them realize the advantages of rational life, which should please them."[49]

In spite of great opposition from old hands who considered Gálvez' ideas crazy, something like his policy was continued through the 1790's, and it worked after a fashion. A hungry Apache was a dangerous Apache; a full one might be harmless.

During the last decade of the eighteenth century, as a result, the citizens of New Mexico enjoyed peaceful relations with practically all the Indians *except* the Apaches, and even with them matters were much improved. For one thing, the Apaches and the Navajos stirred up a private war between themselves which made life easier for the whites.[50] Treaties, rations, and a conciliatory attitude did even more to maintain an equilibrium. Mutual weariness may also have contributed to the unaccustomed calm which descended upon *Apachería* in the years just before 1800. It had been a nightmare of a century for both parties, and they needed a rest.

The uneasy truce lasted for something like twenty-five years—undoubtedly the longest period of peace the region had

[48] *Ibid.*, I, 682–84.
[49] Gálvez, *Instructions for Governing the Interior Provinces*, 43.
[50] Ralph Emerson Twitchell, *The Leading Facts of New Mexican History*, I, 452.

51

known since the Spaniards arrived. As a result, the wealth and prosperity of the settlements increased rapidly. El Paso in particular enjoyed real boom times. Agriculture and stock raising flourished. In 1806, Don Francisco García owned twenty thousand sheep and one thousand head of cattle, which must have been pastured outside the municipal limits of Paso del Norte. The grape industry was flourishing, and "Pass Brandy"—the fiery and potent *aguardiente*—was known far and wide. On March 21, 1807, Lieutenant Zebulon M. Pike, an observant and possibly a willing prisoner on his way to Chihuahua, stopped at the Pass and was entertained by Don Francisco himself.[51] The account which Pike published after his return to the States interested commercially minded Americans, and after a few false starts the Santa Fé trade between New Mexico and the Missouri settlements got under way. The hardier traders ventured as far south as Chihuahua and Durango. One of them, James Wiley Magoffin, became a permanent resident of the border region in 1828, or earlier.[52] Trade was coming to El Paso, and El Paso was ready for it.

Settlers began to edge out into the fertile river-bottom lands so long denied them. In 1824, a number of Mexican families leveled fields and built houses at a place still called Canutillo twenty miles upriver from El Paso. Three years later Juan Ponce de León crossed to the site of present-day El Paso, Texas, took up 140 acres, dug an irrigation ditch, and built up a freighting business as a side line.[53]

Half a century later men looked back on those times as a

[51] Pike, *The Southwestern Expedition of Zebulon M. Pike* (ed. by Milo M. Quaife), 166.

[52] Grace Long, The Anglo-American Occupation of the El Paso District (M.A. thesis, University of Texas, 1931), 32; Susan Shelby Magoffin, *Down the Santa Fé Trail*, xix.

[53] Long, *op. cit.*, 47.

sort of Golden Age. An American Indian agent who respected and befriended the Mescaleros wrote about it in 1863:

> For many years before the independence of Mexico, under the wise policy of the government and the untiring efforts of the Jesuit fathers, they remained at peace, and many of them found employment as shepherds to watch over the immense herds of cattle and sheep that securely fed on every mountain and in every valley of the country. A number were educated at the mission of San Xavier, near Tucson, in Arizona, and others at or near El Paso del Norte, in this Territory. To this day there are a few far advanced in age among the Mescaleros, who can repeat the Catholic prayers in Spanish and who take peculiar pleasure in recounting the events connected with those comparatively happy and prosperous times.[54]

Stray bits of ancient history confirm the idea that the Spaniards and Indians got along with each other for a few years after 1800. Lieutenant Pike, for instance, reported that in the year 1807, when he spent a few hours at San Elizario, all was calm on the Río Grande: "Around this fort were a great number of Apaches, who were on a treaty with the Spaniards. These people appeared to be perfectly independent in their manners and were the only savages I saw in the Spanish dominions whose spirit was not humbled, whose necks were not bowed to the yoke of their invaders."[55]

Twenty years later, however, good will and amity were just a memory. In 1824, the Mexicans expelled the Spaniards and undertook to manage their own affairs. At once there were changes in policy toward the Indians; there were misunderstandings and trouble. Outbreaks began almost at once, and the red men encountered no real opposition. The Mescaleros in par-

[54] *Report of the Commissioner of Indian Affairs for 1863*, 109–10 (Michael Steck to Commissioner William P. Dole).
[55] Pike, *Southwestern Expedition*, 167.

ticular were able to carry all before them. In the 1830's and 1840's they made life all but impossible outside the limits of the larger settlements. Every road was beset, every outlying rancho in constant danger. From the *Jornada del Muerto* to the outskirts of Chihuahua, they took what they wanted and did what they pleased. → *Apaches*

Canutillo was abandoned almost as soon as it was born. Before the thirties were out, the whole El Paso area had been swept clean of livestock, including Don Francisco García's twenty thousand sheep. In the middle forties, the *Paseños* were forced to organize a military company of seven hundred men for the common defense—the hundred dragoons quartered at San Elizario having proved insufficient.[56]

It was probably this military company which administered the only defeat the Apaches are known to have suffered during this period. "About fourteen years ago," wrote Captain John Pope in 1854, "these Arabs of New Mexico, the Apaches, having made a desperate foray upon the Mexicans, retreated with their plunder to these mountains [the Huecos, thirty miles east of El Paso]. The Mexicans surprised and surrounded them, hemming them up in the rocky ravine forming the eastern Tank. Here an engagement took place, in which the Indians were totally defeated and nearly exterminated, only two or three escaping. It is said that upwards of one hundred of them were killed."[57]

The Mexicans were not usually the victorious ones along the northern frontier, however. The new government was unable to cope successfully with all its problems, and the result was ruin and death for settlers in the outlying provinces. "Don Ignacio Zúñiga, commander of the northern frontier presidios, estimated that from 1820–35, 5,000 Mexicans were killed, 100

[56] Long, *op. cit.*, 46.
[57] Pope, *op. cit.*, 69.

settlements destroyed and about 4,000 settlers forced to leave the region. With the exception of the garrisoned towns of Tucson and Tubac, the remaining parts of northern Sonora had become *ranchos despoblados*. And by 1848, even the important town of Fronteras was in the hands of the savages."[58]

In the remaining Spanish settlements farmers carried their arms as they followed the plow. Parties of considerable strength had to be organized when the community needed wood or salt. No cow or horse was safe. An isolated ranch house could expect an Indian scare every few months.

The great old adobe houses still standing in the ancient Spanish towns—Ysleta, San Elizario, Socorro, and San Lorenzo— are reminders of those times in the El Paso region. They are built like the forts they actually were, with tremendously thick walls and few windows. They enclose a central patio, sometimes two of them, with high adobe ramparts all around.

Into those patios at night the cattle and horses were driven for protection, and even then the Apaches were not always balked of their prey. They had a little trick of sending a brave over the wall in the dead of night with one end of a rawhide rope in his hand. A confederate on the outside assisted, and the two of them would use the rope to saw down through the adobe in two parallel lines. The section of wall thus made ready would be eased to the ground, the stock would be driven quietly out, and in the morning the owner would find himself a poorer but wiser man.

So the Mexicans thought of a trick themselves. They put pieces of bone and broken glass into the molds when they made adobe bricks. Such objects found in the ruined wall of an old house today are sure to have been put there to thwart the wily red man and his rawhide rope.

[58] Ogle, *op. cit.*, 29, quoting Don Ignacio Zúñiga, commander of the northern frontier presidios.

55

The situation in New Mexico was perhaps not quite as bad as it was in Sonora and Chihuahua, but on the eve of the American occupation it was bad enough. Three centuries of contact had served only to harden and sharpen the enmity between Indian and Mexican, though it is quite possible that at almost any time during those years of blood and ruin conditions might have been improved. "The views expressed by the earliest Indian agents among the wild tribes of New Mexico are instructive," remarked a New Mexico newspaperman named Ferdinand Andrews. "These views were that notwithstanding the admitted hostile attitude of the Indians, they were nevertheless susceptible, under kind treatment and judicious management, of being effectually tamed and brought to a state of civilization. . . . There is no room to doubt that the adoption of these views would have led to a very different state of things from that which now exists."[59]

[59] Andrews, The Indians of New Mexico and Arizona (MS in the Henry E. Huntington Library), 46–47.

Chapter IV

NO HOPE FOR PEACE
The Americans Take Over

FIRST CAME THE SOLDIERS. General Kearny took peaceful possession of New Mexico in 1846 and the American flag flew over the Governor's Palace in Santa Fé. A little later Doniphan's turbulent Missourians pushed southward into Apache country, reaching the Pass of the North in December, 1847. Already they had encountered the Mescaleros. On November 2, a party of raiders had run off a herd of horses and oxen. The detachment which went in pursuit rode seventy miles before finding the oxen —twenty of them speared to death. The Indians had gone on with the horses and vanished into thin air.[1] This was just a sample of what was coming.

Early in 1849 the gold hunters, California bound, began to work their way from the Texas coast ports across the plains toward El Paso. Their wagons and horses were a constant temptation to the Lipans and southern Mescaleros; and when the stage carrying mail and passengers from San Antonio began making regular runs to El Paso, the warriors felt that another heaven-sent opportunity had come their way. Fort Bliss was

[1] "Diary of Philip Gooch Ferguson," in *Marching with the Army of the West* (ed. by Ralph P. Bieber), 343–44.

established in 1849 to give some measure of protection to the courageous but vulnerable souls who were willing to brave the desert, but not all of them could be saved. The charred wood and twisted iron work of their wagons often told the old story of surprise attack, hopeless defense, and lonely death.

Even Bigfoot Wallace, that sturdy old Indian fighter, used to bring his stage into El Paso stuck full of arrows, and once he had to walk eighty miles to town when the wily redskins got away with his mules.[2]

Danger and difficulty meant nothing to the California pilgrims, who continued to wash across Texas like a tidal wave. At one time in 1849, four thousand immigrants were camped by the river at El Paso, many of them full of stories about the last Indian scare. All along the California trail, but especially westward from the Río Grande, the Apaches were committing mass murder. Reports came in of terrible destruction, "the dead bodies of men and beasts, wagons, packs, arms, &c. being strewed along the road for 5 or 6 days' travel."[3]

The forty-niners were not able to do much about it. Some of them are said to have heard of the prices being offered in Chihuahua for Apache scalps (as much as $200 apiece) and to have sallied forth in quest of Indian hair, but there is no record of their having collected any money.[4]

It was the Western Apaches and the Mescalero bands in the Davis and Guadalupe Mountains who caused most of the

[2] Stanley Vestal, *Bigfoot Wallace*, 248–49.
[3] E. Steen to John H. Dickerson, Doña Ana, N. M., Oct. 20, 1849, Ritch Collection, No. 362. Fred J. Rippy, "The Indians of the Southwest," *Hispanic-American Review*, Vol. II (August, 1919), 363–66, quoting *El Universal* of Chihuahua, notes that all flocks had been destroyed and the citizens were appealing to the central government for protection.
[4] C. C. Cox, "From Texas to California in 1849," *S.H.Q.*, Vol. XXIX (July, 1925), 131.

trouble. The Sierra Blanca Indians tried to keep away from the white man and keep the white man away from them.

Their first contact with Americans, in the summer of 1850, was a bloodless victory. On June 10, Lieutenant Enoch Steen led a detachment of troops out of Doña Ana, fifty miles north of El Paso, to see what was on the other side of the Organ Mountains and the Tularosa Basin. It was the wildest sort of country; the soldiers had little idea of what they were running into, but they feared the worst.

Steen marched 130 miles east into the Sierra Blanca, left his wagons, and turned north to explore the range. After covering 60 miles, he ran into a large band of Apaches under Chief Santana (who later became a great friend of the Americans). The wily Indian succeeded in scaring the army away.

"I was informed," the officer reported, "that there were about two thousand warriors in waiting for me; and my command not being sufficient to engage so large a band of Indians, I thought it more prudent to retire to this place, where I arrived on the morning of the 23rd June."[5]

The White Mountain Apaches never numbered a thousand, including women and children. Santana probably had no more than two or three hundred fighting men, but he made his bluff stick.

There were other soldiers in the country besides the troops on garrison duty. One of the jobs of the Indian-fighting army was to locate and open up lines of communication. From the beginning there was talk of a transcontinental railroad which would inevitably proceed to the Far West through the Pass of the North, and army officers were sent out to do the reconnaissance work. Since the Apaches and the routes of proposed highways and railroads often occupied the same territory, Indian

[5] *Report of the Secretary of War for 1850*, 73 (E. Steen to Lt. L. McLaws).

fighting and exploring often became one and the same problem.

Lieutenant W. H. C. Whiting of the Corps of Engineers left San Antonio in February, 1849, to pioneer "a new route from San Antonio de Bexar to El Paso." All went well enough until he reached the Davis Mountains, where some of the toughest of the southern Mescalero chiefs were at home.

Barring his path was Chief Gomez, "the terror of Chihuahua," with five separate bands of warriors, each under its own leader—two hundred braves in all. Gomez was fierce and insulting throughout the encounter. He demanded to know the reason for this invasion, and when the soldiers were "cool and resolute," both parties dismounted and prepared to fight. Chiefs Cigarrito and Chinonero did not seem as pugnacious as Gomez, however, and a parley was arranged. Whiting's presents brought everybody but the intractable Gomez to a more tolerant frame of mind. Cigarrito even helped the Americans get away toward Limpia Canyon. Gomez pursued them, but they escaped by traveling all night. "Expecting every minute the yell of the enemy," said Whiting, "almost helpless in our exposed position, the wind blowing a gale in chill and furious gusts, the darkness of the night, with the mountain peaks behind us lit up with the glare of fires, combined to render that march one which few of us will ever forget."[6]

Behind the isolationism of Santana and the truculence of Gomez was a very serious situation which few Americans could have been aware of. With the growth of their own numbers and the constant expansion of the white population, resident and transient, the problem of finding a square meal was growing

---

[6] *Ibid.*, 1849 (Report of Lt. W. H. C. Whiting, 284–85). For a fuller account see the "Journal of William Henry Chase Whiting," in *Exploring Southwestern Trails* (ed. by Ralph P. Beiber), 271–81.

more and more pressing in the Indian camps. Washington had agreed in the treaty with Mexico to stop depredations south of the border, which further endangered the Apache's normal way of making a living.

The Indians' predicament was brought to the attention of Brevet Captain A. W. Bowman, an army quartermaster, in 1850. In a report dated April 21, he remarked that so many Apaches were concentrated in the mountainous country that game had become very scarce. This had been true for at least two decades, and during those twenty years they had kept themselves alive by robbing in Mexico. The chiefs told Captain Bowman, "We must steal from somebody; and if you will not permit us to rob the Mexicans, we must steal from you or fight you."[7]

Mulling over what he had learned, Bowman decided that the Americans must "either feed or exterminate the Indians, or prevail upon them to settle down as cultivators of the soil." Before many more chapters of Southwestern history were written, all three methods had been tried.

The wise old chiefs well knew that they had little chance in a prolonged war with the White Eyes. Off in the Sierra Blanca the great leaders Barranquito, Santana, and Josecito must have given much thought to the problem, and early in the game they decided to see what could be done about setting up a firm and reasonable peace. They wanted the agreement to include all their Indian neighbors so that the truce would not be broken by holdouts and fringe groups, who would bring trouble on the main body of tribesmen. A scrap of paper remains to tell us what happened. It is dated June 10, 1850, from the River Pecos, and is addressed to the Governor of New Mexico. It states that the Comanches, Jicarillas, and Mescaleros have met in council for the purpose of making a treaty and propose that "all captives

[7] *Report of the Secretary of War for 1850*, 295–97.

61

in their hands shall be given up and that all in possession of the U. S. shall be given up."[8]

The last thing an Apache ever wanted to give up was his captives, who could be ransomed for money or put to work. Only a real diplomat who meant business would have suggested such a thing. Santana could have made such a gesture, but his "Proposition for Peace" bore no immediate fruit.

His kinsmen farther south made a more impressive beginning. About the middle of September, 1850, a whole band of Mescaleros from the Guadalupe and Davis Mountains under Chiefs Simon Manuel and Simon Porode showed up at San Elizario to see what they could expect from the Americans. They got food and kind treatment, paid a visit to El Paso, where they were likewise well received, and there told Major Jefferson Van Horne that they would come back with their people to make a treaty. The Major was willing to go along with this idea if he could get some tangible encouragement from his superiors. "I presume it is the wish of the government to cultivate friendly relations with them; and, to do this effectually, I should be authorized to issue provisions in limited quantities, and to make small presents to influential men among them," he wrote.[9]

If the Davis Mountain Indians came back, there is no record of it, but they did cause enough trouble here and there to keep the military on the alert. Only the northern bands—the Jicarillas and the Mescaleros—tried to stay out of difficulty. They could hardly have been in worse condition. One officer described their existence as "more filthy than swine and as precarious and uncertain as the wolf."[10] But the chiefs did their best to keep their hungry followers in line.

---

[8] "Proposition for Peace," Ritch Collection, No. 391. The names of both Santana and Barranquito appear on this document.

[9] *Report of the Secretary of War for 1850*, 112–13 (J. Van Horne to L. McLaws, Paso del Norte, Sept. 19, 1850).

In March, 1851, for instance, Lieutenant J. P. Holliday visited a camp of miserable Jicarillas sixty miles southeast of the Manzano Mountains.[11] Francisco Chacon, the head chief, went to Albuquerque to give evidence of the peaceful intentions of his people. He said that Navajos had raided in the vicinity of his camp and that his men had pursued them, killed one, and brought back a herd of sheep.[12]

Governor Calhoun resolved to follow up Chacon's peaceful gesture, and let it be known that he would visit the tribes in eastern New Mexico. On May 16, he reached Anton Chico on the Pecos with some corn for distribution to the starving tribesmen. He learned that a party of Comanches had come in to see him but had been scared off two days before his arrival by "infamous individuals" who spread the story that the Americans were coming to murder all the Indians they could find. Calhoun sent out runners who succeeded in bringing the Comanches back, but he was still in grave trouble.

"During the ensuing day," Calhoun reported, "we had a long talk, in the presence of Colonel Munroe and a number of other persons. During the afternoon the chief, Eagle Feathers, visited me in my quarters, sold to me a captive, manifested perfect satisfaction at all that had passed, and repeated that nothing but *death* would prevent his visiting me again, with chiefs and others, before two moons should terminate their rounds. Between twelve and one o'clock on the morning of the 30th, these Indians fled from the city, leaving behind them their animals, robes, and provisions. So soon as I ascertained the fact, I sent out agents in search of them; only one was overtaken, and he returned and stated that about twelve o'clock at night the chief was called out, by whom he could not tell, and when he returned

[10] *Ibid.*, *1851*, 232.
[11] *Ibid.*, 133.
[12] *Ibid.*

he stated they must run without one moment's delay, as we were preparing to have them killed the next day."[13]

More messengers went out, carrying the property the Comanches had left behind in their flight. Their confidence regained, they offered to come back in, but Calhoun decided that it would be of no use. He was in the country of the *Comancheros* —unscrupulous traders with the wild tribes—and other white rascals who sold the Indians whiskey, bought stolen stock, and in general profited by their ignorance and misery. These men did not want peace and co-operation between the natives and the government. It might spoil their business.

"So long as these wandering merchants are permitted a free and unrestrained access to the wild and roving Indians of this country," Calhoun wrote, "just so long are we to be harassed by them and their allies. . . . Why is it that these traders have no fears, no apprehensions, and pass in every direction through the country roamed by the Comanches, Apaches, Navajos and Utes, unharmed in person and property, when these same Indians show by their conduct a determined and eternal hostility to all Mexicans and others who remain quietly at home?"[14]

It is hard to tell how much of the trouble that was to come could be laid at the door of white men more rapacious and savage than the Indians, but there was never a time when some of them were not promoting one nefarious scheme or another.

Under the circumstances, it was something of a triumph that Calhoun actually signed a treaty with the Jicarilla Chacon and the Mescalero chiefs Josecito and Lobo on April 2, 1851.[15]

The governor's office in New Mexico at this time carried the

[13] *Report of the Commissioner of Indian Affairs for 1851,* 459–60 (Calhoun to Lea, June 30, 1851).

[14] Calhoun to Lea, Oct. 15, 1849, quoted in Keleher, *op. cit.,* 55.

[15] *Official Correspondence of James C. Calhoun* (ed. by Annie Heloise Abel), 314–16.

additional responsibility of ex-officio Indian agent. An extremely able and conscientious man, Calhoun was eager to clean up
the situation in the Indian camps. The best solution, he thought,
would be to confine the tribesmen somewhere remote from
white settlements with at least one hundred miles intervening,
and with white agents and soldiers to manage and control the
new reservations. He had no money to set up any such program,
but he could and did get Congress to appropriate money to pay
four Indian agents for the territory. Early in 1852, the ap-
pointees went to work.

Charles Overman, special agent for the Apaches with headquarters at Socorro, sent in his first report on March 10, and it
was not cheerful. "The Jornada del Muerto is travailed with fear
and trembling," said he, "and the Expressions of Almost every
party that arrives from the lower country add to the impression
that an almost total blockade is maintained on that important
thoroughfare."[16]

Matters were critical everywhere, it seemed. In that same
year (1852) an address was sent to the governor of Texas repre-
senting El Paso as "defenseless,"[17] and John R. Bartlett, leader
of the party sent out to survey and mark the Mexican boundary,
noted that no one could venture alone three miles from the
settlement without running the risk of losing his hair.[18]

Yet at that very time the Mescalero leaders were trying
again to work out some kind of scheme to keep the two races
from each others' throats. Calhoun died in 1852 and his successor as Indian agent, Major John Greiner, another good man,
was eager to co-operate.[19] The record does not indicate who
made the first overtures, but emissaries went back and forth,

[16] Overman to Calhoun, March 10, 1852, Ritch Collection, No. 502.
[17] Long, op. cit., 78.
[18] Bartlett, Personal Narrative of Explorations, II, 384.
[19] Alban W. Hoopes, Indian Affairs and Their Administration, 161–67.

and on June 28 a party of thirty Mescaleros arrived in Santa Fé. Indians and white men got along very well together. Some of the Jicarillas came in to visit their Mescalero kinsmen and saw that they were "behaving very well, well contented." A big dance and celebration followed, which cost the Government $10.25—little enough for such happy results. On July 1 a treaty was signed, after which the Mescaleros went home, well pleased with their presents (cost: about $25) and the outlook for the future.[20]

Greiner wrote triumphantly to his superior in Washington: "For the last *four* months there has scarcely been a complaint of an Indian depredation—the oldest inhabitant has never heard less complaint for the same length of time. . . . A number of chiefs of the Mescaleros, or White Mountains Apaches came to Santa Fé, and were provided for, the Treaty was fully and fairly explained to them—and after some objection to keeping the peace with old Mexico, as required, they at last agreed to do so, and after receiving some presents they returned to their homes highly gratified with their visit to Santa Fé."

In a later paragraph he added: "I have just parted with a Pueblo Indian who has been among them and he states that the Apaches with whom we had just made peace were to meet the Comanches in grand council some time during the next moon at the Bosque Redondo, about six days travel east from here and that they were desirous I should meet them there. If possible I shall do so."[21]

A long first step had been taken toward some degree of tolerance and concord between Indian and American, but the all-important second step was never made. The men of good

[20] "Journal of John Greiner" (ed. by Annie Heloise Abel), *Old Santa Fé*, Vol. III (July, 1916), 220–21.
[21] Report of John Greiner to Luke Lea, Commissioner of Indian Affairs, July 31, 1852, Ritch Collection, No. 540.

will on either side were frustrated by forces which they could not control. With the best intentions in the world, Greiner could not guarantee that white men would never again provoke the Indians to fury and vengeance. Santana could speak for his own people, but not for Gomez in the Davis Mountains and Mangas Coloradas in the Gila country. The signing of a piece of paper was not enough to avert the red storm that was coming.

It was such terrible mischances as the White affair which opened fresh wounds and made a real understanding impossible. E. J. White, a Philadelphian, came to the Southwest in the early fifties with his wife, baby, and two servants to be sutler at Fort Buchanan. Just before his arrival, according to Major Greiner, a detachment of troops at Las Vegas had, "without any sufficient cause or provocation," fired into a band of Jicarillas. The outraged Indians "joined with some Utes and attacked the next train coming from the States, killing Mr. White and others, and capturing his wife and child; and also the stage, with ten passengers, was taken and all killed. A war was the consequence."[22]

A posse was organized to pursue the Indians. They killed seven when they finally overtook them, but Mrs. White was murdered by an Indian woman before the rescuers could get to her. The baby was already dead.[23]

Dr. James A. Bennett, who came to New Mexico as a private in the First Dragoons in 1850, was one of the men who "swore vengeance upon her persecutors" over the dead woman's body.

"After dark," Bennett recounts, "a noise was heard near our camp. At first we supposed it to be an animal of some kind. 3 or 4 of us made an examination through the willow bushes and

[22] *Condition of the Indian Tribes* (1867), 328 (testimony of Maj. John Greiner).

[23] James M. Barney, *Tales of Apache Warfare*, 38–41.

found an Indian child which I suppose was about 8 months old. It was strapped to a board as all Indian babies are. I found it. An old gruff soldier stepped up and said, 'Let me see that brat.' I handed it to him. He picked up a heavy stone, tied it to the board, dashed baby and all into the water, and in a moment no trace of it was left. The soldier's only comment was, 'You're a little feller now but will make a big Injun bye and bye. I only wish I had more to treat the same way.' "[24]

By such acts as this the vicious cycle of murder and revenge was set in motion, and the innocent had to suffer with the guilty. All Indians looked alike to settlers and soldiers. Likewise, an Indian with a grievance or an empty stomach took what he could from any white man who came along.

They came in increasing numbers. The forty-niners had to be fed, and many herds of Texas cattle followed their trail to Arizona and California. Immigrants in covered wagons toiled westward looking for a place to make a living. Newspapermen, lawyers, sportsmen, footloose wanderers—all sorts and conditions of men—passed through *Apachería,* and many of them had harrowing adventures to report. When John C. Reid crossed the desert in the early 1850's, a war party of Davis Mountain Mescaleros caught his caravan at Eagle Springs. Only two of the warriors had rifles, but the rest did well enough with steel-headed arrows. Some of the animals were killed, and several men had to pick those arrows out of their anatomies, but nobody died. The excitement was terrific, however, and Reid came out of it with vivid impressions of the sights and sounds of an Apache battle. Every time one of the braves got in a good shot, he would emit a tremendous *"Bueno!"* (Good!), and in the heat of conflict "their din . . . was a nasal gutteral, squall, whoop, and altogether unearthly noise."[25]

[24] Bennett, *Forts and Forays,* 25.

A white man would hardly have believed it, but in the midst of this seemingly universal warfare the Sierra Blanca Mescaleros were still trying valiantly to keep the peace. On May 31, 1853, Chief Josecito and seven other White Mountain Apaches came in to Santa Fé to report to the *Tata* that their people were doing well—making crops, and hoping that the Governor would keep his promise to set up a fort in their country for mutual protection.[26]

It was the last visit of this kind that the Mescaleros would ever make. Grief and destruction were in store for them. David Meriwether took office as governor in Washington on May 22, 1853, arriving in Santa Fé in August. He brought with him the conviction that he would have to use stern measures with the Indians under his care. He saw two alternatives—feed them or whip them. "The former has been the policy of my predecessors," he said grimly; "the latter has not been effectually tried."[27]

Almost immediately, he had occasion to put his iron-fist policy into operation. The Jicarillas, aggrieved and confused by hostile actions on the part of the military, had already attempted retaliation, and the failure of the government to provide them with promised food supplies excited them further. Trouble broke out in March, 1854, and there was sharp fighting in the Taos region in March and April.[28] In June, there were outbreaks farther south, as one wagon train after another was jumped by Mescaleros at Eagle Springs, and more punitive measures were necessary.[29]

In the light of what we know of these matters now, it seems

[25] John C. Reid, *Reid's Tramp*, 126–27.

[26] Abel, "Indian Affairs in New Mexico," *N.M.H.R.*, Vol. XVI (April, 1941), 343.

[27] Hoopes, *op. cit.*, 172.

[28] *Report of the Secretary of War for 1854*, 32–33.

[29] *Ibid.*, 35.

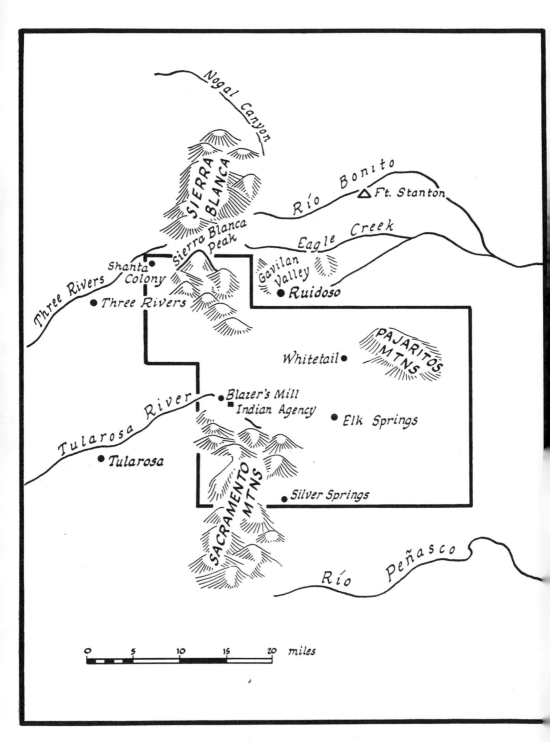

The Present-day Mescalero Reservation

certain that the depredations on the San Antonio road were the work of Chief Gomez and his piratical associates from the Big Bend country, but the Sierra Blanca Mescaleros got the credit. "The depredators are understood to be Mezcalero Apaches from the Sierra Blanca," General Garland reported from his Santa Fé headquarters. "The band numbers about two hundred and fifty warriors, and occupies the country between the White mountains and the Pecos river. It is my intention to send five companies into that country in the course of the present month."[30]

On the last day of June, he reported further that 180 men were actually campaigning in northern Mescalero territory under Lieutenant Colonel Chandler. "This band of Indians has been infesting the road from El Paso to San Antonio, committing murders and robberies," he added; "the steps which I have taken will, it is believed, put an end to their depredations in that quarter."[31]

If, as seems likely, those Mescalero chiefs had been doing their best to keep out of trouble, they must now have felt completely hopeless. But even at that moment, with soldiers pursuing them in their own country, there is no record of any fighting. All the news comes from farther south. In October, there was sharp skirmishing when a band of Apaches attacked a wagon train at Eagle Springs. It is worth noting that the warriors escaped "to the south"—not in the direction of the White Mountains of New Mexico. The troops pursued them, caught them, and killed the chief with six of his men,[32] but this did not stop the depredations. Groups of southern Mescaleros and Lipans had already escaped into Old Mexico and were living in

[30] *Ibid.*, 35 (Brig. Gen. John Garland to Lt. Col. L. Thomas, June 5, 1854).
[31] *Ibid.*, 36 (Garland to Thomas, June 30, 1854).
[32] *Ibid.*, 32–33 (Bvt. Maj. Persiphor S. Smith to Thomas, June 2, 1854).

71

Coahuila and Chihuahua,[33] safe from American pursuit but handily situated for raids on the San Antonio road.

Quite probably a few of the White Mountain people were mixed in with their tougher relatives in these escapades. The wild ones would have scented plunder and slipped away to join Gomez, or do a little raiding on their own. Some of the adventurous ones, however, were busy enough with their own private depredations to have stayed away from bigger trouble. They were stealing horses in their own vicinity, driving them to the camps of their cousins the Jicarillas, and exchanging them for others which could be kept or traded without question. A "brisk trade" of this nature was going on in 1854.[34]

They did this because they enjoyed doing it, and also because they had to pick up a living somehow in times which were steadily growing worse. "These Indians must live," said Agent E. A. Graves; "and when the mountains and the forest cease to supply them with food they will doubtless seek it from those who have it; and if not to be had peaceably, they will attempt to obtain it by force. No animal creature, whether civilized or not, will perish for the want of food when the means of subsistence are within his reach."[35]

Like many Americans at this time, Graves was not much worried about the Indian as a long-term menace. He was of the opinion that it would not take long for all of them to starve to death, and felt no discomfort over the idea. "That this race," he phrased it, "are destined to a speedy and final extinction, according to the laws now in force, either civil or divine, or both, seems to admit of no doubt, and is equally beyond the control

---

[33] *Ibid.,* 54 (Smith to Thomas, June 2, 1854).

[34] *Report of the Commissioner of Indian Affairs for 1854,* 378 (D. Meriwether to G. Manypenny).

[35] *Ibid.,* 389 (Report of E. A. Graves, Indian agent, Southern Apache Agency, Doña Ana, N. M., June 8, 1854).

or management of any human agency. All that can be expected from an enlightened and Christian government, such as ours is, is to graduate and smooth the pass-way of their final exit from the stage of human existence."

The year 1854 was the turning point for the Mescaleros. Under Governor Meriwether the government had grown deaf and hostile. Harried by the army, hungry, and disappointed, the Apaches no longer hoped for peace; before the year was out, actual fighting had begun. The Governor accused the tribesmen of engaging in "open hostilities, robbing and murdering our citizens." Complaints began to come in of cattle stealing over toward the Pecos. In January, 1855, a party of ten Mescalero raiders struck a ranch only a few miles from Santa Fé. They were promptly pursued and exterminated by Lieutenant Sturgis and a company of soldiers.

This time however the military leaders were not going to be satisfied with punitive expeditions. Already a full-scale invasion of the Mescalero country was in motion.

Chapter V

HUNGER AND DEFEAT

The Mescaleros Give Up

In FOUR DAYS it would be January 1, 1855, but the eighty-one men of the First Dragoons were well aware that New Year's would be just another day for them. Fort Thorn, a new frontier post on the west bank of the Río Grande in southern New Mexico, was lonesome enough, but it was certainly better than the wild Indian country where they were going. Hard duty was their lot, however, with pleasures few and far between and death always just across the next mountain. Nobody murmured as the men assembled on the parade ground. Orders were orders, and they had to go.

Captain Richard S. Ewell was in command of the detachment—the same bald-headed, eagle-nosed, dyspeptic Dick Ewell who in a few years was to become one of Robert E. Lee's most reliable generals. His mannerisms made the men laugh among themselves, but his bulging eyes and high voice did not make him any less efficient as an officer, and they knew it.

Of the men who followed him and suffered with him on that winter march, only one added anything to what we know from Dick Ewell's official reports. This was James Augustus Bennett, a twenty-three-year-old private from New York State

74

who had joined the army because he thought it might get him to California. After five years of campaigning he had become a tough professional soldier with wary eyes and a rat-trap set to his mouth. Beneath this tough exterior, however, he retained a thin thread of sentiment and was probably the only man at his post who thought enough of what he was doing to keep a diary.

Captain Ewell watched horsemen and pack animals fall into rank, then squeaked the word of command and led off at a brisk walk toward the crossing of the swift-running river and the snow-blanketed mountains beyond.

The Mescalero Apaches were stealing cattle in the Pecos country two hundred miles to the east, according to the dispatches. The Captain was headed for a rendezvous with units from other forts—each under orders to carry the war to the Indians in their own country.[1] It was a bad time of year for maneuvering in territory which was still marked "Unexplored" on maps, but General John Garland, at headquarters in Santa Fé, apparently believed that the disadvantages of a winter campaign would be greater for the Apaches than for the soldiers. As things turned out, he was quite correct.

Hardship began before the men were out of sight of their home post. At the end of the first day's march Private Bennett made this gloomy entry in his diary:

Dec. 28.—80 men of us under command of Captain Richard S. Ewell left fort: last night camped in the mountains, having traveled 30 miles. In fording the Rio Grande, we lost 3 horses and 2 mules by drowning. We lost 2 boxes of ammunition and some provisions also. Camped beside a small salty lake on a plain. Used some ice for cooking. It is very cold and there is little wood here.

[1] *Report of the Secretary of War for 1855*, 56 (Garland to Thomas, Jan. 31, 1855); Bennett, *op. cit.*, 59 ff. Bennett's dates do not always agree with those in Ewell's report of the campaign, but he supplies much detail.

Three days later, tired and miserable, the command reached Anton Chico, on the Pecos. Even the comforts of this frowsy little Mexican town were denied them, however. A messenger met them with dispatches revealing that the marauding Mescaleros had fled southward. It would be necessary to go down the Pecos and up the Bonito to the Capitans to meet Captain Stanton and Lieutenants Walker and Daniel at the head of twenty-nine dragoons and fifty infantrymen. The combined forces would push into the mountains and try to find some Indians to fight. Captain Ewell swore a high-pitched oath and marched his men southward out of town.

By January 17, the united command had moved south to the eastern slopes of the Sacramento Range, and were heading up the Peñasco into country which their civilian guides had never seen. The busy, noisy little river followed a sinuous valley bordered by juniper-covered hills. Tall pine trees showed richly green against the higher slopes and approached the bottom lands as the men rode farther into the mountains.

Mescalero scouts were watching their every move. This was the second invasion by white men of the country that had always been theirs, and although they were undoubtedly thoroughly scared, they made up their minds to fight the invaders every inch of the way. They made their first attempt at night after the soldiers had gone into camp, attacking with arrows and what firearms they had and trying unsuccessfully to burn the detachment out by setting fire to the dry grass.

All the next day the troops moved up the Peñasco under constant attack.

"The country was broken into high hills with deep ravines crossing the line of march," Captain Ewell wrote when it was all over. "Lt. Moore with some of the best horses gave chase to some Indians on the first open ground, but a winter march of

76

450 miles had reduced the horses too much to catch the Indians on their fresh animals. The Indians gave the impression from their boldness that they were trying to keep us from their families and hoping to bring on a close fight we kept up the march as rapidly as possible.

"During the day some fifteen of them were shot from their horses and carried off by their comrades leaving the ground marked by their blood and at one time after the fall of the boldest they collected on a high hill and set up a lamentation, afterwards becoming bolder in their attack."

At three o'clock on the afternoon of January 18, Ewell came upon the poor homes which the Apaches were trying to defend —a group of tipis on a snow-powdered slope, abandoned and empty. A small valley opening off to the right provided shelter for several more lodges.

Ewell determined to camp there for the night and detailed Captain Henry Whiting Stanton, a good soldier and a much-beloved leader,[2] to reconnoiter the second group of tipis and learn what he could about their departed owners. Ewell's official report described what followed:

> This officer after reaching the point designated charged after some Indians he saw in front and in following up the steep hillsides in the ardor of the chase, became separated from some of his men, badly mounted, which were unable to join when he sounded the rally. After rallying about a dozen of his men, he proceeded up the valley until he became satisfied that the Indians had not retreated in that direction and he started back leading his horses. About ¾ of a mile from camp the valley narrowed, with trees here and there and here he was ambushed and fired into, the first fire killing one of his men.

[2] "Whether on the field or in barracks the Captain was looked upon by his comrades as the very pattern of an officer and gentleman" (Garland to Thomas, Santa Fé, Feb. 28, 1855, Ritch Collection, No. 705).

77

He ordered his party to take to trees but the Indians being in too great force he mounted and directed his party to retreat, remaining in the rear himself firing his Sharps carbine, when he received a shot in the head and was instantly killed.

One of the men with him, when he first charged (Pvt. Dugen Co. 'B.' Ist Dragoons) was dismounted, surrounded and lanced after killing an Indian.

As soon as I ascertained that Captain Stanton was engaged, I ordered Lieut. Moore with a strong party on foot whose approach dispersed the Indians. Lieut. Moore brought in the bodies of Capt. Stanton and the two men killed, and the horse and rifle of the Indian killed by Dugen.

After this the Indians dispersed, and my guides were utterly incapable of tracking them and on the 20th having passed above the sources of the Penasco, I started back, with my horses so worn out that I was forced to lead them to my post. Within five miles of my camp the day of my fight were over 300 newly abandoned lodges.

The infantry were of invaluable service, and towards the last were able to outmarch the Dragoons. The Indians were not aware of musket range until they paid for their experience. . . .

The signal smokes of the Indians on my return satisfied me that they retreated towards the lower range of the Guadalupe Mountains.[3]

Ewell's pursuit of the fleeing Apaches had taken him to the top of the nine-thousand-foot range. It was no place for man or beast, and after camping one night, he headed back the way he had come. Private Bennett made this brief record:

Jan. 21.—Went up the river. Camped last night at its head. Animals are dying fast, 8 to 12 per day. No one of our number has

[3] *Report of the Secretary of War for 1855*, 56–62 (Reports of Gen. John Garland, Jan. 31, Feb. 28; and of Captain R. S. Ewell, Jan. 21, 1855). The quotations are from Ewell's report to Maj. W. A. Nichols, assistant adjutant general, Dept. of New Mexico, dated Los Lunas, February 10, 1855 (contemporary copy in the Ritch Collection, No. 705).

ever traveled this country before. It is nothing but snow and ice. We travelled less than 4 miles before we camped again.

It took two days to get back to the first camp where a dreadful sight awaited the men.

> Came to where we buried Capt. Stanton and the two men. Found the bodies torn from the grave; their blankets stolen; bodies half-eaten by wolves; their eyes picked out by ravens; their bones picked by ravens and turkey-buzzards. Revolting sight. We built a large pile of pine wood; put on bodies; burned the flesh; took the bones away.[4]

The Apaches tried once more to burn the troop out before they left the Peñasco, but the soldiers fired a circle around their camp and got away. It was a sad and weary outfit that slogged up the Bonito past present-day Lincoln and Carrizozo and turned northward toward the Manzanos. At the point of the mountains they crossed over to the Río Grande valley and headed southward toward their home post.

One job still remained to be done before the campaign could be considered finished: Captain Stanton's bones had to be escorted to Fort Fillmore, where he had been stationed. Private Bennett was a member of the detail. He spent a night at Doña Ana, where there was a big dance on the evening of February 15, and went over to Fillmore the next day. What he saw there touched him deeply:

> We rode into the fort. Mrs. Stanton, the Captain's wife, stood in the door awaiting her husband. If a person had one drop of pity, here he could use it. Poor woman! She asks for her husband. The answer is evaded. An hour passes. Her smiles are fled. Her merry laugh is turned to sighs, and tears stain her cheek. Him she loved, she never more shall behold.[5]

[4] Bennett, *op. cit.*, 61–62   [5] *Ibid.*, 63.

79

The Mescaleros, too, were mourning in their comfortless camps, although there was nobody to record their sorrow.

The campaign was a terrible blow to the Apaches. It was the first time the heartland of their domain had been penetrated by a hostile force of such size and effectiveness. Never before had the entire tribe been driven from its tipis and turned out in the wilderness with neither food nor shelter. Never before had they endured such slaughter while the enemy escaped almost unscathed. Their pride was so badly hurt that a small group of die-hards resolved to try once more for a victory. Fifteen of them followed Ewell out of the mountains and all the way back to his home base. On the night of February 23, a few days after the return of the weary dragoons, they attacked a grazing camp twenty-five miles from the post, where four men were guarding the horse herd. The Mescaleros were driven off after a desperate struggle, every one of the guards having been wounded at least four times. Troops from Fort Thorn followed the trail of the fleeing Indians almost to the Guadalupe Mountains, where soldiers from Fort Bliss also took up the pursuit, but the braves dispersed and vanished.[6]

After this one final flurry the Mescaleros resolved to resist no more, but they were lucky to avoid further punishment. General Garland was getting ready to strike again—he had sent three hundred soldiers under Colonel Miles to make the assault—and was prevented only by the interposition of Dr. Michael Steck, the new Mescalero Indian agent. The Apaches came to him first with their plea for peace and he responded by notifying both Garland and Governor Meriwether that he had promised them protection while negotiations were going on. This, Miles re-

[6] *Report of the Secretary of War for 1855,* 55 (Garland to Scott, Feb. 28, 1855).

marked, "was not a little annoying when we were prepared to strike," but his arm was stayed, and the Mescaleros trudged over to Fort Thorn to meet the Governor and ask for an end to their trouble.[7]

Far-reaching changes in their way of life resulted. Fort Stanton, named for the dead officer, was established at the junction of the Ruidoso and the Bonito to keep them in line. The chiefs signed a treaty which confined them to a reservation which has ever since been their home. It took in a strip of land south of Fort Stanton, twenty-seven miles wide and (at that time) extending from the mountains to the Pecos.[8] The treaty under which this land was reserved to them was never ratified by Congress, but nobody explained to the Indians that such ratification was necessary for the treaty to be any good.

They were beaten and destitute, so miserable that even Governor Meriwether was moved by their plight. "When I met the Mescaleros at Fort Thorne for the purpose of negotiating a treaty of peace with them," he said, "I found these Indians in the most destitute condition imaginable. I relieved their immediate wants, and directed Agent Steck to issue to them a limited amount of provisions, from time to time, as they might apply for relief and their necessities seemed to require it."[9]

Meriwether did not, and probably could not, do enough to take care of the situation. If there had been money to keep these poor Indians alive—if there had been any place where they really belonged—if they had had the disposition and the knowledge to settle down to farming, then he could have helped them. As

[7] *Ibid.*, 69–70 (Garland to Thomas, May 31, 1855); 70–71 (Garland to Thomas, June 30, 1855).

[8] Charles J. Kappler, *Indian Affairs, Laws, and Treaties*, I, 870–73.

[9] *Report of the Commissioner of Indian Affairs for 1855*, 186 (D. Meriwether to G. Manypenny, Sept., 1855).

matters stood, there was no way to take care of them, and no way for them to take care of themselves. They were hungry. They had to steal or starve. So they stole.

Michael Steck, the good Pennsylvania doctor who was now in charge of their destinies,[10] reported the depredations more than once, and finally told them not to come back to him for assistance until they had returned the livestock they had taken. This they could not very well do, since the greater part of their booty had been eaten, practically on the spot. When Agent Steck turned his back, there was nothing for them to do but go home to the mountains. They packed up what they had, left the agency at Doña Ana, and headed for the Sierra Blanca. For several months they held out, getting hungrier all the time, and finally began coming to the military post at Fort Stanton in hopes of picking up a few scraps of food. Major Van Horne, commanding the post, noted that "They devour a dead mule with avidity, and eagerly eat up the leavings of dogs."[11]

Lydia Spencer Lane, wife of an officer stationed at Fort Stanton, was there when they ate the mule. It was a sore-backed specimen that had died in the corral. "They cut him up in pieces," she remembered, "carried the meat to their camp, and ate it all up, everything but bones and hoofs. A dead mule is not to be despised when one is starving."[12]

Welcome as this tidbit was, it did not go very far, and the Indians were back at the post almost immediately hoping for

[10] See Keleher, *op. cit.*, 506, n. 137, for a sketch of Steck. He was a sturdy Pennsylvania German, who accepted the appointment as Mescalero Agent in order to bring his ailing wife to New Mexico. He was made superintendent of Indian affairs for New Mexico by President Buchanan, quarreled with General Garland, and fought hard for his Indian charges. Later he made money in New Mexico mines, lost it in railroad enterprises back East, and died a poor man in 1883.

[11] *Report of the Commissioner of Indian Affairs for 1857*, 576 (Steck to J. W. Denver, Aug. 7, 1857, quoting a letter of Maj. Jefferson Van Horne).

[12] Lane, *I Married a Soldier*, 66.

82

more. Major Van Horne told them they ought to go to their agent, and in desperation they finally did. Steck repeated his judgment: No provisions until stolen property was brought in.

"The effect of this course with them," Steck declared, "was that, in two months from that time, they delivered to the commanding officer at Fort Stanton, and to the agent, about forty horses, which have since all been claimed by their owners."[13]

Following orders from the Governor's office (where his refusal to deal with the Apaches until they brought in the horses had caused much criticism),[14] Steck met the band at Fort Stanton in November, 1856, gave them blankets, shirts, knives, tobacco, and provisions, and told them they would get five beeves and thirty *fanegas* of corn every full moon thereafter, as long as they behaved themselves.[15] Almost a year later he was able to report that from the time of this arrangement "not a single robbery in the Territory has been traced to the White Mountain band of the Mescaleros."[16]

Steck was the first agent who took any practical steps to help the Indians make a living. He hired six men to go with the band to La Luz Canyon at the foot of the Sacramentos in the spring of 1856 and get a farming project started. Seventy acres were planted in corn and vegetables, and everybody seemed to be happy and friendly.[17]

food on reservation

The friendliness was partly due to the death of the old chief Barranquito, who appears to have been something of a firebrand. His son Cadete (or Zhee-ah-nat-tsa), who now became spokesman for the greater part of the tribe, told the white men that he was determined to prevent depredations in future.[18]

13 *Report of the Commissioner of Indian Affairs for 1857*, 575.
14 *Ibid.*, 732 (D. Meriwether to G. Manypenny).
15 *Ibid.*, 575 (Steck to Denver).
16 *Ibid.*
17 *Ibid.*
18 *Ibid., 1856*, 732 (Meriwether to Manypenny, Sept. 30, 1856).

Cadete was a great Apache who actually succeeded in keeping most of his people out of trouble, but even the greatest chief could not prevent them from being hungry in those lean times, or keep them from occasional thefts and pilferings. He did his best, however. In August, he brought in ten horses which he told Van Horne his men had taken from thieving Indians. "These people," Van Horne decided, "have all along shown the most friendly disposition, and are doing all they can to prevent the other Mescaleros from depredating."[19]

And now the truth began to come out about those depredations for which the White Mountain Mescaleros had so often been blamed, and for which they had been so severely punished. When Major Thomas H. Holmes took command at Fort Stanton, he heard the standard accusation that they were responsible for the trouble on the San Antonio road. He wrote to General Garland on February 15, 1857, that "after the closest inquiry and strictest investigations, I am convinced that the Indians in this neighborhood are in no way connected with them. This abstinence on their part is entirely to be ascribed to the beneficial influence exercised by means of the small amount the acting assistant commissary of subsistence at this post was authorized by Dr. Steck to issue."[20]

Steck was sure that a firm policy, along with adequate subsistence and good leadership in helping the Indians to make a living for themselves, was the only possible course to follow. He wanted to move all the Apaches to a new reservation on the Gila River, but realized that such a move might be unwise at the time on account of a split which had occurred within the tribe. White bootleggers were active around the reservation, and five or six Indians had been killed in drunken brawls. As a result,

[19] *Ibid.*, *1857*, 576 (Steck to Denver, Aug. 7, 1857).
[20] *Ibid.*

The women were patient and enduring. Left is Indian Mary, well known among the white settlers. Below, the men lived by hunting and raiding.

The Mountain Spirits appeared at the great ceremonial.

one half of the Mescaleros was having nothing to do with the other half. Steck decided that the best course under the circumstances was to open up more and better farm land in Alamo Canyon near the site of present-day Alamogordo, and he persuaded all but two of the chiefs to move over there in the spring of 1858 and get to work. Chiefs Mateo and Verancia, heading a group known as the Aguas Nuevas, said they did not care to join their brothers on account of the recent killings—and besides they had their own farms across the mountains on the Peñasco.[21]

Actually, Steck's worst problem in 1858 was the over-friendly spirit of Chief Gomez and his Davis Mountain braves. They gave "constant trouble" trying to join their White Mountain cousins—probably hoping for a cut of the beef issue. Steck refused to let them come in, well knowing that their marauding ways might be passed on to the young men now busy putting in a crop at the mouth of Alamo Canyon.[22]

Steck's firmness and foresight stabilized the situation for the next two years. The Apaches continued to work their little fields and behaved themselves fairly well. It was becoming obvious, however, that their besetting sin was drunkenness, and that they were at the mercy of rascally white men who lived on the Indian's weakness, crowding in on his small property and robbing him of the pride and dignity which had once been his. The victims yearned for the poison which these bootleggers peddled, and so protected the peddlers. For the next twenty years it was next to impossible to prosecute a whiskey merchant. A tipsy native, when asked where he got the stuff, would reply solemnly, "I found a spring."

[21] Reeve, "The Federal Indian Policy in New Mexico," *N.M.H.R.*, Vol. XIII (January, 1938), 14–62; *Report of the Commissioner of Indian Affairs for 1858*, 195–96 (Steck to Collins, Aug. 10, 1858).

[22] *Report of the Commissioner of Indian Affairs for 1858*, 195–96 (Steck to Collins, Aug. 10, 1858).

Nor was the Apache safe from treacherous attacks of other kinds. He hardly dared show his face near a settlement. In February, 1858, a band of peaceful tribesmen were camped near Dr. Steck's headquarters in the village of Doña Ana. In the Mexican community of Mesilla, a few miles away, a group of militiamen decided that this Indian camp created an intolerable situation which it was their business to remedy, and they made a surprise attack on the unsuspecting Mescaleros. Lieutenant J. W. Alley of Fort Fillmore stated that this "Mesilla Guard" had killed eight or nine Indians, including several women, and afterward "came into town in a condition of semi-intoxication, following women and children who were fleeing there for protection."[23]

A day or two later, one hundred warriors under Gomez (our old friend from the Davis Mountains) came to Doña Ana with the idea of revenging themselves on the men of Mesilla. Dr. Steck persuaded them to go away and let him handle the affair, but before he could take any countermeasures, the army stepped in. The commanding officer at Fort Fillmore seems to have recommended that if the local militia was so anxious to handle the Indian problem, the regular troops would pull out.

This brought the Mesilla citizens to their senses, and 634 of them signed a petition on March 24, 1858, asking that the post be kept in operation and that more troops be sent in. General Garland replied that they had enough soldiers already and told them furthermore, "those of our citizens who perpetrate acts of violence and outrage . . . have no claim to the protection of the military and will receive none."[24]

The Mesilla Guard evidently came to the conclusion, after

[23] *Report of the Secretary of War for 1858*, 284–85 (Lt. J. W. Alley to L. McLaws).
[24] *Ibid.*, 293 (Garland to Charles A Hoppin, James A. Lucas, and others, April 7, 1858).

86

two months of this sort of wrist-tapping, that a mild reproof was all the punishment they need look forward to for killing Indians. On April 10 they tried it again. Just before daybreak a band of them charged into a Mescalero camp at Fort Thorn—killing men, women, and children.[25]

The troops were on them at once. Lieutenant W. H. Wood arrested Juan Ortega, leader of the Guardsmen, and thirty-six of his followers. They were held at the fort—a procedure which brought howls of protest from their fellow citizens. Letters even went off to the Secretary of War complaining that these arrests were "a most gross outrage committed by the officer commanding Fort Thorne."[26]

The Mexicans complained that they had lost two hundred head of cattle and horses in the last six or eight months. The army officers maintained that the Apaches "for the last four or five months have been at peace and on friendly terms with all in the vicinity; have been daily in and about the garrison, quiet and well behaved, and . . . have given no cause for this cowardly outrage."[27]

There is no record that the Mesilla militiamen were punished for the crimes they had committed. Nobody was ever punished for killing an Indian. But the *paisanos* continued to scream about the Indian menace. According to the Mesilla *Miner*, a party of Apaches descended on the little town of San Tomás, below Mesilla, in June, 1860, and attacked the ranch of José Montoya. Everybody was killed but one child, who was taken captive, and one peon who was left for dead. "How long, oh! how long are we to endure these outrages?" wailed the editor. "Will Congress *never* give us protection?"[28]

[25] *Ibid.*, 289 (Lt. W. H. Wood to Maj. W. A. Nichols, April 17, 1858).
[26] *Ibid.*, 290–91 (Justus J. McCarty to the Secretary of War, May 31, 1858).
[27] *Ibid.*, 289 (Wood to Nichols, April 17, 1858).
[28] Mesilla *Miner*, June 9, 1860.

If this raid was as bad as the *Miner* tried to make out (which is doubtful), the perpetrators were probably Gila Apaches. The Mescaleros were neither willing nor able to do much harm at that moment. They were hungry and hopeless. The white man had not been successful in his effort to exterminate them, but his diseases and his whiskey were rapidly getting the job done. They could thank Congress for that. Since the treaty they were living under had not been ratified, the Intercourse Laws did not apply to them. The government could give little protection against the human vultures who preyed upon them.[29]

It must have seemed to a thoughtful Indian in 1861 that the condition of his tribe could not have been worse. "It is not surprising," Commissioner William P. Dole commented, "that very many of them regard their future prospects as utterly hopeless, and consequently cannot be induced to abandon their vicious and idle habits."[30]

And yet if that same thoughtful Indian could have foreseen what was in store for his tribe during the next four years, he would have prayed to White Painted Woman and Child of the Water to keep things as they were.

[29] J. P. Dunn, *The Massacres of the Mountains,* 379.
[30] *Report of the Commissioner of Indian Affairs for 1862,* 12.

Chapter VI

WE ARE MEN AND BRAVES

The Mescaleros Against General Carleton

Civil war breaks out

THE SOUND OF CANNON at Fort Sumter was heard, faint and far away, in the mountains and deserts of New Mexico. It was a bad time for the men in the garrisons scattered about in that vast and lonely land. Southern officers, torn by conflicting loyalties, lay awake nights trying to decide what to do as rumors of the coming change filtered in.[1] It took weeks for news from the East to reach them, but at last it was known that the war was a reality and decisions had to be made.

Some of the loyal officers stayed where they were; some headed for the North. Southern sympathizers worried about the best way to get back to their own people. For some of them the problem was solved when a small army marched west from San Antonio and turned north along the Río Grande, carrying all before it. Fort Bliss at El Paso and Fort Fillmore near Las Cruces became Confederate garrisons—the latter after being disgracefully abandoned by Union forces under Major Isaac Lynde— and the Texans marched northward to triumph at Val Verde and stalemate at Glorieta.

[1] Lane, *op. cit.*, 111–14, gives a firsthand account of the situation of army officers in New Mexico at the outbreak of the war.

Captain B. S. Roberts, in command at Fort Stanton, made no move until he heard that his colleague Major Lynde had surrendered to Baylor's Confederates. As soon as might be thereafter, however, he took his two companies off to Albuquerque—first setting fire to the post. Unfortunately, from his point of view, a rain storm came up after his departure and put out the fire. Although some damage was done, the storerooms contained much useful material which was manna from heaven to the Mexicans and Apaches who were standing about ready to go to work. When Lieutenant John R. Pulliam marched in from Doña Ana to take charge for the Confederates, he found little but ruins and Indian trouble. Fighting broke out between the Southern troops and the Mescaleros almost at once.

There is some doubt about just what happened. Reports from Northern men in Santa Fé make it appear that the Indians took offense at some act or order of the Confederate detachment and started shooting. They "became involved in a quarrel with the Texans that brought on a fight, in which several Indians and some of the Texans were killed," Superintendent James L. Collins wrote.[2]

According to the Confederates, the Mescaleros began it. Four men went out by Pulliam's orders to scout for Union forces in the neighborhood, heading for the Gallinas Mountains just beyond the northern spurs of the Sierra Blanca. Green and over confident, they camped near a spring where they were completely exposed, and the Indians wiped them out in the morning. Only one man escaped—by galloping down "an almost perpendicular mountain" and outrunning the Apaches in a ten-mile chase.

That same evening another band attacked the Mexican

---

[2] *Report of the Commissioner of Indian Affairs for 1861,* 122 (James L. Collins to William P. Dole, Oct. 8, 1861).

settlement of Placitas (later called Lincoln), and Pulliam and his Texans went to the rescue. Five Indians were killed, but the Lieutenant marched back to the ruined fort in a pouring rain, so discouraged that he left the next day for Doña Ana.[3] The Mexicans who had settled in the shadow of the fort knew what was coming and moved out as fast as they could, leaving everything they possessed, including unharvested crops in the field. The Mescaleros were left for a little while in complete and undisputed possession of the mountain region. It was like the old days. There was not an American or a Mexican in the country, and many of the Apaches supposed, as did other Indians throughout the Southwest, that the white men would be too busy murdering each other from now on to interfere with the normal activities of the red men. Bands of warriors headed for the sheep ranches in the Pecos country, for the traditional ambush site at Point of Rocks on the Jornada del Muerto, and for exposed ranches and settlements in the Río Grande valley. Happy days had come again. There would be horses and plunder and—at last—food.

It was probably true at this time, as always, that the wiser heads among the Indians knew that the white man would eventually punish the whole tribe for the sins of its more violent members. But this was no time for counsels of moderation. The young men felt that their hour had come and they meant to make the most of it.

Even so, it was not the Mescaleros in the White Mountains who staged the really important raids and caused the really big trouble. Once again it was the Guadalupe and Davis Mountain bands which did the most damage—holding up stagecoaches, burning wagon trains, and terrifying everybody who came through their country. They seriously threatened the line of

[3] *War of the Rebellion Records*, Ser. I, Vol. IV, 19–25.

communication which the Confederate forces were trying to keep open between El Paso and San Antonio.

Eventually, the military leaders decided that something would have to be done about the southern Mescalero bands haunting that lonely, dusty road, and they agreed to begin by making overtures of peace and friendship. Down in the Davis Mountains at that time were two very tough chiefs named Nicolás and Antonio, lieutenants or war captains of a still bigger leader named Espejo.

Nicolás seems to have been the front or outside man, and was busily engaged in raiding ranches when word came to him that the white chiefs wanted to talk.

Some say that the whole idea originated in Nicolás' crafty mind. Others blame Colonel McCarty at Fort Davis or James Magoffin, one of the Confederate commissioners at El Paso. At any rate, after proper negotiations, there was a happy meeting at Fort Davis between McCarty and Nicolás, complete with toasts and promises of eternal friendship.

The commissioners were anxious to see Nicolás at El Paso, McCarty told him. They wanted to make peace and ask for his help. They would give him many things. He could ride the stage the next day.

Nicolás did it. He took the stage and came on in—probably the only Mescalero who ever rode two hundred miles in such a contraption. No doubt he undertook the trip in a spirit of pure bravado, enjoying the incredulity of his warriors as he told them what he was about to do.

Magoffin and company got up an impressive party for him, with Magoffin himself acting as host and interpreter. Colonel George Wythe Baylor, who commanded the Confederates and hated an Apache worse than he hated sin, was there also, and used to love to tell about it.

Magoffin made a speech. McCarty made a speech. Baylor made a speech. Finally Nicolás, a tall, fine-looking Indian, rose to reply: "I am glad I have come," he said. "My heart is full of love for my pale-face brothers. They have not spoken with forked tongues. We have made a treaty of peace and friendship. When I lie down at night the treaty will be in my heart, and when I arise in the morning it will still be there. And I will be glad I am at peace with my pale-face brothers. I have spoken."

Magoffin thereupon rose and proposed a toast: "Nicolás, our friend."

Completely confident that all was well, Magoffin made arrangements next morning to issue rations and blankets to his new Confederate scouts, and saw Nicolás off on the east-bound stage. Tongue in cheek, Nicolás bade him a warm farewell. But at Barrel Springs, twenty-odd miles out of Fort Davis, he snatched McCarty's pistol from its holster, leaped out of the coach, and disappeared into the brush before the astonished white men could move from their seats.[4]

Next day his band attacked the men guarding the beef herd at the fort, ran off the stock, and killed two of the herders. It was Nicolás' way of telling the Texans how he felt about them and their agreements. He had a chance to make his point more emphatic when Lieutenant Mays with fifteen troopers set out to pursue him.

Mays' soldiers were young Texans, mostly from Lavaca County, who were still feeling their volunteer excitement and seemed willing to fight the war singlehanded. On August 10, 1861, they overtook the Apache band and retrieved one hundred head of horses without a fight. This boosted their martial enthusiasm and they got back on the trail with renewed energy.

[4] Baylor, *Historical Sketches of the Southwest*, 3–6; Carlysle Graham Raht, *The Romance of the Davis Mountains*, 148.

When they caught up again, the Indians were posted in their favorite defensive layout—warriors on both sides of a narrow canyon where there was plenty of cover, and only one road in.

The guide knew what they were up against. "If we go in there," he said to Mays, "not a one of us will come out alive."

"Well, then," replied Mays, "we won't go in."

But that did not suit the boys from Texas. "We aren't cowards," they protested. "Let's go in there and lick hell out of them."

Against his better judgment Mays gave the order to advance. His men charged up the draw, and lasted about ten minutes with at least one hundred cunningly posted Indians blasting away at them. The rescue party, sent out when a Mexican horse herder got away and brought the bad news, could not even find the bodies.[5]

The young men of the Sierra Blanca band did not do so well as their southern cousins. They lost a skirmish near Mesilla on July 25, 1861,[6] two days before Major Lynde's surrender, and thenceforward confined their activities to the mountain regions, where they did considerable damage. The Confederates were too busy to manage them. The United States officials could not get at them while the invading Texans controlled the southern half of the state. Superintendent Collins did what he could by finding an agent for the Mescaleros. This was Lorenzo Labadie, perhaps the best friend those Apaches ever had.

Labadie is almost forgotten now, but in his time he was a distinguished New Mexican. By marriage he was connected with the great Chaves and Baca families, and from his youth had occupied positions of honor and trust. When he died at

---

[5] *War of the Rebellion Records,* Ser. I, Vol. IV, 26 (Baylor to Van Dorn, Aug. 25, 1861).

[6] Twitchell, *op. cit.,* 321.

Puerto de Luna in 1904 at the age of eighty, he was remembered as "a man of many noble qualities."[7] In 1862, he was in his early forties, a man of tremendous energy and tenacity and at the same time deeply sympathetic toward the wronged and the disinherited. As time went on, he came more and more wholeheartedly to the defense of his "poor Indians," but his first report, written from his headquarters at Anton Chico in the Pecos valley on September 25, 1862, was something less than hopeful about them:

> The Mescalero band of Apaches, over whom I have had charge during the year have been in a continuous state of hostility, and have committed heavy depredations upon the people, which they have been permitted to do without any movement being made against them by the military. During the latter part of August, they killed some forty men and six children, and carried a number of children into captivity, some of whom, after keeping them in the mountains for several days, were stripped, and turned loose to find their way back to the settlements.
>
> The property robbed consisted of horses, mules, donkeys, and cattle, besides large numbers of sheep. During the latter part of last year, I was ordered by the superintendent to visit the country of this marauding band, which I did, accompanied by an escort of soldiers, and although I remained a considerable time in the country where the Indians are most generally found, I did not see a single one, they having either secreted themselves in the mountains or moved off south into the Mexican territory. On my return to the agency, I fell in with a party of six Indians, who had in their possession thirty-three head of cattle, which they had stolen; we took the cattle from them, the Indians escaping into the mountains.
>
> In the month of July last a party of eighty men (Mexicans) made an expedition into the country of these Indians in pursuit of stolen property; they returned with four Indian children, cap-

[7] Santa Fé *New Mexican*, Aug. 11, 1904, "Lorenzo Labadie Answers Last Roll Call."

95

tives, and about forty horses and mules, among which were seven of their own previously stolen. The children I took possession of, and turned them over to the military commandant at Fort Union, where they still remain.

About two months ago these Indians gave indications, through the Mexicans, of a desire to make peace, since which time they have not, so far as I am advised, committed any depredations. My experience with the band, however, induces me to receive such propositions with much caution. It will hardly be safe to trust them until they have been punished for past offences, which our present excellent and efficient military commanders seem determined to do, and, as a first step in that direction, it has been determined to reoccupy Fort Stanton. Troops are now moving for that purpose.[8]

The troops which Labadie spoke of were Union soldiers. The brief hour of triumph for the Confederates was over, and they had left the country. The tide had turned against them at Glorieta. They trailed disconsolately down the Río Grande, left their wounded at El Paso for the Yankees to take care of, and disappeared in the direction of San Antonio. In July, 1862, the advance scouts of the California Volunteers reached the river, too late to engage even the rear guard of the Southern forces.

New Mexico was back in the United States, but it was in sorry shape. Torn by the Great Division, fought over by hostile armies, and plagued by Indian uprisings, it obviously needed a firm hand to bring it back to law and order, and General James Henry Carleton, commander of the California Column, took immediate steps to get the job done.

Carleton was an extremely competent and aggressive officer who was always driving himself and his men, a stickler for

[8] *Report of the Commissioner of Indian Affairs for 1862*, 246–47 (Labadie to Collins, Anton Chico, Sept. 25, 1862). For a sympathetic account of General Carleton, see Clarence C. Clendenin, "General James Henry Carleton," *N.M.H.R.*, Vol. XXX (January, 1955), 23–43.

discipline, a man without weakness or mercy, who for the next four years was to be the absolute ruler of New Mexico.

He was a down-East Yankee from Maine, forty-eight years old at the time, spare and durable and ramrod straight in his army blues. His glance was penetrating, his thick hair tended to bristle, his wide mouth, surmounted by a military moustache and flanked by heavy sideburns, drooped at the corners and shut like a rat trap. With his arms folded and his head thrown back, he was a picture of indomitable self-confidence.

He had a heart which could be touched, and a conscience which never slept. He was a Christian and a gentleman; he had friends and loved his family. If he had never come to New Mexico—if he had never had to function as God in a war-torn and distracted country—his determination and organizing ability might have been put to better use. He had intelligence and foresight, driving energy, and a consuming ambition to do well. These qualities had already won him promotion on the battlefield, brought him the leadership of the California troops with the title of brigadier general, and set his name above all others in New Mexico. His trouble was that he could not admit an error, change his mind, or take a backward step. A lesser man would have trimmed his sails and ridden out the storm. Carleton sailed straight on into a disaster which involved not only himself but practically all the New Mexico Indians.

His first problem was to keep his volunteer troops occupied and contented. They grumbled when they found that the Confederates had escaped them. They grumbled louder when Carleton put them to policing and cleaning up the Río Grande villages. Regular troops would have accepted the situation as part of the war's work; the volunteers had rebelled against authority even before they were out of California and might have done so again. Carleton had to find something for them to do.

97

Indians! That would do it! All the tribes were restless and they had been committing many depredations. A full-scale campaign against the marauders would bring glory to the Californians and win the gratitude of the native population. Carleton at once began issuing orders and writing letters—a favorite occupation of his. He wrote well in a rather grandiose manner, and the consumption of paper and ink at his headquarters was enormous.

The Mescaleros were to be humbled first—then the Navajos. With the help of Governor Connelly, he induced Colonel Kit Carson to take command of the troops in the field, and to spearhead the attack with his own New Mexico militiamen.

Carson did not want to do it. He knew the Indians and took no satisfaction from the thought of slaughtering them. He felt that they could be handled without forcing them into a fight to the finish,[9] and, of course, he was right, but he yielded to pressure.

Carleton's order regarding the Mescaleros was dated September 27, 1862: "Fort Stanton, on the Bonito river, in the country of the Mescalero Apaches, will without delay be reoccupied by five companies of Colonel Christopher Carson's regiment of New Mexico volunteers."[10]

On his way to reoccupy the fort, Carson was overtaken by his final instructions:

All Indian men of that tribe are to be killed whenever and wherever you can find them. The women and children will not be harmed, but you will take them prisoners, and feed them at Fort Stanton until you receive other instruction about them. If the Indians send in a flag and desire to treat for peace, say to the

[9] Keleher, *op. cit.*, 279. Keleher's is the best account of the Apache and Navajo campaigns and their aftermath.
[10] Edwin L. Sabin, *Kit Carson Days*, II, 702. Sabin reproduces many official documents relating to the campaign.

98

bearer that when the people of New Mexico were attacked by the Texans, the Mescaleros broke their treaty of peace, and murdered innocent people, and ran off their stock; that now our hands are untied, and you have been sent to punish them for their treachery and their crimes; that you have no power to make peace; that you are there to kill them wherever you can find them; that if they beg for peace, their chiefs and twenty of their principal men must come to Santa Fe to have a talk there.[11]

The complete savagery of this order shocked and embarrassed Kit Carson, but he could do nothing but follow orders. The Indians were in even worse trouble; they had no notion that such barbarity was to be visited upon them. And since they had been behaving themselves and asking for a truce, they were totally unprepared for what was to follow.

They were not prepared either for the attitude of the soldiers, who were, as the saying went, "spoiling for a fight." It made no difference to those soldiers that the Indians were poor and desperate, armed mostly with bows and arrows, hungry and tired. Captain N. J. Pishon, a Californian who found nine deserted camps in the Guadalupes and no Indians, reported to his superior officer that all the men were disappointed, "but none so much as myself, in not getting a fight out of the redskins."[12]

Captain James Graydon was more fortunate than Pishon. In the last days of October he sallied out of newly occupied Fort Stanton on a scout and before long came up with a band of Mescaleros—men, women, and children. The leader was the aged Chief Manuelito, who came on with his hand raised in the sign that he wanted to make peace talk. Captain Graydon obeyed his orders. He fired into the band without warning and with severe execution.[13]

[11] *Ibid.*, 702–703, 847.
[12] Keleher, *op. cit.*, 484–85, 14n.
[13] Sabin, *op. cit.*, II, 703–704.

Manuelito was killed, as was his second in command, José Largo, along with four additional warriors and one woman. In the pursuit which followed, five more Indians were killed and many wounded. Captain Graydon rode back with seventeen captured horses and mules, no doubt congratulating himself on a job well done. What his feelings were when he found that Manuelito was on his way to Santa Fé to ask for peace, the record does not say.

Carson was appalled, and even Carleton had some doubts about this "victory"—especially when word got around that at least one white civilian had made money out of the massacre.

"If you are satisfied that Graydon's attack on Manuelita and his people was not fair and open," Carleton wrote to Carson, "see that all horses and mules, including two said to be in the hands of one Mr. Beach of Manzana, are returned to the survivors of Manuelita's band."[14]

An enveloping campaign was now put into operation against the frightened Apaches. Major William McCleave with two companies of Californians was to go into the Mescalero country through Dog Canyon in the Sacramentos. Captain Thomas Roberts was to take two more companies of Volunteers and enter by way of Hueco Tanks to the south. Carson was to operate from Fort Stanton. Soldiers were thus routed in from three directions, leaving the Indians little opportunity to escape.

Captain McCleave made the first contact at the mouth of Dog Canyon, a well-watered spot and a main highway for Indians going to or from the mountains. Early in November he brought his men to this favorite Indian hangout, and somehow got within range of a camp of five hundred people without being discovered—an unusual occurrence in Apache warfare. He went into action at once. The surprised tribesmen fought back as best

14 *Ibid.*, 705.

General Carleton brought the Mescaleros to the Bosque
Redondo.

The agency near Blazer's Mill in the early eighties.

they could, but seemed more interested in getting away than in wiping out the attackers. Those who were left alive did the wisest thing they could have done. They hurriedly left the camp, hiked across the ranges to Fort Stanton, and put themselves under the protection of Kit Carson.[15]

This placed Kit in a position of still further embarrassment. As a soldier he had to obey orders, but as a man he was not one to shoot into a band of frightened people who were asking for quarter—and the Indians knew it. In November he sent five of them to Santa Fé, accompanied by a military escort and Lorenzo Labadie, their agent. Chief Cadete was their spokesman, and the words of his speech as they were rendered into English still pierce the heart after all these years:

"You are stronger than we," he said. "We have fought you so long as we had rifles and powder; but your weapons are better than ours. Give us weapons and turn us loose, and we will fight you again; but we are worn out; we have no more heart; we have no provisions, no means to live; your troops are everywhere; our springs and waterholes are either occupied or overlooked by your young men. You have driven us from our last and best stronghold, and we have no more heart. Do with us as may seem good to you, but do not forget we are men and braves."[16]

The inflexible Carleton did not allow himself to be moved by Cadete's words. His plans were already made, and he refused to discuss any alternative. At that moment a detachment of officers, acting under orders issued on November 4, was in the Pecos country getting ready to pen the Indians up. A new post, to be called Fort Sumner, had been laid out near a favorite camping place of the Apaches known as Bosque Redondo—

[15] *Ibid.*, 703–704.
[16] Cremony, *Life Among the Apaches*, 201.

Round Grove—a patch of cottonwoods in a broad bend of the Pecos River. All the Mescaleros who wished to co-operate were to go there for settlement. They would be fed as long as they behaved to suit the General. Holdouts were to be run down and killed without parley or delay. Cadete could go back and tell his people that when all were gathered at the Bosque, it would be time to talk about a treaty of peace.[17]

Those were the orders, and that was the way it had to be. The Indians did not want to go into captivity. The New Mexicans who had been running cattle along the Pecos for generations did not want to give up their lands. But New Mexico was under martial law and would remain so as long as Carleton could keep it that way. The first wagon train from Fort Union into the mountain country carried orders to transport to their new home all the Mescaleros who had come in. One by one the lesser chiefs and their bands reported to Carson and were sent to join their fellows. By the beginning of March, 1863, over four hundred men, women, and children were drawing rations at the new post. Less than a hundred had fled west to the wilds beyond the Río Grande to join their remote cousins, the Gila Apaches, against whom the soldiers were carrying on another campaign of extermination. By the middle of the summer of 1863, the colony at the Bosque Redondo was operating under full steam.[18] Fields had been laid out, crops had been planted, housing of a sort had been set up, and everybody—most of all the Apaches— hoped that better times were ahead.

Outside the colony the fighting and killing went on. The Californians holding the Río Grande forts and the posts west of the river had many a skirmish, and some of the die-hard Mesca-

---

[17] Sabin, *op. cit.*, II, 705.
[18] Amsden, "The Navajo Exile at Bosque Redondo," *N.M.H.R.*, Vol. VIII (January, 1933), 45 ff.; Reeve, *loc. cit.*, 261 ff.; J. P. Dunn, *The Massacres of the Mountains*, 384–92.

leros were undoubtedly mixed up in the killing and raiding. There were attacks on farmers, freighters, and soldiers. Horses were run off from Fort Stanton. Captain Pfeiffer lost his wife and a servant girl when they were bathing in the hot springs near Fort McRae on June 20, 1863. Private Nicolas Quintana, on his way from Fort Stanton to Santa Fé, was killed a few days later, apparently by burning at the stake.[19] Nobody knew which Indians were to blame, but some of these things happened in Mescalero country. This was one time, however—perhaps the only time in history—when the sins of the few could not be blamed on the many, since the bulk of the tribe had come in and was practically under lock and key at Fort Sumner.

Carleton's scheme was not a new one. Ever since the Americans had set foot in the Southwest, the citizens, the military, and even the officials in Washington had been crying for a reservation system. The Indians were to be moved as far as possible from white settlements and given a permanent location where they could be watched and herded, and where they could become self-supporting farmers on the American plan. Michael Steck had tried it with the Gilas before the outbreak of the war and succeeded rather well. The Mescaleros had also done some planting under his supervision. Now it seemed that the dream was to be realized and made permanent, and there was much rejoicing in official circles. Even the Indians were willing to make the experiment, and they might have worked their problems out successfully if it had not been for the obtuseness and crookedness of the white man.

The first mistake was made when, in September, 1863, the colony on the Pecos was augmented by the first wave of Navajos. They were sent in as the result of a successful campaign by

[19] Estelle Bennett Burton, "Volunteer Soldiers of New Mexico," *Old Santa Fé*, Vol. I (April, 1914), 386–419.

Colonel Carson and his troops. Eventually there were nearly nine thousand of them on the ground, and as far as the Mescaleros were concerned, that was nine thousand too many.

The two groups of Indians did not get along at all. The Mescaleros were disappointed because they had understood that the Bosque was to be entirely theirs; and as the necessary ditch digging, plowing, carpentering, blacksmithing, and wood-cutting went forward, they resented the presence of the Navajos more and more.

The work had to be done, however, and soldiers and Indians alike pitched in and did it. They built a slaughterhouse; they dammed the river and irrigated their crops. They planted trees. They did everything Carleton issued orders about, and Carleton issued orders about everything. Nobody could say that the new settlers did not try, but all their efforts were in vain as the most amazing series of misfortunes and misunderstandings and meannesses began to plague them.

Farming was a perennial failure. Every year something would happen—worms, borers, blight, hail, floods, drought! The Apaches made a crop in 1863. After the Navajos came, not one successful harvest was brought in.

There was sickness and suffering among the Indians, who were now herded together and exposed to the white man's diseases. Even the healthiest complained about what the alkali Pecos water did to their digestions. They lived in shacks and hovels which were uncomfortable in cold weather. They were practically naked most of the time. Sanitary arrangements were nonexistent and probably would not have been used much anyway by men and women to whom such things had never been familiar or necessary. And when influenza or meningitis struck them, the hospital facilities were completely inadequate.

Dr. M. Hillary, an army surgeon, reported on what he

found in 1865: "The building is a regular tumble-down concern; even rain comes through the roof—in fact I may say the place is only fit to keep pigs in. . . . You can see from my report the vast preponderance of syphilis over every other disease, and which will always be the case as long as so many soldiers are around here, because the Indian women have not the slightest idea of virtue, and are bought and sold by their own people like cattle."[20]

The doctor was not talking about the Apaches when he mentioned these matters. Mescalero women were famous for their discreet behavior. John C. Cremony, who spoke their language and knew them as well as any white man ever has, remarked that "Cases of conjugal infidelity are extremely rare among them, and the girls take no ordinary pride in guarding their purity. . . . On the other hand the Navajoes are extremely loose and sensuous."[21]

Bad water, disease, crop failure—and the end was not yet in sight. Just finding wood to cook with was an increasingly serious problem, and before the period was finished, some of the Indians were going as far as eighteen miles for something to burn and carrying it home on their backs.[22]

When rations were issued, the Apaches, though used to all sorts of unlikely foods, were hardly able to eat what was offered. Agent Labadie reported to his superior in 1865 that his Indians were being fed on the meat of cattle that had died from disease.[23]

[20] *Report of the Commissioner of Indian Affairs for 1866*, 150 (M. Hillary, M. R. C. S., Ireland, Bvt. Capt. and Asst. Surgeon, U. S. Army, to Col. Theo. H. Dodd, Fort Sumner, N. M., Sept. 6, 1866).

[21] Cremony, *Life Among the Apaches*, 244. See *Condition of the Indian Tribes*, 339, testimony of Dr. George Gwyther; "Among the Apaches it [syphilis] scarcely exists at all."

[22] Reeve, *loc. cit.*, 24.

[23] *Report of the Commissioner of Indian Affairs for 1865*, 173 (Labadie to Steck, Sept. 30, 1865).

They could have helped to increase their own food supply, but they were not allowed to set foot off the reservation. Five days after the arrival of the first Mescaleros in camp, they were hungry and asked, through Labadie, to be allowed to organize a hunt. Captain Updegraff said no. Captain Cremony said yes—he would get the Indians back in forty-eight hours. Cremony kept his promise, and the hunters returned with eighty-seven antelope. When Carleton heard of it, however, he refused to have any such act repeated, and would not listen to a request that a party be allowed to go out and make mescal. He wrote to Major Smith, commanding at Fort Stanton, "No Mescaleros have a right, even with a pass, to come back from Fort Sumner into their country to make *mescal*. . . . You will kill every Mescalero *man* that can be found without a passport."[24]

When Dr. Steck became Indian agent for New Mexico in 1863, he visited the Bosque Redondo colony and apparently agreed with Labadie that sending out a mescal party or two would solve some of the Mescaleros' food problems. Carleton heard of that, too, and did not forget it. Months after it happened, he wrote to the commanding officer at the Fort: "About one year since, when Dr. Steck, superintendent of Indian affairs for New Mexico, went to the Bosque Redondo, he caused the Apaches to become discontented, by telling them that they could go to their own country to make *mescal*. If the doctor pursues any such course during his present visit, or talks with the Navajoes in any manner to make them unhappy or discontented, he will be required at once to leave the reservation."[25]

And then there was the trouble with the Navajos. It began the moment the first Navajo set foot on what the Apaches had

[24] *Condition of the Indian Tribes,* 109 (Carleton to Maj. Joseph Smith, May 18, 1863).

[25] *Ibid.,* 109 (Carleton to Smith, May 1, 1863).

understood was to be their own private reservation. Fields had
already been laid out and assigned to them. These fields were
taken away and reassignments were made. Labadie complained
about this. "I laid my claim before the commander of the post,
went to the land, and laid out second boundaries. These have
not been respected. The Navajoes are tilling the ground on the
part of the land laid out for the Apaches. By which causes the
Apaches are oppressed and annoyed, and they are not content
to live together with the Navajoes."[26]

When the crops ripened, according to Labadie, the Navajos
stole what the Apaches had raised:

> During the summer many difficulties have arisen between the
> two tribes—the Apaches in defence of their fields and gardens,
> and the Navajoes in endeavoring to destroy them. The com-
> mander of the post made use of every means to prevent these
> abuses, but without effect. They fought; Navajoes were con-
> fined in the guard house; shots were sometimes fired at them by
> the guard, but all could not prevent them from stealing from the
> Apaches; in fact, their fields were, in some cases, completely de-
> stroyed; and to make matters still worse, as the corn commenced
> maturing, a worm destroyed great quantities, and between
> Navajo Indians and the insect, they left but little to harvest.[27]

When the Apaches had a chance to fight a band of Navajos,
they went at them tooth and nail; and from time to time such
chances occurred. Plenty of Navajos were off the reservation,
and they staged some very impressive raids in the Pecos country. The first big one came in November, 1863, when three hundred warriors passed close to the Fort with twenty thousand
sheep, twelve Mexican captives, and miscellaneous plunder.

[26] *Report of the Commissioner of Indian Affairs for 1864*, 205 (Labadie to
Steck, May 18, 1864).

[27] *Ibid.*, 203 (Labadie to Steck, Oct. 22, 1864).

Captain Cremony and Lorenzo Labadie led twenty soldiers and forty Apaches in pursuit, but the raiders kept ahead for sixty miles and got away when the exhausted pursuers turned back.[28]

A month later the renegades came again and tried to get out of the country with another thousand sheep, but this time the Apaches were ready. Under Labadie's leadership twenty of them got on the trail, caught up within twenty-six miles, and went to work. After four hours of furious fighting, the Navajos fled, leaving twelve of their number dead on the field. One Mescalero was mortally hurt.

An army detachment, sent out to take part in the battle, arrived too late to do any good. General Carleton was nevertheless jubilant about the affair, praised the "zeal and alacrity" of the troops who could not get there on time, and called the attention of the adjutant general in Washington to "the conduct of Mr. Lorenzo Labadie, Indian agent, and to the gallant chaplain of Fort Sumner, the Reverend Mr. Fialon. These two gentlemen, at the head of thirty Mescalero Apache Indians from the reservation at Fort Sumner, (Apaches who, one year ago, were our mortal enemies,) did most all the work, as they were fortunate in being the first to encounter the Navajoes."[29]

Neither the Apaches nor the Navajos had had enough after that one skirmish. Less than a month after their defeat, the Navajos came back for more of the same. Labadie reported what happened:

> On the 4th day of January of this year the Navajoes again returned to avenge their loss. Taking advantage of the darkness of the night, they approached within one mile of the post, and drove off sixty horses belonging to the Apaches, together with

[28] *Ibid.*, 209 (Labadie to Steck, Nov. 25, 1863).
[29] *Condition of the Indian Tribes*, 151 (Carleton to Brig. Gen. Lorenzo Thomas, Dec. 23, 1863).

108

others belonging to the military department. At five o'clock in the morning, in a cold storm, almost insupportable, I again started with sixty Apaches, accompanied by Lieutenant Newbold and fifteen mounted men. After following the trail for nine miles we overtook the enemy, evidently awaiting our arrival, formed in a small valley to give us battle.

We immediately attacked them, and fought from eleven o'clock until sundown, retaking all the stolen stock, except twenty-seven horses. A part of those not recovered had taken a different direction.

There were one hundred and twenty Navajoes in the fight, fifty-two of whom were left dead on the field, and others escaped wounded under cover of the darkness. The Mescaleros are ever prompt to serve the government, and when thus employed are cheerful and obedient as regular soldiers.

In my opinion no tribe of Indians in the Territory have conducted themselves with so much propriety as those now upon the reservation, being peaceful and obedient to all the rules established for their control and government.[30]

General Carleton could not work up much enthusiasm for the Mescaleros. He remarked sourly in a letter to the Adjutant General, "The new superintendent of Indian affairs, Dr. Steck, who has gone to Washington, seems to have a confidence in the integrity of that noted band of murderers which is not entertained by myself."[31]

Yet even Carleton had moments when his frost-bitten heart melted slightly at the suffering and distress of his charges. When the Navajos came in, he noted that "Many of the Navajo women and children which we captured are quite naked, and the children, especially, suffer from extreme cold. . . . It is hard to see them perish. Will the War Department authorize the quarter-

[30] *Report of the Commissioner of Indian Affairs for 1864,* 202 (Labadie to Steck, Oct. 22, 1864).

[31] *Condition of the Indian Tribes,* 143 (Carleton to Thomas, Nov. 15, 1863).

master department here to buy some cheap blankets for the destitute children, and to issue condemned clothing to these Indians until they can get a start at the Bosque Redondo towards clothing themselves?"[32]

The fact is that this stern New Englander was making a one-man crusade out of his Indian project. He called it "this great work,"[33] and made himself believe that "The Indians on the reservation are the happiest people I have ever seen."[34] The plan had to succeed. He would not have it any other way; and his indignation knew no bounds when anyone disagreed with him, or questioned his ideas.

He took the most meticulous care of every detail and issued the most minute instructions about how things were to be done. He had his adjutant send down a "small sack of apricot seeds, which the general desires to have planted at once."[35] He sent to St. Louis for a thousand-pound bell "to be used as a signal for hours of labor and repose for the Indians."[36] The cost was to be defrayed out of what the Indians earned by selling straw and fodder to the cavalry. He worried about putting Indian prisoners to work at picking up scattered grain to be used for seed in the fields where the crops were ruined year after year.[37]

"You must pardon me for suggesting all these details," he wrote, after sending a particularly picayunish batch of instructions about house building, "but my anxiety is so great to make this powerful nation, which has surrendered to us, as happy and as well cared-for as possible under all the adverse circumstances which encompass us, that every idea looking to this end which

---

[32] *Ibid.*, 226 (Carleton to Thomas, Dec. 12, 1863).
[33] *Ibid.*, 175 (Carleton to Maj. Henry D. Wallen, April 9, 1864).
[34] *Ibid.*, 192 (Carleton to J. P. Usher, Aug. 27, 1864).
[35] *Ibid.*, 219 (Ben C. Cutler to Maj. Wm. McCleave, March 10, 1865).
[36] *Ibid.*, 230 (Carleton to McCleave, July 24, 1865).
[37] *Ibid.*, 233 (Carleton to McCleave, Aug. 9, 1865).

comes into my mind I send to you, fully believing that you will enter into the spirit which animates me for their good."[38]

There was nothing he did not think of, and everything he thought of he fought and pleaded for with all his strength and authority. The Indians must have religious training, and he pulled wires until he succeeded in making Fort Sumner a chaplain post. Then a letter went off to Bishop Lamy: "I beg respectfully that you will name some clergyman of energy, and all those qualities of patience, good temper, assiduity and interest in the subject so necessary in one who is wanted to teach the Indian children now at Fort Sumner, not only the rudiments of an education, but the principles and truths of Christianity."[39]

The Most Reverend Bishop replied that he would send Father Fialon, who was soon to return from France.[40]

A little later, Carleton was wrestling with the Secretary of the Interior over the need for a school building. He had no reply and returned to the attack in 1865, pointing out that there were three thousand children on the reservation, growing up a little too naturally to suit him. "The education of these children is the fundamental idea on which must rest all our hopes of making the Navajoes a civilized and Christian people."[41]

It is an insoluble question whether Carleton's zeal came from his determination to have his own way or from his real concern for the Indians. His letters show a growing tendency to think of the Navajos and Apaches as suffering mortals rather than as hostile savages, and he could actually plead with his superiors in Washington, "For pity's sake, if not moved by any

[38] *Ibid.*, 208 (Carleton to Brig. Gen. Marcellus M. Crocker, Oct. 31, 1864).

[39] *Ibid.*, 112 (Carleton to Lamy, June 12, 1863).

[40] *Ibid.*, 116–17 (Carleton to Capt. Joseph Updegraff, June 23, 1863).

[41] *Ibid.*, 224 (Carleton to the Secretary of the Interior, March 30, 1865). Aurora Hunt, in her life of *Major James Henry Carleton*, 285, says schoolrooms were built in 1864, and some of the Indian children were induced to attend.

other consideration, let us, as a great nation, for once treat the Indian as he deserves to be treated. It is due to ourselves, as well as to them, that this be done. . . . They have fought us gallantly for years . . . they threw down their arms, and, as brave men entitled to our admiration and respect, have come to us with confidence in our magnanimity."[42]

Just three days after these words were written, when Dr. Steck suggested that the Navajos be allowed to go back to their own country, he flared up and went on the other tack. "This was positively forbidden by myself. . . . The Navajoes should never leave the Bosque, and never shall if I can prevent it." What the Indians wanted was of no consequence, he insisted. "They have only to await our decisions."[43]

When, in 1865, Ganado Blanco and Barboncito, Navajo chiefs, with a dozen lesser Indians, did try to leave the reservation, Carleton ordered everybody into the field, enlisted civilian troops, and became as excited as if the whole tribe had risen in arms.[44]

No one could advise or remonstrate with a man who was as touchy and peremptory as General Carleton, and the Indian Service was at loggerheads with him almost from the first. Superintendent Collins, a brave and efficient man, kept the peace by giving the General his own way (Carleton would have called it co-operation). Collins was out in 1863, however, and when Dr. Michael Steck took charge, the temperature went up immediately. Steck had been working with Indians for a long time, and had a mind and a tongue of his own. He disagreed with Carleton on basic issues, and said what he thought.

In the first place, he never liked the Bosque Redondo idea,

[42] *Condition of the Indian Tribes,* 166–68 (Carleton to Thomas, March 12, 1864).

[43] *Ibid.,* 168–69 (Carleton to Thomas, March 19, 1864).

[44] *Ibid.,* 227–28 (Carleton to Maj. Wm. H. Lewis, June 19, 1865).

and he liked it less when Carleton moved the Navajos in. Steck felt that there was not enough farm land to support nine thousand people at the Bosque, and he knew about the hostility between the Apaches and the Navajos. It seemed to him that if Carleton wanted to set this thing up, he had better be the one to keep it going. The Indian Bureau gave him little money to spend, and he saw no reason why he should feed the Indians, although Carleton insisted that the army was not there to run an Indian commissary. They sent critical letters to Washington abusing each other, and some stiff communications went back and forth between them.

The man caught in the middle was Agent Labadie, who talked in vain about "the sorrowful situation of my Indians," and "the good conduct observed by them during the time they have lived on the reservation."[45] Word came to Carleton that there was something crooked going on in the matter of supplying beef to the prisoners. Labadie was supposed to be in on it, with a Captain Morton of the post garrison. Morton was brought before a court martial and cleared, but Labadie did not fare so well.

> I felt it to be my duty to order that Mr. Lorenzo Labadie, Indian agent for the Mescalero Apaches, be required to leave the reservation at the Bosque Redondo. He has, without a doubt, been engaged in buying cattle which had been delivered at Fort Sumner for subsistence for Indians. Captain Morton was not found guilty on the specification charging him with sending government cattle to Labadie's herd; but in General Crocker's opinion, as well as in my own, there can hardly be a doubt that Labadie and he were concerned in defrauding the government. ... I beg, respectfully, that the Secretary of War ask of the Secretary of the Interior that Mr. Labadie be removed as Indian agent. He is not fit to hold office under the government.[46]

[45] *Report of the Commissioner of Indian Affairs for 1864*, 205 (Labadie to Steck, May 18, 1864).

[46] *Condition of the Indian Tribes*, 223 (Carleton to the Assistant Adjutant General, March 22, 1865).

113

Labadie was escorted from the post in March, 1865, and moved the agency to his ranch just north of the military reservation. "My departure," he said, "caused great excitement and sorrow among both the Navajos and Apaches, both tribes having placed in me from the beginning the love, confidence and respect that an agent seldom obtains among the Indians."[47] He insisted that his removal was the result of his protest about the kind of meat the Indians were getting.[48] One would like to believe him. His concern for his "poor Indians" and his confidence in their good qualities should have come from the soul of an honest man.[49]

All through the war years, Steck, Labadie, and the other officials had made no headway against the all-powerful Carleton and his troops. Their suggestions, when they felt called upon to make any, had been ignored or rejected. Unless their conduct pleased the General, they were in danger of being run out of the very establishments which they were supposed to manage.

Such a situation was a public scandal and could not long endure. By 1864, Carleton had accumulated an impressive roll of enemies who were clamoring for his removal. They pointed out that the state was no longer in the theater of war and that martial law had long since ceased to be necessary. Judge Joseph G. Knapp of Mesilla bitterly resented Carleton's demand that all citizens who had to travel must do so under a military pass. As a judge, Knapp felt that his functions must go on whether the army approved or not, and he took his complaints as far as Washington. Dr. Steck likewise protested to the highest

---

[47] *Report of the Commissioner of Indian Affairs for 1865*, 173 (Labadie to Delgado, Sept. 30, 1865).

[48] *Ibid.*

[49] Labadie was discharged with a clear record the following year, when there were no longer any Apaches at the fort (Reeve, *loc. cit.*, 266), but was acting as agent in 1868 (*Report of the Commissioner of Indian Affairs for 1869*, 244–45).

114

officials he could get to listen. All he got out of it was a request for his resignation.[50]

Meanwhile the New Mexican press had taken up the quarrel, with the Santa Fé *New Mexican* leading the cry against military government. Carleton seldom had trouble in ignoring criticism. In his view, people who disagreed with him were either uninformed or crazy. But even his thick skin was penetrated at last, and on December 16, 1864, he journeyed down to Las Cruces to make a speech defending his actions—a speech which he had printed as a pamphlet and distributed where it would do the most good. Judge Knapp charged into the fray with a flaming answer to Carleton's arguments, and New Mexico soon found itself up in arms, either for or against Carleton—mostly against. The state legislature memorialized the President of the United States asking for a more capable officer; and some of the California troopers, now out of uniform, made public expression of their ill will toward their former commander.[51]

Carleton stood firm through it all and held the line for two more years (he was relieved on September 19, 1866), but his empire crumbled steadily. The Mescaleros at Bosque Redondo began giving up the long contention with hunger and despair. In March, 1864, Chief Ojo Blanco went out with forty-two of his people. At the urging of Lorenzo Labadie he came back after several months' absence, but his fellows slipped away in increasing numbers. A census taken a few months later showed nine hundred Apaches and Navajos missing from camp. Carleton felt obliged to set up a more rigorous system of passports and renew his order that any male Indian caught off the reservation would be killed.[52]

[50] Keleher, *op. cit.*, Chs. 6 and 7, tells the whole story in detail. Hunt, *op. cit.*, 248–52, adds other details.

[51] Keleher, *op. cit.*, 444–58.

[52] Reeve, *loc. cit.*, 265.

The exodus continued nevertheless, and blood flowed once more in the Mescalero country. A number of small raids occurred in 1864: two horses run off from a farm on the Bonito in May,[53] a wagon train cleaned out below the Gallinas Mountains in August,[54] and a party of soldiers ambushed in the Sacramentos toward the end of the same month.[55]

A group of Navajos caught one of these bands at work and tried to revenge themselves for their two previous defeats at the hands of Labadie's warriors. Early in August, 1864, the Navajo chief Delgadito Chiquito discovered the Apache raiders near Alamogordo with much contraband livestock. What Delgadito Chiquito was doing away from the reservation we do not know, but he sent off a messenger to Fort Stanton for soldiers and got ready to fight.

When the soldiers arrived, the fight was over and the Navajos had not triumphed. One of their men was dead, and three were wounded. The Mescaleros had left five hundred sheep and thirteen burros, but every warrior got safely away.[56]

The misery which brought these things to pass finally came to the knowledge of the national Congress. In June, 1864, $100,-000 was appropriated for food, clothing, and implements to be used at Bosque Redondo. Though it came late in the day, this measure might have saved the situation had it been honestly and efficiently administered. But politicians found opportunity for graft in the project. There was much delay, and when the goods finally arrived on the Pecos just before Christmas, the Indians had been cheated again.

Dr. George Gwyther, who was there, was still indignant when he wrote about his experiences in 1873: "No language can

[53] *War of the Rebellion Records,* Ser. I, Vol. XLVIII, Part I, 903.
[54] *Ibid.,* 905.
[55] *Ibid.,* 906.
[56] *Ibid.,* 905.

do justice," he said, "to the ingenuity with which some parties had managed to relieve their stores of a large quantity of rusty, old-fashioned, unserviceable, and unsalable plows, soft-iron spades, rakes and hoes, knives and hatchets, coarse, gaudy calicoes and muslins, and thin, flimsy, shoddy clothes and blankets. I particularly recollect the blankets, because I took one pair of them to the scales, and by accurate weight found they weighed 4½ pounds; and as a single government blanket, such as is issued to troops, weighs 5½ pounds, and costs $4.50, the reader can judge of the honesty of an invoice which charged $22 per pair for such articles."[57]

The odor of scandal was so strong in New Mexico that Congress was forced to take still further action. In January, 1865, a joint resolution was proposed, setting up a full-scale investigation of the condition of the Indian tribes. A subcommittee journeyed to Santa Fé and began hearings on July 4, under the chairmanship of Senator James R. Doolittle of Wisconsin. Carleton stole a march on the members on that date by bringing military government to an end in New Mexico, but he could not cover up or explain the starvation and misery and mismanagement which had been the lot of his Indian wards since 1863. In fact, he did not try. He simply fell back on his original contentions: that the Indians had caused much trouble; that something had to be done about them; and that the army was the agency best qualified to take care of the problem. If there had to be an Indian Bureau, let it take orders from the War Department.

Other witnesses filled in the picture—and it was a dark one —but not all the testimony was anti-Carleton. Kit Carson himself, addressing the committee by letter, agreed with Carleton's view of the situation. And some of the experts contradicted each

[57] Gwyther, "An Indian Reservation," *The Overland Monthly*, Vol. X (February, 1873), 129.

other completely. One man swore, for instance, that the Bosque Redondo Reservation was unhealthy and injurious to man and beast.[58] Another (an army doctor) said he regarded it as "the healthiest place I ever lived in."[59]

So it went. And when the testimony was all in, the committee packed up its papers, went back to Washington, and filed its report, while the Mescaleros stood around and looked at their blighted, ruined fields day after monotonous day with nothing to do and nothing to look forward to. They had long talks with Captain Cremony about the things the white man said were true—that the world was round, for instance—and Cremony did his best to satisfy their curiosity.[60] But they were at the end of their endurance. It began to be obvious that death was much better than decaying in this vile, unbeautiful place, surrounded by enemies and pushed about by soldiers.

Everything came to a head in the summer of 1865. It was the worst year New Mexico had known for generations. Frost, hail, blight, drought, destroying insects—all seemed reserved for this particular time. Supplies had long since run out, and on account of wartime conditions in the East, none could be obtained. Carleton ordered the bread ration cut to three-quarters of a pound per day, and the meat ration to one pound per head. "Every ounce of food should be carefully husbanded," he cautioned. "Famine literally stares the people of the Territory in the face this year."[61]

A little later he was forced to reduce the ration still farther. Human beings could take only so much of this and the Indians grew very restless. Yet for some time the head men counseled

---

[58] *Condition of the Indian Tribes,* 335 (testimony of Percy Ayers).
[59] *Ibid.,* 339 (testimony of Dr. George Gwyther).
[60] Cremony, "The Apache Race," *loc. cit.,* 207.
[61] *Condition of the Indian Tribes,* 229 (Carleton to McCleave, July 18, 1865).

patience. If a few left the reservation, they would be followed and killed. If everybody left at once, the whole tribe might get away.

In secret councils the plan evolved. No white man knew anything about it, and no white man knows anything about it yet. Just before winter set in, in 1865, they were ready. On the third of November, during the night, every Apache who could travel arose and vanished. In the morning only the sick and the crippled were left,[62] and within a few days they vanished also.

They were not pursued. How could the soldiers chase a whole tribe at once, and in all directions?

The Navajos now saw how things were going and planted less and less in the years that followed. They were sent home in June, 1868, leaving the bare bones of the Bosque Redondo community as a monument to the stupidity and greed of the white man.

[62] Only nine were left (*Report of the Commissioner of Indian Affairs for 1866,* 149).

Chapter VII

BACK TO THE WILDS

The Mescaleros Choose Freedom

WHEN THE MESCALEROS left the Bosque Redondo en masse, they well knew what the consequences would be and were willing to pay the price. There would be no rest, no peace, and no help from anybody. Nevertheless, any fate was better than stagnation and captivity. Death was far better. They could not foresee what was in store for them, but one thing they were certain of: they would never come back to the Bosque.

Cadete is said to have told the military authorities that his people were leaving (he did not say when) and to have left word that they would come in whenever a reservation should be set up for them, where they could live in some sort of endurable circumstances. Having had much experience with the penuriousness, indecision, and corruption of the white man's government, he knew well that he might have to wait a long time, but he left the door open.[1]

They used the old Apache trick of scattering to confuse pursuers. Some headed for their ancestral home in the Sierra Blanca—others for the Mimbres country to the west or the Davis

---

[1] *Report of the Commissioner of Indian Affairs for 1871*, 400 (A. J. Curtis to Gen. John Pope, Sept. 12, 1871).

Mountains to the south where their cousins were lying in wait along the San Antonio road.[2] A large portion of the tribe forded the Pecos and struck out into the pathless immensity of the Texas plains—straight into the country of their hereditary enemies, the Comanches. There is evidence to show that some of them actually joined Comanche war parties,[3] but what happened to the bulk of the tribe—where they camped, how they lived, whether they came back to the Sierra Blanca—these are matters that do not appear in the record, because there was no record in which they could appear. For all practical purposes, the Mescaleros vanished for something like seven years. They were always being blamed for depredations in their old country, but if the depredators were Mescaleros in fact, they must have been splinter groups far removed from the main body of the tribe.

Around the settlements, along the wagon roads, and throughout the desert country, there was sporadic raiding and killing. Only one man in New Mexico could be sure no Indians would come near him. This was Labadie, ejected from the Bosque Redondo in 1865, before the Mescalero exodus, but back again at his futile job after a brief stay with the Jicarillas at the Cimarron Agency. He described his situation in 1868: "This agency is located at Agua Negra, New Mexico, and the Indians comprising it are all Mescalero Apaches, numbering about 525. They never visit the agency and have been at war with the government since November 3, 1865. . . . No appropriations have been made for them for several years, and consequently this superintendency has been unable to do anything with them."[4]

[2] William Edgar was besieged for four days in Limpia Canyon in 1866 by a party of Southern Mescaleros, Lipans, and Indians from the Bosque Redondo (see *Outing*, Vol. XXXIX (January, 1902), 381–83).

[3] Carl Coke Rister, *Fort Griffin*, 109, 183, 187, mentions Comanches and Mescaleros together.

[4] *Report of the Commissioner of Indian Affairs for 1868*, 160 (N. M. Davis to N. G. Taylor, Sept. 15, 1868, quoting Labadie).

The next year (Labadie's last, before leaving the Indian Service for good) saw no change. "I have the honor to inform you that during the time that has elapsed since my last annual report, the Mescalero Apaches under my charge have not visited this agency," Labadie said, and he went on to plead, one last time, for some sort of intelligent approach to the Apache problem. "For a long time past my recommendations have been very frequent, urging the department to take some measures to establish these Indians upon reservations in their own country."[5]

Labadie's was the voice of one crying in the wilderness. It would be years before the Mescaleros would have a place that belonged to them, more years before they would be delivered from hunger and the fear of sudden death, and decades before they could hold up their heads and face the future with hope. There was an almost impassable gulf between them and the white men who controlled their destinies. Hardly a one, from the commissioner in Washington to the employees at the agency, had any conception of the traditional pattern of the Indian's life and thought—or any patience with it. He was a filthy, treacherous savage who had to become civilized overnight or take the consequences. If Washington had provided understanding, or funds, or even a consistent policy, some progress might have been made. But for years there was no money available, except to pay soldiers for shooting Indians; no real interest in helping them to find their own way; no long-range program of any kind.

Preyed on by crooked traders and brutal settlers, exasperated by broken promises and mystifying changes in policy, hungry, and resentful—it is no wonder that the Indians struck back in ways that were familiar to them. Yet even in the worst times, the great leaders of the Mescaleros tried to endure their sufferings with patience and keep their people out of trouble.

[5] *Ibid.* (Labadie to E. S. Parker, June 30, 1869).

Chief Santana—he was old Chief Santana in 1867—was one who was willing to try. He had tried in 1850 (his name was on the "Proposition for Peace" which came to the governor in that year),[6] and probably kept on trying as long as there was any hope of success. When all efforts proved useless, and the white soldiers invaded his homeland in the winter campaign of 1855, he took up his weapons, as any man would have done, and fought as hard as he knew how. The army officers knew his caliber, and they betrayed feelings of considerable relief when a report came in that he had been killed in the skirmishing. The report was, of course, erroneous.

Santana had been a leader of great authority among the Mescaleros since about 1830, but his importance increased considerably after the death of Barranquito in 1857. He kept himself and his people as far away from the white man as possible, however, and never achieved, or cared for, any great renown outside the tribe.

He may have gone to the Bosque Redondo with the rest of the Mescaleros, but his name does not appear in the reports and records, unless he was one of the chiefs Captain Cremony mentions by their Indian titles. (These matters are hard to learn about now, because after an Apache dies, his fellow tribesmen think it is bad luck to mention his name—a fact which interferes with the transmission of history from one generation to another.) He may never have gone to the Bosque at all. In 1867, two years after the tribe broke out and headed for the wilds, he was certainly camping far back in the valleys of the Sierra Blanca, keeping away from everybody.

It was at this moment, when Santana had undoubtedly given up all hope of better relations between red men and white, that his opportunity finally came. It arrived in the person of

[6] "Proposition for Peace," *loc. cit.*

123

Dr. J. H. Blazer, who was as great a man in his way as Santana himself. The relationship which grew up between these two valiant gentlemen is evidence enough that friendship and forbearance could have flourished in *Apachería,* instead of bloodshed and enmity.

Blazer was not a native of the Southwest, and he never saw an Indian until he was almost forty years old. Born in Pennsylvania in 1828, he grew up on an Illinois farm, studied dentistry in St. Louis, and joined an Iowa cavalry regiment when the Civil War came along. Severely wounded, he was let out for disability and became sutler to his regiment. In 1865, he was discharged at Shreveport. The supply service which he had operated in his capacity of sutler left him with considerable equipment on hand, including a train of four six-mule wagons. He arranged to buy the whole train, packed it with his leftover supplies, and set off on a trading trip to El Paso. He got through safely, disposed of his load at a profit, and in the spring of 1867, was on the road again, this time with a cargo of Chihuahua corn for the military posts in New Mexico.

What he saw on that expedition revived the dream which haunts every born frontiersman—the dream of settling down in some favored spot still untouched by civilization. One place in particular caught his eye: a sawmill in the heart of the Mescalero country on the Tularosa river, strategically located beside the road from the Pecos to the Río Grande—a main wilderness highway.

The mill had been in operation for a long time and had supplied timber for Spanish and Mexican settlements throughout the region. Formerly known simply as *La Maquina*—"The Machine"—this place now became Blazer's Mill, where settlers and soldiers could get pine lumber sawed out of the native timber, just as the padres had obtained their doors and vigas a century before. The little settlement had folded up when the soldiers left in 1861, but Blazer found a couple of partners, looked up the owners, and bought the whole enterprise. Eventually he became sole proprietor—the only one of several owners and operators who was able to make the business pay.

He was the friend of everybody in the Territory—a man to be trusted and confided in. He never took sides in the feuds and fights which plagued his neighbors, but kept open house for travelers, ran the post office, acted as forage agent for the military, and was a licensed Indian trader. A big, blue-eyed, solidly built man who talked slowly and spoke the truth—he was one of the very few white men whom the Mescaleros trusted and accepted as their friend.

As the doctor passed the story on to his children,[7] he met Santana soon after he settled at the mill. Word came to the chief at his hideaway somewhere back in the mountains that a strange white man had settled at *La Maquina*—a different sort of white man—one whom everybody respected. Santana decided that he wanted to know more about this phenomenon, but he did not go himself to find out. He sent one of his women to visit the mill and bring back a report. When she returned, he questioned her minutely about Blazer.

"He is as tall as you," she told him, "and as heavy, and he looks old, for his hair and beard are white, but he is not old for his eyes are not old and his face is not old where there is no beard, and he moves quick and easy like a young man. He talks slow but he thinks fast and the other men think he is very wise.

[7] A. N. Blazer, the Doctor's son, lived and died on the reservation. He learned Apache, had long talks with the old men of the tribe, and was anxious that the facts should be preserved. Several of his articles were printed, and he left behind him when he died a book-length manuscript called "Santana, the Last Chief of the Mescaleros" (in the files of the Mescalero Indian Agency). See also his "Blazer's Mill," *New Mexico*, Vol. VI (January, 1938), 20, 48–49.

His legs and his arms are long and his body is short, so that when he sits down he looks short and when he stands up he looks tall."

"But does he talk straight?"

"Yes, I think he talks with one tongue."[8]

Santana determined to go and see the Doctor himself, and so they met. Blazer was impressed by the chief, who was unusually large for an Apache, well muscled, with a broad, calm face and great dignity of manner. Santana was equally impressed, and from that time on they were friends. Before long the other tribal leaders came to trust and depend on Blazer almost as much as Santana did.

The three most important men among the Mescaleros at this time were Santana, Cadete, and Roman—all sons or nephews of the irascible old Barranquito, who had died in 1857. Cadete is mentioned as Barranquito's son and successor by commentators in that year. The others may have been his half-brothers or cousins. (In Apache kinship terminology all cousins are brothers.)[9]

Each one of the three left his mark on the pages of history. Santana may have been the most powerful of the three, but, as we have seen, he avoided the spotlight. It was Cadete who had most to do with the whites, and he was regarded by them as the real leader of the tribe. He was popular and sociable among his own people (he is said to have had seven wives) and had a gift for diplomacy and negotiation. Undoubtedly he was subtle and shrewd. Cremony says that "he was not, so far as personal bravery goes, the leading warrior of his band; but he was the most dexterous thief."[10] He was also an Indian philosopher, and it was he who gave Cremony the conversation-stopping answer,

---

[8] Blazer, Santana, *loc. cit.*, 36.

[9] A. N. Blazer says the men were half-brothers; Percy Bigmouth believes they were cousins.

[10] Cremony, *Life Among the Apaches*, 43.

quoted in the introduction to this book, explaining why Indian children should not attend white schools.

Roman, the third member of the ruling group, is heard of occasionally in news stories and dispatches of the post–Civil War period. He was apparently a good run-of-the-mill minor chief, but not in the same class with Santana and Cadete.

All three of these leaders, it would seem, were willing and perhaps anxious to get along with the Americans, but there were ambitious and hot-headed Apaches who would not stay in line. More and more white men were filtering into the country—prospectors, trappers, outlaws, and travelers of various kinds. It was pleasant and profitable for renegade tribesmen to murder them or chase them out. In time, however, the raiders began to set their sights higher, and in the spring of 1868 they began a series of bigger raids in the Tularosa region. A war party swept through the country on March 11, killing eleven men and two women and running off two thousand sheep and some other stock. A cavalry detachment took three days to get organized, then set off in pursuit and followed the trail to the Guadalupe Mountains. The soldiers never saw an Indian, of course.[11] A month later came the Round Mountain fight, which may have saved the little town of Tularosa from destruction.

On the flood plain a mile from the mouth of Tularosa Canyon, this small Mexican community had struck root. The first settlers had come in 1861, when the *placita* of Colorado on the Río Grande above Las Cruces was swept away by a flood. These refugees, with some other Mexican families, organized at Mesilla and moved a colony into the Mescalero domain. The rich soil and plentiful water supply seemed worth the risk to the Durans, the Carillos, and the other families. Their first settlement close up against the foothills was too vulnerable to Indian

[11] *Record of Engagements with Hostile Indians*, 7.

attack, and in 1862 they moved to the present site of Tularosa.[12]

Sometimes they paid in blood for their boldness, but they hung on. For twenty years they posted sentries while they worked in their fields and orchards, and men carried their guns as they plowed. The Indians, who were more curious than hostile, pestered them constantly. One corpulent brave tried to crawl through a window one time to assist some of the women with their bread-making. He got a can of hot lard in his face, and his screams scared off all the Apaches within hearing.[13]

On April 17, 1868, a four-mule team with a wagonload of supplies came down from Fort Stanton, on the way to Fort Selden in the Río Grande valley. Six men under Sergeant Glass rode as escort. Five miles from Tularosa the soldiers turned back, thinking the wagon was out of danger. Near an isolated peak called Round Mountain, ten miles up the canyon from the town, they ran into a party of Indians and a fight started.[14] One soldier went back to Tularosa for help. The others took cover in an old fortification a mile west of the peak and held out in the hope that reinforcements would soon come.

The Mexicans did not let them down. Twenty-six of them arrived on the run, and the fighting went on for several hours around the old fort. Johnny Patton, a veteran of this encounter, used to come back to Mescalero in the summer time (he spent his winters in an Old Soldiers' Home in California) and talk about the old days. He said that the Mexicans brought their horses into the enclosure, threw them, and tied them to keep them out of harm's way. The Apaches shot their arrows high so that they would fall inside the walls, and they killed every last

[12] "Tularosa," *Río Grande Republican*, June 2, 1888; Nov. 16, 1889.
[13] Jane Clayton, Tularosa (in the files of Tularosa High School).
[14] Meadows, "The Round Mountain Fight," Alamogordo *News*, Jan. 30, 1936. Meadows thought Cadete was the Indian leader. The *Río Grande Republican*, June 17, 1882, gave San Juan credit for leading the tribesmen.

animal. Only one man was hurt, however. His name was Nieves, and, as the skinniest man in the crowd, he should have suffered no damage, but an arrow went through his wrist.

When the fighting was at its height, a huge old Apache, armed only with a spear, jumped up on the wall and probably would have carried the fight to the besieged had he not absorbed several ounces of lead and lost his scalp to the defenders. Nobody could imagine why an Apache would do such a foolhardy thing. Perhaps he meant to inspire his fellow warriors to make a supreme effort.

Finally the men in the fort began to need water, and during a lull in the fighting a sixteen-year-old boy wormed his way down to the Tularosa River, only a few yards away. The Indians did not see him leave, but did catch sight of him as he hurried back up the hill to rejoin his friends. They apparently thought he was the advance guard of reinforcements. There was a brief flurry of gesture and debate; then it was all over. The Indians were gone. The Mexicans went home fully convinced that they had saved their town from an all-out attack.

The Apaches themselves tell an entirely different story. It starts with a woman named Hah-nan-guh (Clarence Enjadi is her grandson). She was a medicine woman, in close touch with the supernatural. Before this trouble came, she had a dream in which she was told to go to a cave in the mountains. For four days she went. In the cave she saw painted figures dancing—the Mountain Spirits. On the second day she took some people with her and told them to wait at the mouth of the cave—maybe someone would come to them as a sign. While they waited, a bear came by, very close to them. One of the men picked up a rock to throw at him. The rest told him not to do it, but he threw the rock anyway and it hit the bear. The animal turned around, looked at him, and left. When Hah-nan-guh came out, she asked

129

if they had seen anybody. They told her about the bear. She said to them, "That was the person who was coming to you for a sign."

This was a bad beginning for whatever was to happen, but the woman continued to go to the cave, washing herself and combing her hair beforehand and putting on perfume from a plant that she knew about. They mixed this perfume with marrow from deer bones, and the scent lasted a long time. On the fourth day she came out covered with yellow pollen; she bore a message from the Mountain Spirits. It was the will of the supernaturals that they should make peace. If they would do just as she said, everything would be good. They were to take a dancer and two singers and go to Tularosa. There would be four shots fired at them, and if they did not get scared and run, it would all come out all right. The man who had thrown the stone at the bear must take no part in the proceedings, or it would be very bad for him.

They went down the valley and came to Tularosa. They were fired on, as prophesied, but they stood their ground—all but the dancer. He got scared and ran. It was no use going on after that, so they began the return journey. That was when they ran into the wagons. The soldiers shot at them and took refuge in the fort. The Apaches all started hurrying away, but one of their number fell, and was dragged inside the walls. When they stopped to see who was missing, it turned out to be the man who had thrown the stone at the bear. There was no fight; it was all a mistake about their being hostile.[15]

Whatever the facts of this locally famous battle, the Mexicans thought they had won it and marched triumphantly back to their homes. There was a big dance in town that night, with the scalp of the dead Mescalero figuring prominently in the fes-

[15] Percy Bigmouth, July 28, 1956.

tivities. The more sober citizens decided that, in gratitude for their deliverance, they ought to build a church.[16] The chapel beside the main street of Tularosa today, set back among lush fruit trees and shrubs, was begun that same year, and the names of the Indian fighters are recalled to the memory of the worshipers by an inscription attached to the rear wall.

The band involved in the Round Mountain fight numbered perhaps two hundred men, women, and children. The bulk of the tribe under Cadete were in all probability far out on the buffalo plains, from which they returned three years later.

The raiders were back at work within a month. Early in May they ambushed a wagon train at the San Agustín Pass over the Organ Range, but were unsuccessful. They killed only two soldiers and lost five of their own number. In August they tried it once more at the same place, engaging a troop of cavalry in a fight which was not reported in detail.[17]

Three times in the fall of 1869, the troops were out after hostile bands. Men were killed and wounded on both sides, but most of the time the Indians got away with their spoils.[18]

Some of the mischief was done by Comanches. A war party of this tribe came through the country in December, 1869, and burned Blazer's Mill. The attack came early in the morning when the men were all near the house, and nobody was killed. Blazer's livestock was driven off, however, and he had to build a new mill.[19]

In the fall of 1870, the renegade Apaches were back on the job. There were raids in June, in October, and in November[20]—with detachments pursuing the Indians into the Guadalupe Mountains, according to what was becoming a familiar pattern, and losing them there.

[16] Parish Records, St. Patrick's Church, El Paso, Texas.
[17] *Record of Engagements*, 19, 23.
[18] *Ibid.*, 23, 25.   [19] Blazer, "Blazer's Mill," *loc. cit.*, 20.
[20] *Record of Engagements*, 27, 29.

During these perilous times, about the only safe place in the Mescalero country was Blazer's Mill. Dr. Blazer gave Santana the credit. It was he who kept the wild Apaches away and meted out drastic punishment to raiding bands which came too close to the reservation.[21] And just as Santana stood by his white friends, they did their best to take care of him.

In the winter of 1876, the time of the great epidemic, the chief caught the smallpox and retired to his tipi with his two wives. The women were frightened and wanted to get away, but he kept them beside him, where he thought they belonged, at the point of a gun. They waited till he fell asleep; then they ran as fast as they could to Dr. Blazer, who had Santana brought in and put to bed in his own house. There he nursed him through the worst of the disease, but when the crisis was past and the chief was on his way to recovery, something called Dr. Blazer away. Santana rose up and stalked back to his lodge, where he contracted pneumonia and died.[22] He was the last real chief of the Mescaleros.[23]

[21] Blazer, Santana, *loc. cit.*, Santana's name is mentioned in 1873 when a group of citizens made affidavit that the Mescaleros had stolen some horses. Superintendent L. Edwin Dudley, who was at Fort Stanton, reported the matter to General W. R. Price. Price "immediately arrested Santa Ana, and a younger brother of the principal chief, Roman." (*Report of the Commissioner of Indian Affairs for 1873*, 264.)

[22] *Ibid.*, 146–48.

[23] As A. N. Blazer told the story, Santana's brothers, Cadete and Roman, who had always lived amicably with him and followed his lead, were now rivals for the headship of the tribe. According to tribal custom, they had to fight it out in a "duel by stealth." They were taken to two springs about fifteen miles apart; each was given weapons, food, and water; and they were allowed four days to find each other and fight to the death. Neither ever came back. Roman was found dead near the place where they had left him; Cadete had tied himself on his horse and got as far as Fresnal Canyon, where the searchers came upon him.

This is such a good story that one wishes it were true, but since Santana died in 1876, Cadete and Roman could not have fought for the succession. Cadete was murdered in 1872. Percy Bigmouth says he had been to Mesilla to see Colonel Fountain and was returning with his interpreter when he was killed. The interpreter and his horse disappeared and were never seen again. Superin-

While all this was going on inside the tribe, unsuspected by outsiders, the ponderous wheels of government had begun to turn in a new rhythm. General Ulysses S. Grant was sincerely anxious to settle the Indian problem once and for all, and when he became president, there was much surveying, reporting, and recommending. A joint special committee, appointed in 1865, completed its mission "to inquire into the condition of the Indian Tribes."[24] The Indian Peace Commission dug a little further into the problem in 1868.[25] On April 10 of that year, Congress paved the way for action by appropriating two million dollars to be spent in pacifying the hostile tribes and starting them on the road to self-sufficiency.[26] A Board of Indian Commissioners was set up, composed of public-spirited and substantial citizens, to keep an eye on expenditures and observe conditions on the reservations. The members had no real power, and their earnest efforts were, in the end, not too productive; but until the board was abolished in 1933, they did the best they could.

One of the bright ideas which came out of all this mingling of brains was that better Indian agents could be engaged if the churches were given a voice in the selection. A request for recommendations was sent to the Society of Friends. By the sum-

tendent Dudley noted in his report for 1873 (p. 263) that Cadete's death was attributed to Mexicans "against whom he had recently given evidence on a trial of them for selling whiskey to the Indians." The Santa Fé *New Mexican* for November 25, 1872, notes Cadete's death "under mysterious circumstances" in La Luz Canyon.

Roman survived both Cadete and Santana. Dr. Howard Thompson, who came to the reservation in 1885, advised the Indians to stay away from the white communities, where an epidemic was raging, but some paid no attention and died as a result. Roman was one of them. Bigmouth and a large band of Mescaleros headed for the Sacramentos in bitter weather ("so cold that the horses could not urinate; it froze on them in balls") and came through unscathed. (Percy Bigmouth, Sept. 8, 1955.)

[24] Elsie Mitchell Rushmore, *The Indian Policy During Grant's Administration*, 13–14.

[25] *Report of the Commissioner of Indian Affairs for 1869*, 4.

[26] Rushmore, *op. cit.*, 27–29.

133

mer of 1869, the Quakers were running sixteen of the Indian agencies throughout the country. In 1870, other religious groups were invited in—their share of the field depending on the number of Indian missions they already had in operation.

It took a little while for these changes to filter downward to the Mescaleros, and meanwhile, for a brief time, the army took charge of the Indian posts in New Mexico. In 1869, Lieutenant A. G. Hennissee was detailed to take care of the Sierra Blanca Apaches. He began his work with great vigor and earnestness, recommending to his superiors that the Fort Stanton Reservation be re-established, and actually going so far as to negotiate with some of the Indian leaders about coming in and settling down.

During the month of October, 1869, Post Commander Chambers McKibbin of Fort Stanton captured two Mescalero women, who were treated kindly and sent out again to tell the tribesmen to come in. Four months later, in February, 1870, a minor chief named José La Paz brought a small band to the fort and dallied more or less seriously with the old idea of raising crops.

A. N. Blazer, the Doctor's son, gives Santana the credit: "In 1870 Santana was successful, to some extent, in his efforts to have his people adopt civilized methods. Some crops were raised, largely by military details, but the Indians were induced to accompany the soldiers and did a small part of the work. The corn produced was bought for the cavalry at high prices to encourage the farmers, and to Santana's great relief, no considerable amount was available to be made into *tu-lipa*."[27]

Hennissee kept trying to get more Apaches to come home. He sent José La Paz off to the Comanche country to see if he could round up any of the tribesmen who had fled in that direc-

[27] Blazer, Santana, *loc. cit.*, 132.

tion from the Bosque. He was back on April 12, with about thirty of the fugitives and a message from Cadete that he and his people wanted peace—that they would come in as soon as the grass was high enough to take care of their animals when they crossed the Staked Plains. Hennissee spent some time, in the days that followed, trying to persuade Washington to do something about the returning exiles.

"If the Indians were established on a reservation," he wrote, "the influence of bad men (of which there is no scarcity in this country) would be in a great degree broken; and the Indians would have more liberty to hunt. At present they are compelled to depend almost entirely upon the food issued by the Department, as they are afraid of scouting parties when they are away from the immediate vicinity of their established camps. . . . The Indians who now receive food from the Department seem to be as well satisfied as it is reasonable to expect them to be, under the circumstances, the allowance of food per day to each Indian being only one half of one pound of corn and one half of one pound of fresh beef."[28]

The Lieutenant had no time to go far with any of his schemes for Indian betterment. Early in 1870, the army was out of business on the reservations again, as the churchmen prepared to take over. Robert S. Clark was appointed agent for the Mescaleros, but something cooled him off before he ever saw an Apache. A. J. Curtis, a Unitarian, took his place and reached Fort Stanton, with Superintendent Nathaniel Pope, on June 10, 1870. The two men stepped into an absolutely virgin field of operations. "I found neither record, buildings, nor property of any kind belonging to the agency," Curtis reported. He did find a few Indians, with a prospect of more to come.

[28] *Report of the Commissioner of Indian Affairs for 1870* (Report of Lt. A. G. Hennissee, Aug. 31, 1870).

On July 5, word reached him that Cadete and his people had arrived at the Pecos and were camped near Seven Rivers. Curtis decided that a hospitable gesture was in order and set out immediately, with a guide, an interpreter, and a wagon loaded with provisions and presents. A week later he found the Indian camp deserted and trailed Cadete into the fort, wondering every minute if he might not be running into traps and ambushes.

There was a big council then, with speeches and good resolutions and much happiness all round. Cadete "called upon heaven and earth to witness" that they wanted a lasting peace. "I then made a treaty," Curtis said, "on the following terms: that they should be protected and provided for by the Government, should have a school for their children, and land to cultivate; also that they should be allowed to keep their stock and all the property then in their possession, if they would remain on the reservation and live at peace, to which Cadete and head-men of the tribe agreed, and said it was good, again calling upon heaven and earth to witness that they were now at peace and would remain so."[29]

Fragments of the tribe were still scattered about—with the Western Apaches in the Mimbres country and the Comanches on the Staked Plains—but Cadete said they would all be in by the following fall. They would have their reservation; everything was going to be friendly and peaceful at last.

Cadete's dream might well have been realized, for Washington was laboring as never before to bring about a better day. Mr. Vincent Colyer, a Quaker and a passionate defender of the abused aborigine, had received a presidential commission to come to the Southwest, visit the Indians of all tribes, and establish them on the reservations which had so long been talked

29 *Ibid., 1871* (Report of A. J. Curtis, Sept. 18, 1871).

136

about. He arrived in the Southwest in the spring of 1871, carried out his mission, and reported on his findings.

In his opinion, Indian affairs were in a mess, and he did not hesitate to lay the blame where he thought it belonged:

> This report shows plainly that, according to the records of the Indian Department, the Apache Indians were the friends of the Americans when they first knew them; that they have always desired peace, were industrious, intelligent, and made rapid progress in the arts of civilization; that their ill-will and constant war with the Mexicans arose from the fact that the Mexicans denied them any rights to the soil as original occupants, and waged a war of extermination against them; that the peaceable relations of the Apaches with the Americans continued until the latter adopted the Mexican theory of "extermination," and by acts of inhuman cruelty made them our implacable foes; that this policy has resulted in a war which, in the last ten years, has cost us thousands of lives and over forty millions of dollars, and the country is no quieter nor the Indians any nearer extermination than they were at the time of the Gadsden purchase; that the present war will cost the people of the United States between three and four millions of dollars this year; that these Indians still beg for peace, and all of them can be placed on reservations and fed at the expense of less than half a million of dollars a year, without the loss of life.[30]

To the soldiers and to many of the citizens, Colyer was a starry-eyed idealist who did not know what he was talking about. Even before he arrived on the scene, some of the pioneering white people were practically up in arms over the report that Colyer was going to feed and protect the Apaches. On July 30, Dick Hudson, who was probate Judge of Grant County and later developed the hot springs at what is now known as Faywood, forwarded a set of resolutions to Nathaniel Pope, super-

[30] Colyer, *Peace with the Apaches of New Mexico and Arizona*, 3.

intendent of Indian Affairs for New Mexico. These resolutions had been adopted by a group of citizens from the Mimbres country at a mass meeting held on July 19, 1871, and read in part as follows:

> *Resolved,* That the people of Grant County, New Mexico, organize themselves into a posse and follow their stock to wherever it may be, and take it by force wherever found, even if it be at sacrifice of every Indian man, woman, and child, in the tribe.
>
> *Resolved,* That if opposed by Indians or their accomplices, be they Indian agents, Indian traders, or Army officers, let them be looked upon as our worst enemies and the common enemies of New Mexico, and be dealt with accordingly.[31]

In this spirit Colyer was received by a good many citizens of New Mexico and Arizona, and the army officers resented his mission almost as much. Over in Arizona, General George Crook was getting ready to start a full-size campaign against the Apaches in his vicinity, and was much disgruntled when he had to stop the proceedings. "When I received my mail," he wrote in his autobiography, "I discovered that Mr. Vincent Colyer had been sent out by the 'Indian Ring' to interfere with my operations, and that he . . . was going to make peace with the Apaches by the grace of God."[32]

General John Pope likewise betrayed some impatience, when Colyer's visit put a stop to his plans for campaigning against the New Mexico Apaches. "I had proposed beginning some scouts against them this summer," he reported rather grumpily, "but the arrival of Mr. Vincent Colyer . . . made it proper for me to suspend any hostilities against them."[33]

[31] *Ibid.,* 8.

[32] *General George Crook, His Autobiography,* (ed. by Martin H. Schmitt), 167.

The Indians in general were glad that something was going to be done for them, and at most places they came in promptly and gladly when the desert telegraph brought them the word. Over in the Mimbre country the Gila Apaches were pretty nervous about Dick Hudson's threats, and it took a long time to get them rounded up on a reservation far from Dick's property. But at last they came.

Colyer by-passed Mescalero entirely, merely remarking that the Mescaleros had been at peace for a long time, and authorizing the establishment of a reservation for them in their old country near Fort Stanton.

It was not until two years later, on May 29, 1873, that Washington officially made the Mescalero reservation a reality.[34] In the meantime, however, they had their homeland back *de facto* if not *de jure*. They had an agent to look out for them. Supplies were issued at regular intervals. The army was there to keep the peace. What more could an Apache want?

It turned out that the Apache was exactly where he had always been—just as hungry and in just as much danger as ever.

[33] *Report of the Secretary of War for 1871*, 36 (Report of Gen. John Pope).
[34] Kappler, *op. cit.*, II, 870.

Chapter VIII

PEACE WITH DISHONOR

The Mescaleros Settle Down

"**W**E WILL HAVE our reservation in the mountains," Cadete had prophesied, "and that will be good." Cadete was a poor prophet.

The first difficulty was that the Mescaleros could not be sure how much they owned, or whether they really owned it. The reservation was set up by executive order—not by treaty. Congress never ratified the transaction, and nobody knew whether the arrangement was really permanent or not. Executive orders had been set aside before. Furthermore, no survey was made establishing the boundary lines. This fact worried the officials, who complained perennially that the Indians had not been settled upon "a defined reservation secured to them."[1] It worried the Indians still more, because they were likely to be shot at if they wandered out of their own territory.

To complicate the situation further, a number of white squatters had possessed themselves of patches of arable land while the Apaches had been penned up at Bosque Redondo and during their years of wandering afterward. Under the law these

[1] *Report of the Commissioner of Indian Affairs for 1873*, 275 (Report of S. B. Bushnell, Sept. 1, 1873).

people could claim government land which they were putting to profitable use. When their claims conflicted with those of the Indians, some higher authority had to be called in to pass judgment. That meant time, money, and trouble.

White men who crowded in on the Indians under such circumstances were apt to be pretty tough specimens. Some of them peddled whiskey, or what passed for whiskey, and took everything the Indians had in exchange. Others ran gambling games in their houses and got what little the tribesmen had left. The agents could do nothing to remedy the situation, for their authority stopped at the squatter's boundary line. "It is here under his very nose," one indignant agency head complained, "that the Indian gambles away his property; and, when the agent interferes to protect the Indian, he is notified that he (the settler) is on his own land, and not on the reservation."[2]

In time most of these squatters were bought out, scared out, or otherwise disposed of, but for years they were the cause of a large proportion of the headaches which the agents had to endure. The Apaches never understood how a white man could legally be domiciled on their reservation. They crossed his fields when they felt like it, and if he had something they needed or wanted, they felt justified in taking it. Then the agent had another problem to solve.

A typical report sent to Washington during the seventies indicated that the Indians took about as much punishment as they handed out. "I have in one instance received a complaint from a farmer," so ran the story, "stating that the Indian horses had entered his fields and done some damage, and while riding to the spot in order to investigate the matter, I found his stock feasting on the Indian's garden."[3]

[2] *Ibid.*, 1876, 106 (Report of F. C. Godfroy, Aug. 18, 1876).
[3] *Ibid.*, 1877, 155 (Report of F. C. Godfroy, Sept. 1, 1877).

141

The squatters had one advantage—they were always backed up by all the white settlers in the vicinity, who never ceased to accuse the Indians of murder and larceny and to recommend that they be moved to the Indian Territory or some other place equally remote.[4] They stole from the Indians and killed them without compunction when opportunity offered, in some cases even raiding the Indian camps with a ferocity which outdid anything the Apaches had to offer. In the years between the end of the Civil War and the outbreak of the Apache troubles in 1879, there was enough of this sort of thing to make it a wonder that the Indians did not retaliate more often, or leave the reservation in a body and go to Mexico, as some did.

With a full stomach and a warm blanket, an Apache could have taken a stoic view of his plight, but even those things were denied him. "These Indians have no treaty with the United States," said Commissioner Walker in 1874, "nor do they receive any annuities. They are, however, subsisted in part by the government, and are supplied with a limited quantity of clothing when necessary."[5] This obviously meant that the United States was niggardly as usual in all expenditures except those considered necessary for punishing and killing the natives. The Apaches were not given enough food to live on or enough clothes to keep them warm. They had to hunt or steal in order to live, and their reservation did not include enough territory for successful hunting. On October 20, 1875, another executive order took account of this situation and extended the reservation into the Sacramento Mountains to the south,[6] which helped matters some—but not enough.

Tough white men and short rations—those were perils which a Mescalero could see and feel. But he was in greater

[4] *Ibid., 1876, vii* (Report of Commissioner J. Q. Smith).
[5] Francis A. Walker, *The Indian Question,* 232.
[6] Kappler, *op. cit.,* I, 872.

danger from something outside his comprehension: namely, the crookedness and corruption of the people who were supposed to provide his meager necessities. Even before the tribe returned from its long exile on the Texas plains, the wily white man was hatching his nefarious schemes.

In 1871, Major L. G. Murphy and Captain Emil Fritz, former members of the California Column, had set themselves up as post traders at Fort Stanton. Both of them were to attain notoriety later in the Lincoln County War (starring Billy the Kid)—Murphy as the leader and subsidizer of the group of cattlemen who opposed John Chisum and his friends, and Fritz as the maker of the last will and testament which triggered the whole affair.[7] These gentlemen knew that they could make a good thing of Indian contracts if they played their cards right, and they started by turning on all their charm for Superintendent Nathaniel Pope and Agent A. J. Curtis, who came to the fort in 1872 to set up an agency for the Mescaleros.

Pope and Curtis swallowed the bait. The reports they sent off to Washington glowed with admiration for the Fort Stanton traders. Pope wrote that the establishment of peace was entirely owing to "the good management on the part of the commanding officer of that post and the persistent efforts of Hon. L. G. Murphy and Major Emil Fritz, citizens of Lincoln County. The Indians are being supplied with beef and corn temporarily, at the contract rates for those articles at that post."[8]

Curtis bowed even lower before the great men. "They have several times, at their own expense, sent out clothing and other presents, with messengers to communicate with the tribe, and on one occasion sent a team and wagon laden with presents into

[7] For a full account of these matters see Pat F. Garrett, *Authentic Life of Billy the Kid.*

[8] *Report of the Commissioner of Indian Affairs for 1872,* 371 (Report of Nathaniel Pope, Oct. 10, 1872).

the Comanche country, to induce them, if possible, to come in and make peace. These efforts were at last crowned with success, and the Government not only, but the people of this county as well, are largely indebted to these gentlemen for the important results obtained by their efforts."[9]

The first result of the diplomacy of Messrs. Murphy and Fritz was a magical multiplication of the number of Indians who were being fed and clothed (at contract rates) at the fort. Superintendent Pope reported in the fall of 1872 that between 500 and 600 Mescaleros had come in. A year later the number had jumped to 830, and had been further increased by the arrival of 440 Aguas Nuevas (members of a Mescalero subdivision), 350 Lipans, and 310 Southern Apaches. All of the later arrivals were supposed to have come in from the Mimbres country, attracted by the government's liberality in issuing supplies at Fort Stanton.

Pope merely reported to Washington that the Indians at Fort Stanton now numbered "over eighteen hundred, being an increase of about fifteen hundred since the date of my last annual report." Eventually the count went as high as 2,679–"a rapidity of increase," Agent Curtis remarked, "which leaves rabbits, rats, and mice in the shade."[10]

To what extent Superintendent Pope and Agent Curtis were aware of or involved in these shady transactions, we do not know. But before the year 1872 was out, L. Edwin Dudley was in the superintendent's office at Santa Fé, and S. B. Bushnell was in charge of the Mescaleros.

During the last days of December, 1872, Dudley paid the Mescaleros a visit and was appalled at what he discovered. Murphy and Fritz, he found, had "taken entire possession of Indian

[9] *Ibid.*, 401 (Report of A. J. Curtis, Aug. 31, 1872).
[10] Reeve, *loc. cit.*, 27.

affairs" at Fort Stanton. The agent was a mere pensioner of the firm, with no accommodations except what they chose to offer him, and with no business "except to approve vouchers made for him by these men."[11]

The Indians were, of course, completely neglected. There was no school for the Indian children, although Cadete had asked for one when he came in from the plains. There had been no appropriation for implements or seeds, and farming was at a standstill, although the chiefs had expressed a willingness to go to work. Six or seven hundred Apaches were rotting in idleness, unable to do anything for themselves and afraid to leave the vicinity of the fort for fear of violence from white squatters and bands of "scouts." This was the "better day" that Cadete and his people had dreamed of.

Dudley did the best he could to straighten things out, but it took almost a year to make even a beginning. Agent Bushnell, who arrived at Fort Stanton in March, 1873, found Murphy and Fritz too much for him to handle. A building had been purchased from the firm for the agent's use, but he could not occupy it. It was not until Dudley made a second visit in the following September that enough pressure could be applied to give the agent possession of his own quarters, and then Dudley had to threaten to clean the place out personally if it was not vacated within twenty-four hours.

Setting his jaw, he next tackled the beef issue—the focal point of reservation graft. No more meat was apportioned on the hoof. Regular weekly issue of dressed beef became the new rule. On issue day the Indians were rounded up in a corral and given tickets for their rations. "By this means," Dudley remarked, "I hope to prevent fraud, and to secure the Govern-

[11] *Report of the Commissioner of Indian Affairs for 1873*, 263 (Report of L. Edwin Dudley, Nov. 15, 1873).

ment against paying for rations that are neither supplied by the contractors nor received by the Indians."[12]

The new system undoubtedly interfered with the undercover business carried on by Murphy and Fritz, and before long they left the post. Murphy set up a store in Lincoln, but he continued to take a deep interest in the Indian business. His successor as post trader, Captain Paul Dowlin, carried on in the Murphy tradition. He had a license to sell liquor, and the Indians continued to drink it. Agent Crothers thought there was some connection. When he found that he could do nothing to remove Dowlin, Crothers removed himself, taking his agency first to Copeland's ranch, eight miles from the post, and finally to South Fork, forty miles away, with headquarters at Blazer's Mill.[13] This was the beginning of the present-day Mescalero headquarters.

Having defied the Murphy gang, Crothers had now to face the consequences. These men controlled the courts, and the simplest way for them to get back at an enemy was to have the law on him. Crothers found himself facing trial in the District Court as soon as they could think up something to accuse him of. He had issued more rations than there were Indians, they said, and had used government property in setting up a hotel. He was actually indicted on a charge of running a hotel without a license, but the District Attorney would not prosecute the case. The sound of angry voices finally reached Washington, and Congressman John McNulta was sent down as a special investigator to look into the matter. His report was favorable to the agent, but in the spring of 1876, Crothers resigned.[14]

---

[12] *Ibid.*

[13] Reeve, *loc. cit.*, 273.

[14] *Report of the Commissioner of Indian Affairs for 1875*, 38–39. Congressman McNulta praised Crothers' handling of the Indians but criticized the business management of the agency.

It seemed that the Indian agents of this period were either weak or wicked. Indian Commissioner J. Q. Smith commented, in the year of Crothers' retirement, that the great need in the service was for "thoroughly competent agents."

> When it is considered that these men must take their families far into the wilderness, cut themselves off from civilization with its comforts and attractions, deprive their children of the advantages of education, live lives of anxiety and toil, give bonds for great sums of money, be held responsible in some instances for the expenditure of hundreds of thousands of dollars a year, and subject themselves to ever-ready suspicion, detraction, and calumny for a compensation less than that paid to a third-class clerk in Washington, or to a village postmaster, it is not strange that able, upright, thoroughly competent men hesitate, and decline to accept the position of an Indian agent.[15]

It was almost as true of the agents as it was of the Indians that they must either starve or steal.

Crothers' successor, Fred C. Godfroy, furnished a good illustration of how things were apt to go. He was an able man who went at his job with energy and enthusiasm, trying to get to know his Indian charges, visiting them daily in their camps, and encouraging them to get busy and do something for themselves. He complained bitterly about bootleggers and squatters. He mourned over his quarters, rented from Dr. Blazer, and his lack of funds. But he was cheerfully confident that the Indians could be helped—that they showed "a great desire to please" and were "willing workers."

Unfortunately, he allowed himself to be taken into camp by Murphy and his business partner, J. C. Dolan, the latter having the beef and flour contract for the agency. Before long Godfroy was being labeled "the Presbyterian fraud," and was

15 *Ibid.*, 1876, iv.

answering charges of boosting the head count of the Indians for the benefit of his friends. The inspector who came down to look into the mess thought Godfroy was a good administrator but had been guilty of questionable practices. He was out in 1879.[16]

The kind of thing that might have happened was reported in the Las Cruces newspapers: "On Sunday morning Dr. O. H. Woodworth seized in Mesilla fifteen bales (about 2,000 pounds) of smuggled Mexican blankets. They were shipped by Indian Agent Purroy [Godfroy?] from Fort Stanton and were found in possession of Ira M. Bond, who claimed he knew nothing about them."[17]

Godfroy even seems to have been a partner of Pat Coghlan, the "King of Tularosa," who bought stolen stock from Billy the Kid and sold it to the government.[18] What chance did the poor Indians have against that sort of thing?

In the long run, however, the Mescaleros suffered most from two other groups of white men: soldiers on the one hand and desperadoes on the other. From 1872 until the outbreak of the Apaches in 1879, they were in continual danger from one or the other of these groups, and sometimes from both simultaneously.

So far as the soldiers were concerned, Indians existed only to be fought with and killed. It was impossible for most army officers to regard an Apache as anything but a "hostile"; to think of him as an abused and ignorant human being was a mental leap which only a handful of soldiers were capable of taking. They honestly believed that force was the only thing an Indian could understand, and that it was absolutely necessary to in-

[16] Reeve, *loc. cit.*, 273–76.
[17] Las Cruces *34*, Jan. 1, 1879.
[18] F. C. Godfroy to S. A. Russell, Jan. 10, 1880 (letter in the files of the Mescalero Agency). Godfroy presents a claim for loss of stock "belonging to myself and Mr. Coghlan at Three Rivers Range."

flict "punishment" (which meant killing any of the tribesmen they could catch up with) every time a "depredation" was committed or reported.

Lieutenant A. G. Hennissee, agent for the Mescaleros in 1869–70, called his charges "the worst Indians in the country," and declared that "talk and promises do not amount to anything among these treacherous and suspicious beings."[19] General Pope, commanding the Department of the Missouri, added a year later that he considered the Apaches a "squalid, cowardly race, divided into innumerable small bands, acknowledging no common authority. . . . It is much to be doubted from the character and habits of these Indians, whether they can be brought to live on a reservation at all, unless, indeed, they are furnished with everything they covet."

Pope wanted to do away with Fort Stanton entirely and move the Mescaleros to some remote place, "far away from lines of railroad and river navigation," where they could luxuriate in their barbarism without hurting anybody but themselves.[20]

The soldiers were brave and conscientious men, of course, and many of them laid down their lives in line of duty. As we look back after sixty or seventy years, however, we can see that their harshness was not always necessary, nor was their cause always just.

General Pope himself was not proud of the army record. In 1875 he could write:

> It is with painful reluctance that the military forces take the field against Indians who only leave their reservations because they are starved there, and who must hunt food for themselves and their families, or see them perish with hunger.

[19] *Report of the Commissioner of Indian Affairs for 1870*, 623 (Report of Lt. A. G. Hennissee, Aug. 31, 1870).

[20] *Report of the Secretary of War for 1870*, 8 (Report of Gen. John Pope).

It is revolting to any humane man to see such things done, and far more so to be required to be the active party to commit violence upon forlorn Indians, who, under the pressure of such necessity, only do what any man would do under like circumstances.[21]

Revolting or not, such things were done time and again. The pattern was set when Superintendent Dudley made his second visit to the Mescaleros, in the fall of 1873. On his arrival at Fort Stanton he found a body of horsemen waiting for him—six troops of cavalry under Major W. R. Price. The Major had received, so he said, sworn complaints from "a large number" of citizens who said the Mescaleros had stolen their horses. He had come to recover the stock and punish the Indians, and was anxious to get started. Dudley demurred, explaining that the Indians did not know the boundaries of their own reservation because such boundaries had not been determined; that they honestly believed the country was theirs and the white settlers owed them an occasional gift by way of tribute; that the whole thing could be settled peaceably by explaining things to the Indians and warning them that they would have to stay within bounds (wherever the bounds were).

Price argued that he had come a long way to do this job, and he wanted to do it. Dudley weakened and wrote him a letter giving him carte blanche to "take such means as you think proper, to recover property previously stolen, and to prevent further depredations." The date of this communication was September 3, 1873.[22]

Price went happily to work. First, he arrested Santana and Roman and told them they would be held as hostages until the

---

[21] *Ibid.*, *1875*, 76 (Report of Gen. John Pope).

[22] *Report of the Commissioner of Indian Affairs for 1873*, 264 (Report of L. Edwin Dudley, Nov. 15, 1873).

stolen horses were returned. The Indian encampment thereupon fell into great excitement. Two hundred Mescaleros immediately decamped for parts unknown. Dudley heard that some had gone back to the Comanches and some to Old Mexico,[23] but enough stayed in the vicinity to enable Major Price to do what he had come for. The report of his activities read: "One officer, in command of about 60 cavalrymen, succeeded a few days since in attacking a single rancheria and killing all its inhabitants, seven persons, men, women, and children. Owing to the peculiar state of feeling in this Territory this is regarded as a very important military achievement."[24]

Price could not find any more Indians, or his military achievement would undoubtedly have been greater.

There was worse to come, as the soldiers combined with squatters and settlers to harass their red brothers. The white men around the reservation continually brought in charges that the Mescaleros were stealing horses. The center of their activities was supposed to be on the Pecos River some seventy-five miles from the fort, but reports came in from all directions. Agent Crothers looked into these accusations and thought that most of them did not hold water.[25] Nevertheless, the propaganda campaign against the Apaches continued. It made no difference that the horse herds of the Indians were being systematically raided. No white thief was pursued or punished, but all the Mescaleros had to suffer for the sins of a few.

Their punishment took the form of mob action. In the fall of 1874, a gang of white thugs crept up on a Mescalero encamp-

[23] Mescaleros were still with the Comanches in the late seventies, when the campaigns against the Plains Indians were at their height. See Rister, *The Southwestern Frontier*, 181, 186, and *Fort Griffin*, 109, 183.

[24] *Report of the Commissioner of Indian Affairs for 1873*, 265 (Report of Commissioner Edwin P. Smith, Nov. 15, 1873).

[25] *Ibid.*, 1875, 329 (Report of W. D. Crothers, Sept. 30, 1875).

ment, fired into it, and killed several women and children. The Apaches could not fight back, being completely surprised and practically without arms. They did not pursue when the raiders drove off their horses, and they did not get their animals back.

The "citizens" repeated this performance a few months later, in January, 1875. The Indians were, of course, terrified and distracted. Unable to recover the stolen property or bring the white thieves to justice, Major Clendenin, post commander at Fort Stanton, encouraged the tribesmen to pitch their tents within gunshot of the fort, where he could guarantee them protection. He was not able, however, to take away their fears and forebodings.

Rumors reached them that the killers were coming back. The chiefs asked Crothers what they should do. He told them to stand their ground—with the soldiers behind them, they could hold their own. They thought it over. Finally a delegation came to ask Crothers if they might spend the night in the mountains and come back the next morning. Crothers agreed, not anticipating the wild flight which followed. Within thirty minutes every Indian had gone to earth. They were completely terrorized.

They did not come back the next morning—nor the next. The army officers assumed that they were off the reservation and must be pursued and punished. Ten days after their departure Captain E. G. Fechet was sent out to find them, and luck was with him. After a march of a few hours, he came upon a Mescalero band camped in a canyon. To the surprise and consternation of the Apaches, they now found themselves in worse danger from their protectors than from their enemies. Captain Fechet ordered his troops to fire on them.

There was no fight. The Indians scattered and ran, leaving everything they had—clothes, blankets, horses, and tents. Fechet burned everything but the horses. Those (fifty head) he sold at public auction by order of his commanding officer, for about seven dollars apiece.

In reporting this incident, Agent Crothers commented, probably without intentional irony: "There was also a child of about eight months left on the grounds. It was taken by Captain Fechet and kindly cared for."

Crothers sent an agency employee and "two citizens" out to look for the remnants of the band. After a two weeks' search they found them—starving. "On their return," said Crothers, "it was heart-rending to see a class of human beings so destitute of the absolute necessities of life; many of them almost naked and bearing marks of an outraged class of human beings. In Council the chiefs apologized for having left the reservation, as they had said prior to leaving that they would be back next morning; but said that when they got out into the mountains the evening that they left, their women and children were so frightened that they were compelled to continue their tramp all night, feeling they were pursued by the raiders; that they had no intention of committing depredations on the citizens; that their leaving was to save the lives of their women and children. They felt they had been wronged; that they had been driven from their homes when on their own reservation; that the "Great Father" did not want them to retaliate or to take revenge for the wrongs that had been committed against them; nor have they."[26]

In fear of their lives, two good-sized bands of Mescaleros kept on running after this massacre, not stopping for breath until they were on the other side of the Mexican boundary.[27] Crothers sent messengers to tell them to return, but they dared

---

[26] *Ibid.*, 330.
[27] M. E. and Catherine H. Opler, "Mescalero Apache History," *N.M.H.R.*, Vol. XXV (January, 1950), 26: "From later reports it seems likely that the bands which had deserted the agency were those of Natsile and Pinoli."

not trust anyone and stayed out until J. A. Lucero of Las Cruces brought them back in August, 1876. He charged the government $1.50 a head for his services.[28] Long before the tribe was united, however, Congressman McNulta had made his inspection of reservation affairs and concluded that the Indians were "in no degree at fault in this affair."[29]

Still the raiding of the Mescaleros' scanty possessions went on. In 1876, the agent made a count of their horses (their only wealth) and found, to his surprise, that the herd included 597 horses and 122 mules, "notwithstanding the constant raids made on them by the Mexicans, many of whom have more need of a reservation and military to restrain them than these Indians."[30]

Most of the trouble came from a band of horse thieves with headquarters at the Mexican town of Boquilla, seventy miles from the reservation, who made a business of stealing everybody's animals (including those of the Mescaleros) and then "raising the hue and cry of 'Apache' to cover their own depredations." Crothers recovered some stock from this town, assisted by a detachment of soldiers, and the citizens took it upon themselves to run the robbers out. The band moved a little farther away—to Puerto de Luna.[31]

In July, 1876, the gang had worn out its welcome again, and the citizens of Puerto de Luna notified Agent Godfroy that he could come and get a number of Mescalero horses which they had taken from the thieves. Morris J. Bernstein, the agency clerk, set out with four Indians to reclaim the stolen property, and three other Apaches, who had lost horses during the months preceding, joined the group on the road. The commanding offi-

[28] *Report of the Commissioner of Indian Affairs for 1900*, 288 (W. M. Luttrell, "A Brief History of the Mescaleros").
[29] *Ibid., 1875*, 39.
[30] *Ibid., 1876*, 108 (Report of F. C. Godfroy, Aug. 18, 1876).
[31] *Ibid.*

cer at Fort Stanton refused to send a military escort, but the party went on anyhow, into what they knew to be dangerous territory for them.

For perhaps the first time in history, the Apaches found a party of citizens who were willing to do them justice. A public meeting was called at Puerto de Luna, and although all but two horses and two mules had been "reclaimed," the reclaimers were ordered to bring the animals into town to be inspected. Ten deputies and Bernstein's Indians went out to see that the job was done. Horses came "pouring in from all sides." The Apaches claimed ten head, and were given seven to which they appeared to have clear title. One more horse was picked up at Fort Sumner, and the side trip to this town may have saved Bernstein and his company from serious trouble, for they learned later that the thieves had set up an ambush on the main road to waylay them and get the horses back.

The fact that Lorenzo Labadie, onetime agent and friend of the Mescaleros, was living at Puerto de Luna and took a prominent part in this unprecedented attempt to do right by the Apaches, may explain why such a thing happened at all.[32]

The next year, 1877, the robbers—or others like them—were back on the reservation. The agent called them "Texans," and many of them probably were, but in New Mexico at this time almost any unruly white man was a *Tejano.*

On July 20, 1877, they came to Godfroy with straight faces and asked permission to look over the Indians' horse herds, to see if any of their brands were represented. The agent gave his permission, they made their inspection, and took their leave with great courtesy, saying that they had found nothing belonging to them. The next night they surrounded the smallest of the Indian camps, fired into it without hitting anybody (an unusual

[32] *Ibid.*

piece of luck for the Indians), and got off with thirteen horses. Nothing was done about it, although if the raiders had been Indians, the soldiers would have been after them at once.

On August 11, probably emboldened by their previous success, the Texans tried it again just before dark and got off with a good portion of the herd held at the agency, including two government mules.

Godfroy had no arms and no permission to organize a pursuing expedition, but as soon as it was possible to get across the mountains to Fort Stanton, a detachment of fifteen cavalrymen started in pursuit of the thieves. The pursuit was fruitless; heavy rains had washed out the trail, and that was that.[33]

The country was in an increasingly precarious condition as the seventies drew to a close. The guerrilla bands which fought each other during the Lincoln County troubles were riding about, seeking whom they might destroy. The white men and women at the agency were terrorized more than once,[34] and there were many dead Indians and missing horses before those bad times were over.

Some of the Mescaleros' difficulties, we must admit, were home-grown. In 1876, they threatened to carry on a private war among themselves. It started with five Gila Apaches who had married Mescalero women and were living as members of the tribe.[35] They seemed to get along well enough with their hosts until the evening of August 1, when a large quantity of *tiswin*

[33] *Ibid.*, 1877, 157–58 (Report of F. C. Godfroy, Aug. 15, 1877).

[34] Agency Clerk Bernstein was killed by outlaws in August, 1878, and agency personnel were afraid there would be more trouble for them. Lieutenant Colonel N. A. M. Dudley wrote to Godfroy on August 6, offering to send arms and provide a refuge for the women of the agency (letter in the agency files). See *Report of the Commissioner of Indian Affairs for 1878*, 107 (Report of F. C. Godfroy).

[35] One Navajo, one Comanche, three Jicarillas, and five Gilas were living with the tribe at this time.

156

turned up in the main camp, with the usual consequences. Two of the outsiders tangled with some of the Mescaleros, of whom one was killed and two were liberally cut up. Suspecting that their absence might be welcomed, the two Gilas stole some horses and left with great haste.

The next day six Mescaleros, relatives of the murdered man, asked the agent for passes to visit the Gila Reservation at Ojo Caliente. Godfroy thought he knew what they had in mind and refused to let them go, but they went anyway, and by that time the rest of the Gilas had seen the handwriting on the wall and vanished in the wake of their brothers. Godfroy notified Agent Shaw at the Gila Agency and told him to arrest any Mescaleros he found, lest the rift "involve the whole tribe in a war."[36] No Mescaleros were arrested.

A few months later a terrible smallpox epidemic broke out on the reservation. Many Indians were struck down, from Chief Santana to babes-in-arms. Godfroy had started a one-room school, but the disease left him with only a few pupils.[37] He tried to control the sickness by scattering the Indians out over the reservation, and this may have helped some, but the Mescaleros lost a great number of their people.

In the spring, when the epidemic slackened, Godfroy tried to start some farming and thought he had good success. Nautzile, a powerful leader who had been hard to corral and who had come in to the agency only the year before, got in a garden at Twin Springs in the Sacramentos, and, in his annual August report, Godfroy wrote that he was anticipating a fine crop of potatoes.

A year later all the good work had been undone again. The Mescaleros were restless and alarmed. The Lincoln County feud

---

[36] *Report of the Commissioner of Indian Affairs for 1876,* 107.
[37] *Ibid., 1877,* 157 (Report of F. C. Godfroy, Sept. 1, 1877).

was breaking out into open warfare, and the Apaches were suffering the fate of all innocent bystanders. Some had lost their horses; others, their lives. "Two of the bands, Estrella's and Peso's, have almost all left the agency," said Godfroy, "and are only visiting it when they are very hungry and needy. I have used my utmost endeavors to allay their fears, and when almost successful, the military, with Navajo scouts, attacked them, and killed some and took one child prisoner."

It seemed to the Mescaleros that there was nobody whom they could trust, and they remained suspicious and withdrawn. When Special Agent Frank Warner Angel came to make an official count of the tribe, many of the Apaches refused to come in. One band, camped only half a mile from the agency, sent word that if Mr. Angel wanted to make a count, he could come to their camp. He did not come, and no count was made.[38]

So matters stood just before the troubles of 1879 set the Apache world ablaze. There was some raiding going on, but most of the reports of depredations came from farther south.[39] The Mescalero leaders had kept their people in line to the best of their ability, and had put up with much more persecution and harassment than they had inflicted. In the years between 1872 and 1879, they had been repeatedly driven away from their homes, many of them had been murdered in cold blood, and most of them had been blamed for sins they had not committed. The heritage of these Indians, as usual, was fear and danger, and the end was not even in sight.

[38] *Ibid., 1878,* 107 (Report of F. C. Godfroy, Aug. 22, 1878).
[39] *Record of Engagements,* 75–76. Six engagements involving Mescaleros were reported in 1877, five in 1878. Every one was in the Fort Davis–Río Grande country.

Chapter IX

THE BLOODY BORDER

Victorio Takes the Warpath

Now came Victorio, the great war chief—a fierce-faced, long-haired fighter of great ability who had learned his tactics from the mighty Mangas Coloradas himself. Ironically enough, Victorio may not have been an Apache at all. There is a tradition in northern Mexico and the border country that he was a Mexican captive, who came into the tribe as a little boy and rose to eminence by sheer personal force and fighting ability.[1] However that may have been, he passed for a Mimbres or Gila Apache of the Warm Springs band. Their people were his people; their gods were his gods.

Ever since Colyer's mission in 1871, Victorio and his tribe had been in constant turmoil. Colyer located them on a reservation they did not like. Climate, food supply, water—everything was wrong, according to them. They were intractable, inde-

---

[1] According to old residents of Chihuahua, Victorio may have been a Mexican, taken as a child from the Rancho del Carmen, belonging to Don Luis Terrazas. Rufino Padilla, after four years' captivity among the Apaches, brought back the story that Victorio bore a great physical resemblance to the father of this stolen child. Bertha Montes has followed up the legend in Chihuahua. Her manuscript, "Last of the Great Chieftains," dated May, 1948, is in possession of C. L. Sonnichsen. The old Mescaleros also have heard that Victorio was a Mexican (Crookneck and Willie Magoosh, Feb. 5, 1955).

pendent, and indolent, and there was much tension between them and the army officers who were sent to keep them in line. Soon after their new reservation was set up, they walked away from it and went to the Chiricahua reserve in Arizona.

There they stayed, resisting all pleas and threats, until the government gave in and established another reservation for them in central New Mexico at Ojo Caliente, or Warm Springs, in a valley called Cañada Alamosa. This they regarded as their real home—the place where they belonged and where they wanted to be—and they were happy.

Had they been allowed to stay there, all might have been well. But no! Washington decided on a policy of "concentration" (the Indians never understood what that meant), and the Warm Springs Apaches were told that they would have to move farther west to the San Carlos Reservation.

The official reason given by the Commissioner of Indian Affairs was that the Warm Springs band was aiding and abetting the rebellious Chiricahuas, whose reserve had been abolished in 1876. Apparently without hesitation, or any real consideration of the consequences, the powers in Washington returned the Warm Springs Reservation to the public domain and told the Apaches that they might consider San Carlos their home in the future.

In May, 1877, 453 of them were led, or driven, to San Carlos. They were desperately unhappy from the start. The arid landscape was ugly and unpleasant to these mountain people; they did not like the Indians who were already established there; they yearned for liberty. On September 2, about 300 of them left in a body and took to the wilds. They were pursued and brought back, or came in when food looked better than freedom, but they were so disconsolate and restless that the officials decided to undo what they had done. The bulk of the band—260 people—received permission to go back to Warm Springs.

Their happiness over this move was short-lived. The order was changed again, and before they were well settled in their old home, the troops came to escort them to San Carlos once more. This was in August, 1878. Victorio, their leader, made up his mind that he would put up with no more of this shilly-shallying. At the head of eighty men he departed for the mountains.

Apparently the band divided. In December, old Chief Nana appeared at Mescalero with sixty-three men[2]—hungry, cold, and anxious to be taken in. Victorio had gone to Mexico with the rest of the runaways, but in February he came back to Warm Springs for a visit. His talk was about the warriors who had joined the Mescaleros, about how much better off they were, and how strongly he was tempted to join them. For once the white officials were willing to agree with him—anything to get him to settle down. But when an order actually came to move him over to the Tularosa country, he showed symptoms of panic and headed for the hills again. It was not until June 30 that he finally arrived at Mescalero, followed by thirteen fighting men.[3]

Almer Blazer, the Doctor's son, just back from a prospecting trip, saw them at a mountain water hole and got to the agency just behind them.[4] They were already in conference with Agent S. A. Russell, and full of ideas about what they wanted to do. First of all, they wished to settle down with the Mescaleros and receive rations as the rest did. Russell, a good man but quite incapable of decisive action, said he could not agree to such a

---

[2] *Report of the Commissioner of Indian Affairs for 1900*, 289 (Luttrell, "Brief History of the Mescaleros").

[3] *Ibid., 1879, xxxviii*, (E. A. Hayt, commissioner).

[4] A. N. Blazer, "Beginnings of an Indian War," *New Mexico*, Vol. XVI (February, 1938), 39.

thing without authorization from Washington, and they would have to wait.

For a few days they loafed around the agency, getting hungrier and more belligerent, and spreading a good deal of propaganda among the wilder Mescaleros. They let it be known that they were thinking about seizing the government stores and going off on the warpath.

Finally Chief San Juan, who had been doing his not-too-effectual best to exercise leadership in the tribe since the death of Santana, brought Victorio and his followers to Dr. Blazer, saying that something would have to be done. Blazer knew what to do. He gave the newcomers a fat steer of his own, and contributed the flour, sugar, and coffee to go with it.[5]

A week went by without incident. Then somebody turned up with a supply of *tiswin;* there was a big drunk, and a Mescalero got killed. The visiting Apaches were blamed for both the liquor and the casualty, and things were a little less than calm at Mescalero.

About that time a further complication arrived in the shape of a party of men from Silver City, who were ostensibly on a hunting expedition. The group included a judge and the Grant County prosecuting attorney, however, and Victorio, who was under indictment for murder in Grant County, became nervous. Perhaps under the influence of the *tiswin,* he approached Agent Russell again. According to Almer Blazer, he ended by pulling Russell's beard and threatening to take what he wanted out of the stores without further ceremony.

The old Mescaleros remember what happened. "They were drawing rations," Solon Sombrero says, "but the men kept telling them to wait. Victorio caught on after a while. He knew they were getting ready to do something to him. He had seen those

[5] *Ibid.*

men around. He tore up his ticket and threw it at Russell. He said, 'There are other things besides rations. I will live. In three days we will leave.' His men had been making *tiswin*. He told them to give away what they had for the Mescaleros to have a celebration with.'"[6]

Russell was frightened by Victorio's display of ugly feelings, and sent off at once to Fort Stanton for troops to protect him. A detachment was dispatched with all speed, and as the soldiers approached the mill, a bugler sounded a call. Victorio and his men heard it in their camp a short distance from the agency, and that was all it took to start six years of savage warfare.[7] In a matter of minutes they were mounted and on the road.

Dr. Blazer was about to go out for hay needed by the cavalry mounts which he knew were on the way from the fort. Victorio came to him and told him they were afraid to stay any longer, finally shaking his hand solemnly in farewell. It was the last white hand he would shake in the few months that remained to him.

Running Water and Manchito, Mescaleros, were with him when he left—perhaps a few others. They were the first of an assortment of Mescalero braves who joined Victorio's band. Although the tribe as a whole was not mixed up in the events of the next few years, some of the restless ones could not resist the temptation to follow a successful leader in the old raiding pattern. And, as usual, the peaceful ones who stayed at home and behaved themselves had to pay for the crimes of their brothers.

Victorio started his campaign of death and destruction before he was well out of the Mescalero Reservation. In Temporal Canyon at the foot of the mountains, his men killed two sheep herders and made off with their horses. Then they headed west

---

[6] Solon Sombrero, June 8, 1955.
[7] Paul Blazer, July 28, 1956.

across the San Andres into the Gila country, killing and burning as they went, while the soldiers saddled up and clattered off in pursuit.

Many a book has been written about the campaign against Victorio; thus only the highlights need be sketched in here. Victorio swung southwest through New Mexico with the cavalry at his heels. He circled through Mexico below El Paso and came back into the States in the Big Bend region, where he was joined by a party of Mescaleros under old Chief Caballero.[8] How many of them were from the Fort Stanton reservation it is impossible to say, but since estimates of their number run as high as three hundred,[9] many of them were probably from Alsate's band in the Davis Mountains.

Victorio's sojourn in the United States was very brief this time. The Tenth Cavalry and Baylor's Texas Rangers were maneuvering to get at him, and he ducked back into Mexico. On September 4, 1879, he suddenly appeared in New Mexico near Ojo Caliente, his native place, where a cavalry post had been set up.

Eight privates were on herd duty that day. After an eighteen-month drought there was not much grass, and the weather was hot and discouraging. The men kept within sight of the post but allowed themselves to drift into thoughts of things far away. Without any warning Victorio was upon them with sixty warriors. In five minutes all the herders were dead or the next thing to it, and the Indians were off in a cloud of dust, with forty-six horses.[10]

---

[8] Wellman, *The Indian Wars of the West*, 365-74. W. M. Luttrell's "Brief History of the Mescaleros" (*op. cit.*, 289) says: "In March, 1880, Caballero had offered to go out and induce Victorio to come in and surrender, in which plan he failed to succeed."

[9] Wellman, *op. cit.*, 166.

[10] *Report of the Secretary of War for 1880*, I, 86.

Victorio,
the great war chief.

Nana,
Victorio's successor.

COURTESY MRS. EMMA B. THOMPSON

Leaders before 1900:
Nautzile (above),
and San Juan (right).

The post was practically dismounted, but Major Morrow started in pursuit with all the force he could muster. Several times he skirmished with the raiders, but never could bring them to a decisive action. They split up into small bands, lived off the Mexican sheepherders who were all over the region, and laughed at pursuit. Major Morrow had to turn back, his force completely used up. In February, Colonel Edward Hatch, down from Santa Fé to try to keep things going, reported that Morrow's command was "entirely unfit for service, having lost nearly all his horses from casualties, exposure, and want of forage."[11]

When the cavalrymen did succeed in coming up with Victorio, he made them regret it. Colonel N. A. M. Dudley caught him on September 18. The braves took cover behind rocks and cacti. Dudley could not dislodge them, and they got rid of eight men and thirty-eight horses for him. Then, like shadows, they were gone.

By this time 150 men from Hillsboro and the Black Range country had taken up the trail, eager to put an end to the massacring of their neighbors. Victorio paused briefly to pick off eighteen of them, and then hurried on.[12]

The citizens of Mesilla and the little Mexican communities in the valley near by heard of the slaughter, assembled a company of twenty volunteers, and started to the rescue. On October 13, when they were well into the Black Range, they saw three horses near the road and went over to pick them up. It was an ambush. Before they knew what was happening, one hundred Indians fired from their hiding places, killing five of the Mexican volunteers and an American named W. T. Jones. The militia retreated to a near-by ranch and sent for help. The

---

[11] *Ibid.*, I, 93 (Report of Col. Edward Hatch).

[12] "Apaches in Ambush between Hillsboro, Lake Valley, Killed 18. Frontiersmen Buried in Single Grave on the Spot Where They Fell," El Paso *Times*, March 1, 1942.

Apaches let them go and turned their attention to two supply trains which were creaking unsuspectingly toward Mason's Ranch. Eleven men were killed; one woman and one child were taken captive. When more volunteers arrived, the warriors had departed toward the Florida mountains and were soon across the border in Mexico.[13]

While all this was going on, something like panic reigned at the Mescalero Agency. Russell confidently expected that Victorio would come back. On November 9, Lieutenant G. W. Smith wrote to the post adjutant at Fort Stanton, "The danger I apprehend here is from Victorio's men on their return. . . . Cannot get anything reliable from the west."[14]

Russell called frantically for more troops to protect the agency. Lieutenant Colonel P. F. Swaine replied, "I am powerless to comply with your request to send you a force for the protection of life and property at the Agency. The effective strength of this command is out operating against the Indians who have left your reservation."[15]

A wave of horrified expectation swept over the citizens when Lieutenant Smith sent a telegram to everybody at Tularosa on Nov. 25: "A party of Mescalero Apaches left the Reservation yesterday and after killing an ox and fifteen head of sheep packed the meat on six horses which they had just stolen and moved south. From the fact of the meat being largely in excess of their present needs, I think this is only a foraging party for a much larger force waiting for their rations today (issue day) to be joined by them and take the field *en route* to Old Mexico."[16]

---

[13] Mesilla *News*, Oct. 18, 1879, clippings in possession of Mrs. Frank Barger, El Paso, Texas.

[14] Letter in the files of the Mescalero Agency.

[15] Swaine to Russell, Nov. 10, 1879 (files of the Mescalero Agency).

[16] Lieutenant G. W. Smith to the Citizens of Tularosa (files of the Mescalero Agency).

word Victorio was back

The suspicion that Victorio was back changed to certainty when Lieutenant Colonel Swaine at Fort Stanton received a telegram from Fort Bayard dated December 1, 1879. It stated that Fred Asbecks and William Mann, miners, had been chased out of the Sacramento Mountains on November 5, by Victorio and a war party of Apaches, Comanches, and Lipans. "Mann knows Victorio well and saw him in person," the telegram said.[17]

Scalps sat uneasily on many a head when that word got around, and fear begot contention between soldiers and civilians. The army had always blamed the Indian agents for giving the Apaches too much rope; the agents were always complaining of the inefficiency and wrongheadedness of the troops. Now tempers flared as letters went back and forth between Agent Russell and some of the officers. Lieutenant G. W. Smith wrote as follows:

Station Det Co "H" US Cav.
TULEROSA N. M.
Dec. 2, 1879

Mr. S. A. RUSSELL
  US Indian Agt
    Mescalero Apache Indian Agency
      MAJOR.

I have the honor to acknowledge the recpt of your letter and in reply to yr remark, that you appreciate your (my) offer of assistance *"after"* the return of the Indians who have just left your Reservation for a raid of theft and murder I desire to be *distinctly* understood that the offer referred to, which I have repeatedly given you is made subject to your call at *any time* you may need my men and myself.

You ask if it would not be better to follow the Indians *"immediately."* Certainly, I answer it would and I would be glad to do it if the "immediately" came within from 12 to 24 hours of their departure from the reservation, and left a reasonable chance of

[17] Files of the Mescalero Agency.

167

overtaking them. There is not a Chief on yr Reservation who does not know when a party of your murderers will leave, where it is going and all about it, and if the Chiefs entertained any other than the most treacherous feelings of hatred toward you, and of which I have fully informed you, they would let you know when these murdering thieves are about to leave, you could easily notify me and there would be some small chance for an officer to "arrest" them as you desire, but you may fully depend upon it, that an "arrest" means a calibre 45 bullet, and that a bench warrant even, issued by my much esteemed friend Judge Bristol, would not stop it.

If you had studied the Indian from the saddle—not the rocking chair you would have learned that instead of his movements being "encumbered" (as you seem to suppose) by extra horses, they are on the contrary facilitated and hastened by all the extra horses he can steal. This talk about "arresting" and "convicting" the brutal Apache whose hands are now reeking with the blood of the noble men, devoted women and innocent and lovely little children of N. M. is a fatal folly and you ought to know it, and at the next "departure" which will in all probability soon occur, if you will come down here, I will give you a sample Cavalry ride on a trail toward Old Mexico, which, long before it (the ride) is ended, will convince you that, talk is one thing and work is another when dealing in the rampant state with the fiends whom you hold in a fancied control in the quiescent state, whilst issuing them rations and clothing to trade for arms and ammunition with which to murder peaceful citizens. I have warned you of your danger and can do no more than repeat the warning and tell you that you can trust a dead Apache; but God help you for he only can, if you trust a live one. I will come to the helpless people of the Canon if I have to crawl on my hands and knees to do it. Do your duty in telling me to come and I will do mine in coming.

I am Sir
Very Respectfully
Your Obt. Svt.
G. W. Smith—
Lt. Commdg.[18]

Eventually the panic subsided, when word got around that Victorio was actually catching his breath in Chihuahua. Nevertheless, accusations and rejoinders continued to fly back and forth as the citizens assessed the damage and tried to find somebody to blame for what had happened. The Mesilla *News* lambasted General Hatch and Major Morrow, accused them of fighting an Indian War in "parlor rooms," and blamed them for the loss of life because they had issued no warnings to the civilian population.[19]

Major Morrow fought back in the columns of the Santa Fé *New Mexican* on November 22, declaring that he had engaged Victorio twice in the Black Range, and that he had "whipped him thoroughly and chased him out of the country."[20] The country newspapers replied with editorial catcalls and attributed Victorio's break for old Mexico to the pressure exerted by the Las Cruces and Mesilla volunteers.[21]

While this was going on behind him, Victorio had holed up in the Candelaria Mountains in Chihuahua, not far from the El Paso highway, where he could see what was happening on the plain below and where a natural tank or reservoir of fresh water was always available.

Fifteen Mexicans from the little town of Carrizal came out to try to persuade him to move on. He ambushed them in a narrow canyon and killed every one of them. The date was November 7, 1879.

When the men failed to return, a band of friends and neighbors went out to see what had happened. Victorio wiped out this second group in the same place.

---

[18] *Ibid.*
[19] Mesilla *News,* Oct. 18, 1879.
[20] Ritch Collection, No. 1886, "Notes Concerning the Fight of Maj. A. P. Morrow with Victorio, Santa Fé, Nov. 22, 1879."
[21] Mesilla *News,* Oct. 18, 1879.

In desperation, the Mexicans sent an SOS to Paso del Norte. Ten of Baylor's rangers, stationed at Ysleta, were permitted to enter Mexico and lend their assistance. The Indians were gone when the Rangers and Mexicans arrived at the scene of the double massacre, but the story was easy to read.[22]

In January, 1880, Victorio was back in New Mexico west of the Río Grande, standing off troops in brief flurries of gunfire— at the head of the Puerco River and in the San Mateo Mountains—holding his own very well in the skirmishes, and maneuvering easily through country so rough that it broke down cavalrymen and horses in a few days' scouting.

Again the smoke rose and dead men lay on the ground. James K. Hastings was a small boy in the mountain mining village of Chloride, while these things were taking place. "The saddest sight I ever saw," he says, "was on a Sunday morning when two soldiers came down the street in our town, the end of the coach line, driving two broken-down cavalry horses hitched to a coach filled with bullet holes and covered with human blood. The Apaches had jumped the coach about sunrise, near Ft. Cummings, a six-company post. The Indians had hid behind the tall yucca stumps and killed every mortal on the coach. . . . Our mail the next day, from those mail sacks, showed plenty of blood on it."[23]

Victorio's supply service was too well organized for the soldiers to beat him. His men could ride their horses to death, cut their throats, eat them if they had to, and find replacements at the nearest ranch. Mexican sheepherders, with whom they had a very good understanding, would get arms and ammunition for them and provide them with mutton.[24]

---

[22] Raht, *op. cit.*, 233–66; Baylor, *loc. cit.*, 37–42.
[23] Hastings, "A Boy's-Eye View of the Old Southwest," *N.M.H.R.*, Vol. XXVI (October, 1951), 290. Hastings came to Chloride in 1880.

170

It has been said that these Apaches should have had no real chance—that they represented the Stone Age making a stand against gunpowder.[25] But while they were able to put their hearts into it, those Stone Age warriors (with the help of a little gunpowder of their own) outfought the United States Cavalry and all others who had the temerity to go after them.

All this was bad for the morale of the Mescaleros at the agency. News was always coming in of some feat accomplished by Victorio, and many a substantial Indian had long, long thoughts of the spoil and glory he was missing.[26] Before the winter was over, a number of ambitious braves had joined the outlaws—perhaps as many as sixty. These were the wild ones. The real tribal leaders stayed at home. Sam Chino, who lived at Mescalero in dignity until his recent death at the age of 102, was one who kept his head. He joined the Indian police force when it was established in the early eighties and spent his life

[handwritten margin note: Some left, some stayed]

[24] *Report of the Secretary of War for 1881*, 197 (Report of Col. Edward Hatch).

[25] Wellman, *op. cit.*, 366; *Report of the Secretary of War for 1880*, 197 (Report of Col. Edward Hatch). The best account of the equipment and tactics of the Apache warrior in these campaigns is Lummis' "Apache Warrior," *op. cit.*, 113–19.

[26] While the bad Indians were trying to get away, others were trying with small success to come home. Among those who left the reservation in 1875 when the "Texans" shot up their camps was Polonio, a brother of Chief San Juan. In February, 1879, Polonio's son-in-law José Maria wangled permission from Agent Godfroy to hunt him up and bring him back. Five months later they came in—José Maria, Polonio, two women, and three children. By this time Russell had succeeded Godfroy. Knowing nothing of the arrangements, the new agent threw the entire band in jail. In an interview, Godfroy said that he knew Polonio but declared that all arrangements for bringing him back had been made after he left the agency. Resentful over this raw deal, the Indians retained Colonel A. J. Fountain to help them. Fountain took statements from everybody and raised as much dust as he could, threatening to bring Agent Russell into federal court "if the facts relative to their arrest and imprisonment can be reached in no other way." Before it was over, the Commissioner of Indian Affairs had to take a hand. He wrote to Russell, instructing him to turn the Indians loose if they had told the truth. (Fountain's letter to Russell, dated October 11, 1879, with statements by the Indians involved, is in the Mescalero Agency letter file, as is Commissioner E. A. Hayt's, dated October 22.)

trying to influence his people in the right direction.[27] Nautzile, "an exemplary Indian and a true friend of the Government," kept his young men at home and refused to be seduced by the glitter of Victorio's success.[28]

The good conduct of these men made little difference to the army officers who were having such conspicuously bad luck in suppressing Victorio and his renegades. All the Mescaleros, they thought, were aiding the outlaws, and all the Mescaleros must suffer for it. In the spring of 1880, they evolved a scheme for reducing the whole tribe to impotence—a scheme which some white men still blush to think about.

[27] Mrs. Tom Charles, "Sam Chino Helped Direct Mescaleros," El Paso *Times,* Feb. 24, 1952.

[28] *Report of the Commissioner of Indian Affairs for 1880, xliv* (E. M. Marble); 129 (S. A. Russell, Aug. 16, 1880). Russell says that 250 Mescaleros, including women and children, were with Victorio by April 1, 1880.

Chapter X

THE ARMY MOVES IN

The Disarming of the Mescaleros

ACTING ON THE THEORY that an Indian without a gun or a horse would have to be a good Indian, the military men began to cast about for a way to dismount and disarm the Mescaleros. They intended to round up every pistol and every pony on the reservation.

It would be a ticklish job, of course. Violence might—probably would—break out, and consequently many soldiers would have to be brought in. It was necessary to keep the scheme absolutely secret, for if one Indian suspected what was afoot, all their plans would go for naught. After six months the officers ironed out most of the difficulties and came up with a satisfactory set of arrangements.[1]

Mescalero was to be the center of a far-flung tactical pattern which would bring troops in from every direction like spokes to the hub of a wheel. Secret orders were sent to forts along the Río Grande, and even farther west. Negro troops of

---

[1] The army went through channels in setting up the plan. On February 24, 1880, E. R. Platt, assistant adjutant general, wrote from Leavenworth, Kansas, that a letter had been received from the Secretary of the Interior consenting to "the dismounting and disarming of the Mescalero Indians." (*Report of the Secretary of War for 1880*, 99.)

the Tenth Cavalry were notified to move up from their posts in Texas. The rendezvous was set for the morning of April 12, 1880.

In order to make sure that the Indians would be present, some sort of instructions had to be sent to their agent, but even he was not to know everything that was going on. Colonel Hatch wrote to Russell on March 23, 1880, asking him to have the Indians collected, with all their stock, on April 12. He indicated that troops were on the way from Texas, but disarming was not mentioned. "I shall be forced," Hatch concluded, "to consider all Indians not at the agency hostile."[2]

Russell did as he was told and by April 10 had all the Apaches camped within an hour's ride of his headquarters.

Meanwhile the great envelopment had begun, with soldiers converging on Mescalero from all directions. Since the Negro cavalrymen from the Texas forts were farthest away, three companies of them were on the road by April 1. They followed three separate routes, the better to scout the Guadalupe and Sacramento Mountains, and each one had brushes with Apache bands scattered through the wild highland country.

Company K had what it considered a special bit of luck. It marched through the Guadalupes and up the east slope of the Sacramentos, striking pay dirt at a place called Shakehand Springs. The report reads: "April 9th struck the camp of a small party of Mescaleros on Shakehand Springs, N. M. Killed one buck, captured four squaws and one child, released from captivity a small Mexican boy (Cayetano Segura) aged 11. Captured twenty-one head of horses and mules and destroyed their camp. Distance marched 417½ miles."[3]

The important fact about this "strike" was the discovery of

[2] *Report of the Commissioner of Indian Affairs for 1880,* 129 (Report of S. A. Russell, Aug. 16, 1880).

[3] Major E. N. Glass, compiler, *The History of the Tenth Cavalry,* 100–101.

174

a large quantity of government-issue supplies at the Indian camp—proof positive to the officers that the Indians were using their rations to live on while making war against the United States. It is hard to see the logic of this attitude, since the Apaches were in their own country, had a right to the supplies issued to them, and were not making any trouble. They did not attack the troops; the troops attacked them. The military authorities, however, felt that this was the final bit of evidence needed to justify the proposed disarming.[4]

While the troops from Texas were thus occupied, cavalry detachments, reinforced by Indian scouts from Arizona, were closing in from the west. The Indians were ignorant of what they were in for, but Russell's order to come in to the agency was enough to let them know that something was in the wind. A large band of their fighting men concentrated at a wild and inaccessible spot in the San Andres Mountains known as Hembrillo Canyon. Victorio himself may have been maintaining a field headquarters there, though Nana is also said to have been the leader.[5] Before long, they found themselves involved in an unusual bit of military action which has never been described in detail by historians of the Indian wars.

Knowing of Victorio's presence in Hembrillo Canyon, Colonel Hatch determined to route his troops past this spot on their way to Mescalero, hoping to surround and annihilate the band. He was sure that "nearly every Mescalero warrior" was there. Much careful planning was necessary beforehand:

[4] Rister, *The Southwestern Frontier*, 186–90, takes this view, as does Colonel M. L. Crimmins, "The Mescalero Apaches," *Frontier Times*, Vol. VIII (September, 1931), 554—both agreeing with Hatch and his fellow officers.

[5] Colonel Hatch, in his account of the fight, assumes that "Victoria" was in charge. After the battle, the newspapers decided that Nana was the man (Santa Fé *Era Southwestern*, April 15, 1880, clipping in possession of Robert Glass Cleland, San Marino, California).

Major Morrow, with his command, was brought up to Palomas and there met a train of supplies—boots, shoes, clothing and rations—which he was greatly in need of. McLellan was brought down to the same point from the San Mateo mountains, where he was scouting. Hooker, Ninth Cavalry, with one hundred men was sent by Anaya Springs to go through the pass of the northern point of the San Andreas, and came down on the east side of those mountains. Carroll, Ninth Cavalry, with scouts and one hundred men, had been ordered to come up from Fort Stanton to Embryo Cañon, to attack, when hearing the principal attack, which I had decided to make from the west side of the mountains, and for this purpose brought up Morrow's command on April 4 to the Aleman.[6]

It was a good plan. Aleman was a station in the heart of the *Jornada del Muerto,* just under the west slope of the San Andres. By dropping over the crest, Hatch would find himself in the midst of the Apaches. The troops coming in from the east and the north would cut off their retreat. It was too bad something had to go wrong at the worst possible moment. Hatch continues:

Unfortunately the water at this place [Aleman] is obtained from a well of great depth, brought to the surface by means of a force pump, which broke down when needed. Knowing we could not find water for the animals in Embryo Cañon 35 miles distant, it was of the greatest importance they should be watered, and with a scant allowance moved out McLellan and the Indian scouts at dark, and as the command could obtain water during the night and morning sent them forward by companies as rapidly as watered. McLellan arrived, with the Indians, his command of the Sixth Cavalry, and detachment of the Ninth Cavalry, at daylight on the morning of April 8. Coming over the first range of mountains, he discovered Captain Carroll, surrounded by Indians, within a semicircle upon hills of higher range. Carroll was then fighting. The hostiles had thrown up rifle pits on the crest

[6] *Report of the Secretary of War for 1880,* I, 94–95.

176

of this range, covering three-fourths of a circle around Carroll's command, where nature had not furnished them with shelter; they had left their rifle pits and were moving down the ravines in strong bands with the intention undoubtedly of destroying Carroll. There was no time to be lost, and McLellan, realizing this, at once charged with his entire force, taking the hostiles by surprise, driving them back, and keeping up a very heavy fire as they retreated up the cañons. Captain Carroll, who had been seriously wounded, gave up the command to Lieutenant Cusack, Ninth Cavalry, who at once charged, with his command, and claims that he inflicted great damage upon the Indians.[7] The command came up gradually during the day. The Indians at dark had been driven into their works on the upper range and beyond, when the command moved forward, throwing the scouts to the rear of the hostiles, who fled. The command was then brought back to the horses and mounted and obliged to go out by Embryo Cañon. It was not well on the trail until nearly dark when it was discovered that the hostiles were in large number and nearly all going towards the Mescalero Agency. The command marched until half past two o'clock the following morning over the gypsum beds known as the White Sands, and at daylight moved up to water near Tularosa.[8]

The country was full of people that night. George Sligh was a boy at the time, living in White Oaks. He and his father were coming over the San Agustín Pass while the fight was going on thirty miles north. They had a wagonload of El Paso whiskey and beer to sell to the soldiers at Tularosa, and were still traveling when night came on. Presently they noticed lights wavering in front of them—then more lights behind them. Then they began to hear voices. They drove off the road, tied their horses to the wagon wheels, and lay out in the brush, praying that the

[7] Hatch estimated that three hundred Apaches were in the band and that thirty were killed. A. J. Fountain and others scoffed at this report in the columns of Las Cruces *34*, declaring that fifty-three Indians were present and that only one was killed (June 23, 1880).

[8] *Report of the Secretary of War for 1880*, I, 95 (Hatch).

animals would be still and not give them away. The lights went off into the distance. It was the Indians heading for Dog Canyon after the battle, using torches to keep together.

Next day, in Tularosa, Sligh saw the disgusted Negro soldiers of Carroll's command and heard them talking about the fight. Some of them were soaking their feet in the *acequia* which brought water from the mountains into the village, and one declared, "I ain't never going up no canyon again for no officer. If they let me fight them the Indian way, I fight them, but I ain't going up no more canyons."[9]

In spite of the interruption at Hembrillo Canyon, the army timetable was working perfectly. The troops sent in for the disarming arrived at Mescalero from all directions "within an hour of the time assigned," Hatch noted. This was too much for the Indians, who were prepared to see some troops march in but had no idea there would be more than a thousand of them. Practically instantaneously they all disappeared from the vicinity of the agency and secreted themselves so successfully that Russell was able to find only one camp—that of his trusted Indian friend, Nautzile. From him Russell learned that a rumor had passed among the tribesmen to the effect that the soldiers had come to take them to San Carlos. Nautzile himself was so scared that he would go to the agency for a talk with Colonel Hatch only on condition that Russell would stay with him every minute until he was back in his own camp. This Russell promised to do, and Nautzile came in, to be convinced by Colonel Hatch that no harm was intended to him or any other Apache.

That evening Russell himself heard for the first time what the army had come for, and he was indignant about it. "If the Indians had known this," he told Hatch, "they would not have been here. They relied upon me as their friend and came in

[9] George Sligh, Feb. 26, 1948.

cheerfully and promptly when I told them to. They had no reason to expect anything of this kind, and I will not be a party to such a deception."

"In that case," Hatch replied, "I will turn my own Indians loose on them."[10]

They argued until Hatch finally accepted the suggestion that Russell be allowed to try to collect the arms and horses belonging to the Indians, with the understanding that everything would be returned after peace had been restored. Hatch "readily assented" to this proposition. In the light of what followed, it is hard to believe that he had any intention of keeping his promise, but his consent served to keep Russell quiet. Hatch merely stipulated that the Apaches would have to come in close to the agency to a place he would select. Russell, in his innocence—or perhaps more accurately, his helplessness—agreed to that. This was on April 12.[11]

There were some four hundred Indians on the reservation, mostly women and children. Nautzile and San Juan, with the aid of Chiefs Griego and Roman, went out on April 14 to herd them in. The date of the disarming was moved forward to April 16.

The Indians grew more and more alarmed, and they had reason to be. Colonel B. H. Grierson, riding in through the Sacramento Mountains on April 14, came across a camp on the Tularosa which he surrounded and prepared to attack at daybreak. A messenger from Agent Russell arrived just in time to prevent a massacre. The unsuspecting Apaches, mostly still in their blankets, were there by permission of the agent on a hunting expedition.[12]

---

[10] *Report of the Commissioner of Indian Affairs for 1880*, 130 (Report of S. A. Russell, Aug. 16, 1880).

[11] *Ibid.*

[12] Wellman, *op. cit.*, 383.

This band escaped by the skin of their teeth, but two of their fellow tribesmen were not so lucky. Just after daybreak on the morning of the sixteenth, firing was heard near the agency. The Indians were thrown into near panic, and when they learned that Lieutenant Charles B. Gatewood had killed two Apaches who were "driving off stock," they became terribly alarmed. One of the dead Indians was Nautzile's father. He and his companion had been sent out by Russell to bring in animals which had strayed away from the agency.

Russell rode out to the camp and quieted the uneasy tribesmen as best he could, but some of the men left and did not return. Thus there were only sixty-five adult males on the ground when the disarming started.

When Hatch told Russell he was ready, the agent, with Captain Steelhammer and an interpreter, led a company of soldiers to the Indian encampment. Russell called the men around him and told them that they were to be disarmed but that they could give their guns and horses to him, to be returned after the troubles were over. A few came forward and handed over their guns. Others on the outskirts of the group began to drift away.

"Captain Steelhammer and I both appealed to them not to leave," Russell stated later. "Nautzila, the principal chief, went out among them and endeavored to get them to come back again. Very soon it became evident that those who had left would not return, and the troops opened fire on them."

The first shots were not fired in anger. Hatch had sent a detachment of his soldiers some distance away from the agency to intercept fugitives. It was agreed between him and Colonel Grierson that, in case of emergency, three shots would be the signal for the reserves to come in. When he saw that some of his intended victims were leaving, Hatch began to feel the need for

180

Apache Agent
W. H. H. Llewellyn.

COURTESY MRS. TOM CHARLES

Agent James A. Carroll.

COURTESY MRS. IRVING MCNEIL

Issue day at the commissary in the 1890's.

more men. The signal shots were fired, and no more was needed to throw the Apaches into panic. They broke for the wooded hill north of the agency. The soldiers held their fire until the escapees were clear of the women and children; then the shooting began in earnest. Fourteen Indians were killed.[13] Twenty-five kept on running. The rest were brought back as prisoners.

Russell's report said, dsecribing the events which followed:

> The Indian camp was about one-third of a mile from the agency. After the occurrence mentioned above, Colonel Hatch ordered all of the Indians to be brought to the agency; soon as they arrived here they were dismounted, placed under guard, searched for arms and ammunition, and their horses corraled. In this hurried removal, and the search that was made by soldiers, the Indians lost much that was valuable to them and not contraband. The next morning the Indian horses to the number of 200 or more were sent to Fort Stanton, and the Indians put in the corral, where the old manure was 3 to 5 inches deep. This produced so much sickness among them that they had soon to be removed. This was after Captain Steelhammer and I had repeatedly reassured them that those who remained faithful and did as he requested would be well treated, and their horses put in my hands. In addition to the animals that were sent to Fort Stanton, a good many were CONFISCATED by the military. I am credibly informed that of the horses sent to Fort Stanton there are but 42 left, the others having died, been killed, or claimed by citizens.[14]

The Mescaleros who ran were now vulnerable in the game the soldiers were playing. They were pursued, and some of them did not get away. An extract from the report of Company

---

[13] *Record of Engagements,* 95, says ten were killed; *Report of the Commissioner of Indian Affairs for 1880,* 130 (Report of S. A. Russell). Russell says fourteen.

[14] *Report of the Commissioner of Indian Affairs for 1880,* 130 (Report of S. A. Russell).

L of the Tenth Cavalry reads: "Left agency April 20th for Silver Springs on fresh trail. Overtook party of four or five in number same afternoon and killed one Indian and captured five horses."[15]

Other detachments did even better: "Between the head of the Rio Fresnal and Rio Alamo Lieutenant Mills with his Indians attacked a small party of Mescaleros, killed them all and captured twenty-odd head of stock. Lieutenant Mills's action is worthy of notice."

Agent Russell boiled over as he thought, four months after it happened, of all this unnecessary and unpardonable cruelty:

> Colonel Hatch claimed that the Indians broke faith with him by leaving their camp, and thus justified his course afterwards. It is true that a part of them did leave (through fear). Did this justify the harsh treatment given them? A few of the Indians that left at the time voluntarily returned; they, with those that did not leave, are still held as prisoners. Four months have passed since they were placed under guard. They often ask, "For what are we held as prisoners? How long are we to be confined because others did wrong? Will we be paid for our horses?"[16]

These were questions which by now the Indians should have been ready to answer out of past experience. But the Indians never completely gave up hope. The white men talked so much about justice and keeping promises—perhaps some day they would keep their own.

Poor nervous Mr. Russell must have seemed to them the

[15] *Report of the Secretary of War for 1880,* I, 100 (Report of Maj. A. P. Morrow, May 1, 1880).

[16] *Report of the Commissioner of Indian Affairs for 1880,* 130. Many citizens of New Mexico were horrified at what happened in connection with the disarming. S. H. Newman, editor of Las Cruces *34,* visited the agency on June 23 to see for himself what was going on. On June 26, his paper printed a set of resolutions blaming the army for the Indian trouble and asking for the removal of Hatch. The issues of April 2 and May 5 carried more information about the disarming.

only white man who cared whether they lived or died. By the time of the disarming he actually had a school building erected and twenty-five little Apaches in the seats, although neither they nor their parents were enthusiastic about education. And because the men were kept under guard when they should have been planting crops, Russell and the agency employees took care of that task for them, hoping they would be released in time to do their own cultivating.

Week after week the soldiers camped at the agency, and the Indians dared not take a long stride in any direction for fear of punishment. On August 21, they addressed a petition to Hatch asking for more freedom. Hatch's reply, dated September 3, 1880, said that the request for "increased limits is favorably considered . . . the Indians to be present as they promised every seven days. The Company of Infantry to remain at the Agency, and the companies of the 9th Cavalry with Lieutenant Cusack to scout the Reservation and adjacent region."[17] Later instructions stated specifically that the Indians could go out eight miles from the agency, but must not approach white men on ranches and must keep off the roads.

It was not until January, 1881, nine months after the horrible episode of the disarming, that an order was issued to remove the troops from the reservation.[18] The old Indians have not forgotten, and will never forget, that miserable time. The killing—the confinement—the breaking up of families—they remember it with quiet bitterness.

[17] John S. Loud, capt., 9th Cavalry, and assistant adjutant general, to S. A. Russell, Santa Fé, Sept. 3, 1880, files of the Mescalero Agency.

[18] J. A. Manye, acting post adjutant at Fort Stanton, to Russell, Jan. 17, 1881. On January 17, Lieutenant Walter L. Finley, commanding troops at South Fork (Mescalero), wrote to Russell that he would suspend execution of the order to remove troops until he received instructions from Fort Stanton. The removal must have occurred shortly after this, however. (Both letters in the Mescalero Agency files.)

Old Crookneck, ninety-nine years old as this is being written, says his father and mother took off for Mexico and stayed for a long time. What sticks in his mind especially is the thought of that horse corral where his people were left day after day in six inches of manure.[19]

[19] Crookneck, Feb. 5, 1955.

Chapter XI

PEACE AT LAST

Victorio Goes Under

Iᴛ ᴛᴏᴏᴋ ᴏɴᴇ ᴛʜᴏᴜsᴀɴᴅ sᴏʟᴅɪᴇʀs to subdue half that number of more or less peaceful Mescaleros. Two thousand cavalrymen, plus rangers, militiamen, and indignant ranchers, could not catch Victorio. After the fight at Hembrillo Canyon, he headed for the mountains across the Río Grande, pursued by soldiers who were careful not to get too close.[1] Back in his old haunts he soon had the whole country in an uproar.

Thirteen herders were done to death and 100,000 sheep were scattered during the last days of April in the Mogollon Mountains.[2] Cooney's mining camp in the same district was attacked on April 29.[3] Terrified citizens sent frantic letters to the governor, complaining of the "*terribiles incurciones que los Barbaros Apaches han cometidos desde Mediado del mes de abril*

---

[1] *Report of the Secretary of War for 1880*, I, 96 (Report of Col. Edward Hatch): "I had sent Captain Purrington with three companies the morning before to the Rio Grande, to watch 'Victoria' and follow up a large party who were going that way. He reports he came up in sight of the Indians at the river, but does not explain satisfactorily why he did not follow and attack, stating that he was obliged to go down the river to Palomas, where his wagons had preceded him." Captain Purington (*ibid.*, 101) said he turned back because he had no pack mules or rations.

[2] Denver *Tribune*, May 4, 5, 1880 (dispatches from Santa Fé).

[3] *Ibid.*, May 4, 1880.

sobre los pastorias de ganados menores mayores y Caballadas"—
the terrible depredations which the savage Apaches have committed since the middle of April upon the herders of big and
little bands of sheep and horses.[4]

The soldiers got on the trail at once, but Victorio kept ahead
of them. He was not even seen by any United States force until
May 24, when Captain H. K. Parker, chief of scouts, found his
hide-out in the Black Range. During the night of the twenty-
third, Parker and his Arizona Indian scouts surrounded Victorio's camp. "We creeped all night," Parker said, "and daylight
found us in fifty yards of his camp. The 30 scouts in rear of camp
opened on them at daybreak, killing several men, women, and
children."

All day the fighting went on. After their first panic, Victorio's men settled down grimly to the business in hand. To
Parker's horrified surprise, they made the ten women in their
camp expose themselves to the fire of the soldiers while the men
dug in. Parker had sixty men against Victorio's thirty, plus the
unusual advantage of surprise. Parker estimated that he killed
about thirty men, women, and children before lack of water
forced him to withdraw. He got away with seventy-four of the
Apaches' horses.[5]

The Territorial press seized upon this victory with loud
cries of joy. The army was not popular in New Mexico, and
Colonel Hatch was a special target from 1879 on. After Parker's
victory, a report from Washington came in to the effect that
reinforcements were on the way to join Hatch's command. One
newspaper advised the government to "trot the troops back. . . .
A million under him [Hatch] would not whip Victorio—while it

---

[4] Jesus María Chávez to Lew Wallace, Socorro, May 2, 1880 (Ritch Collection, No. 1895).
[5] *Report of the Secretary of War for 1880*, I, 99–100 (Report of H. K.
Parker, May 26, 1880).

is a notorious fact that H. K. Parker, at the head of sixty-one Apache scouts almost wiped out his entire band. Hatch and his troops had better go into summer quarters and leave Victorio to be dealt with by Parker."[6]

It was the reasoned opinion of most New Mexicans that the soldiers would never be able to do anything with Victorio—that the only way to finish him would be to let the Apache scouts handle it.

Victorio did not wait for the newspapers to conclude their argument. He headed straight for Mexico, where he picked up recruits and horses, and was back in Texas by the end of July.

Now began the greatest man hunt the border country had ever seen. Mexican troops were moving in Chihuahua. At least two thousand United States soldiers were deployed in southern New Mexico and West Texas. The Texas Rangers, local militia companies, and posses of citizens stood ready to take the field. Victorio, with less than two hundred warriors, was met with gunfire wherever he turned. They chased him back across the river on July 31, but he returned within four days, dodged two detachments of troops, and rode for the Guadalupes. This time the soldiers had outthought him and had an ambush ready. He fell into it—got out of it—and fell into another. Each engagement cost him a few men. The pressure was too great; by the middle of August he was headed for Mexico again.

And now the Mexicans and Americans did what they might well have done before—they agreed to combine forces and co-ordinate the attack. Following a carefully worked out timetable, several columns of American troops went into Mexico, beginning about the tenth of September. It was a big operation, and the noose drew tighter and tighter around the harried Apaches. Victory seemed to be in sight at last—but this was one campaign the soldiers were not destined to win.

[6] Santa Fé *Era Southwestern*, June 1, 1880.

Just when Victorio had been driven far south of El Paso into the Tres Castillos Mountains—when all avenues of escape had been put under observation—at that moment Colonel Terrazas, in command of the Mexican forces, sent word that "it would be objectionable on the part of his government for American troops to advance farther into the interior."[7]

To the frustrated American officers, it seemed obvious that Terrazas thought he had the situation in hand and did not wish to share the glory.

By the time the United States troops began to withdraw on October 10, Victorio was already finished. On October 9, the Mexican forces surrounded him and began the death struggle. While the Apaches were making their last stand, their ammunition all used up, a Tarahumare marksman got his sights on Victorio and brought him down with a miraculous long shot. When it was over, Victorio and eighty-six warriors were dead; eighty-nine women and children were captives.

Only a few members of the band got away. The largest group belonged to a scouting party which had been sent out under Nana before the battle started. Eight months later, in July, 1882, this remnant of Victorio's little army embarked on the last and bloodiest of the Apache raids—a raid of death which equaled, or perhaps exceeded, Victorio's exploits.

Nana was the last great chief of the Warm Springs band. Although he was seventy-three at this time, he had married Victorio's daughter and was prepared in skill and cruelty to step into his father-in-law's shoes. He was, it is true, half-blind and terribly crippled by rheumatism. Lieutenant Gatewood called him a "palsied, aged and decrepit chief, who was barely able to

---

[7] Colonel M. L. Crimmins, "Colonel Buell's Expedition into Mexico," *N.M.H.R.*, Vol. X (April 1935), 133–49. See Frank P. Lockwood, *The Apache Indians*, 222–23, for a different version of Victorio's end, based on a manuscript written by General Thomas Cruse.

accompany the squaws and children in their forays."[8] But once in the saddle he could ride his seventy miles and more a day; and, like Victorio, he was a master strategist.

During the days when the Warm Springs Apaches were struggling to keep their reservation and taking to the hills every time an attempt was made to take them to or keep them at San Carlos, Nana had gone to the Mescaleros and was living with them when Victorio took up his brief residence at the agency. Perhaps he was an adviser to Victorio during the raids of 1879— some of the army officers thought so[9]—and he was certainly with Victorio part of the time in 1880, remaining with him at Tres Castillos until just before the end.

Nana and his thirty fighting men probably spent that winter in Mexico. By June, 1881,[10] however, they were camping in the New Mexico mountains within reach of the Mescalero Agency. Paul I. Wellman is one who assumes that they were still eager to fight the white man and that they were spending this quiet interval getting ready to go on the warpath again.[11] There is evidence to show, however, that some of the band wanted to surrender—and were not allowed to.

By this time W. H. H. Llewellyn had become the Mescalero agent. He noted in his first year's report that some highhanded tactics had been used in dealing with these weary warriors:

It seems that some few months since a Lieutenant of the

---

[8] Lieutenant C. B. Gatewood, "Campaigning against Victorio," *The Great Divide*, Vol. XI, No. 4 (April, 1894), 102; Crook, *op. cit.*, 241 ff. General Crook gives Nana's age as seventy-three.

[9] Gatewood, *op. cit.*, 102.

[10] *Report of the Secretary of War for 1881*, 117, says that Nana crossed the Río Grande near Fort Quitman about July 13 and made his way "without discovery" to the mountains near Mescalero. "Here he was joined by twenty-five Mescaleros from that reservation."

[11] Wellman, *op. cit.*, 393.

United States Army then stationed here, gave a written permit
to three Indians at this agency to go to Old Mexico and bring
back here a party of their friends whom they claimed had left
at the time of the Victorio troubles. This party were due here
three weeks ago, and at that time attempted to come in but were
chased and driven into the mountains thirty miles from the
agency to the south. Since that time they have made, according
to the statement of one of the packers for the scouts, who is now
at this agency badly wounded, three ineffectual efforts to get
into the agency, being prevented each time by the scouts and
soldiers; finding that they could not return to the agency, as they
had been led to believe they could, they commenced to go on
the warpath. I learn on good authority that there are about
seventy Indians in this party.[12]

The increase from thirty to seventy in Nana's enrollment
was due to the arrival of volunteers from Mescalero. Victorio's
force had included Comanches and Navajos, according to news
stories of the time,[13] but Nana's group seems to have been all
Apaches. The soldiers who were on the watch for such things
knew that Mescalero man power had gone to strengthen Nana's
troop, and were sure that his camp was somewhere near by in
the mountains. Peso and Choneska, leading Mescaleros, acted
as scouts for the soldiers, but could not, or at least did not, succeed in locating the hostile camp.

One white man came a little too close to it for comfort. He
was Tom Keeney, an old pioneer who had a homestead up in
the mountains behind present-day Alamogordo. John Meadows,
another salty character who had been out with the scouting parties looking for the hide-out of the renegades, reported the episode many years later. John saw Keeney come into Tularosa one
afternoon on foot with his bed roll on his back. This was suf-

---

[12] *Report of the Commissioner of Indian Affairs for 1881*, 4–6.
[13] Denver *Tribune*, May 4, 1880 (dispatch dated Santa Fé, May 3).

ficient cause for wonder since Keeney was notoriously averse to any kind of physical exertion. Meadows inquired about it.

"Well, John," Keeney replied, "you know that place of mine up in the hills? I went up there this morning to do some assessment work—thought I'd stay a few days, so I sent the boy back with the team and wagon to La Luz. About the time I got the cabin cleaned up, I saw a shadow in the doorway and there was old Comesco. I've been friends with Comesco for many years, so we shook hands and I fixed dinner for us. Afterwards we had a smoke and a talk, and I asked him where them renegade Injuns was.

" 'I just come from their camp this morning,' Comesco says.

" 'Comesco, you and I have been friends for a long time.'

" 'Yes, you and me have been friends for years, and always will be.'

" 'Comesco, if them wild people took a notion to come down here and kill your old friend, what would you do?'

" 'I wouldn't let your enemies kill you. They will never kill you.'

" 'What would you do to keep them from killing me?'

" 'Why, I would come down and kill you myself and wouldn't let your enemies do it.' "

"John," said Keeney to Meadows after letting this sink in, "how did I know but that was what he was there for right then? I rolled my bedding up, left my provisions, and got out of there damn quick."[14]

Apparently the renegades were ripe for trouble by this time and Keeney may have got out with no time to spare. They were ready to go to war when, on July 17, they left their mountain camp and followed the ancient Indian highway down Dog Canyon to the valley floor. At the mouth of Alamo Canyon, near by,

[14] Meadows, Alamogordo *News,* Feb. 13, 1936.

they ambushed two soldiers, wounded one, and got away with three mules. Two days later Lieutenant Guilfoyle and a detachment of the Ninth Cavalry almost caught up with them—almost, but not quite—near the White Sands, just after they had killed three Mexicans.[15]

The soldiers figured that thirteen Indians were involved in this minor massacre—Nana's main force must have been somewhere else.

Patiently the troops toiled across the desert on the trail of the raiders. On July 25, somewhere in the San Andres Mountains, they finally caught up, and there was a skirmish. Triumphantly the troop commander reported that he had "captured two horses, twelve mules, many blankets, and all the Indians' provisions; two of the hostiles were shot and believed to be killed; the others crossing the Río Grande six miles below San José, killing two miners and a Mexican in the flight."[16]

Once across the river, the band took up the old weaving dance, murdering as they went. Through July and August the old raider and his band kept in the lead, riding as much as seventy miles a day, fighting rear-guard actions when they had to and always coming out on top.

The bloody little scenes unreeled like a horror film: four Mexicans killed in the foothills of the San Mateos; thirty-six Indian-hunting ranchmen, eating their dinner in Red Canyon of the San Mateos, surprised and shot up (one man killed, seven wounded, all their horses driven off); one Mexican killed as the Apaches left the canyon—so it went!

August 3 the troops caught up at Monica Springs, capturing eleven head of horses and wounding a couple of Indians.

[15] Wellman, *op. cit.*, 394.
[16] *Record of Engagements*, 99.

August 11—Two Mexicans killed and two women carried off at La Cebolla.

August 12—Captain Parker and nineteen Negro soldiers of the Ninth Cavalry caught up again twenty-five miles west of Sabinal. Result: one soldier killed, three wounded, and one missing. Parker thought the Indians lost about the same number, but his detachment, "incumbered by their wounded, were unable to pursue."[17]

August 13—more fighting near Cuchillo Negro. More damage to the troops. Lieutenant Burnett wounded; two enlisted men and six horses killed. "The hostiles lost several killed."

August 18—another encounter fifteen miles from McEvers' ranch in Hillsboro country. "Lieutenant G. W. Smith, Ninth Cavalry, with a detachment of twenty men, struck the hostiles. . . . The Indians were defeated after a very severe fight, in which Lieutenant Smith and four of his men were killed; a party of citizens, under command of George Daly, joined Lieutenant Smith in the fight, and Daly was killed."[18]

It was Daly's own fault that he lost his life. The troops and civilians were closing in on Nana when the wily Indian general led his braves into Gavilan Canyon. Lieutenant Smith ordered a halt, but the miners would not stay back, and Smith could not let them go in by themselves. One volley finished Daly and Smith. The rest of the white men got away as fast as they could.[19] Smith was the officer who had written the indignant letter to Agent Russell two years before, when Victorio went out.

By now the country was swarming with soldiers, and Nana decided that it was time to retreat. Toward the end of August

---

[17] *Ibid.*, 100.
[18] *Ibid.*
[19] El Paso *Times*, March 1, 1942.

he slipped across the Mexican border and studied war no more. One historian sums up his achievement:

> In less than two months Nana, handicapped by age and physical disabilities, led his handful of braves over a thousand miles of enemy territory, maintaining himself and his followers in the country as they went. He fought eight battles with the Americans, winning them all; killed anywhere from thirty to fifty of his enemies, wounded large numbers more; captured two women and not less than two hundred horses and mules; eluded pursuit by more than a thousand soldiers, not to mention three or four hundred civilians—and did it all with a force which numbered only fifteen warriors at the start and never exceeded forty braves.[20]

General Pope, commanding the Military District of the Missouri, paid grudging tribute to the skill of the Apache general:

> The difficulties of the country, among the almost inaccessible mountains of that region, were very great, and the Indians scattered themselves so much when closely pressed that it was necessary to hunt them down almost individually in the rough and difficult country south and west of Fort Craig, but it can be truly said that the troops did everything that was possible, and pressed the Indians so closely and persistently from so many directions that they had no time to rest, and finally were driven across the Mexican line. . . . As the Indians remounted themselves with stolen horses wherever they could find them, and scattered through the mountains by twos and threes whenever closely pressed, to unite again at points well known to them, and as it was therefore necessary to scatter the troops considerably to follow up the trails, it happened that whenever the troops met the Indians the forces were not unequal generally, and the fights were correspondingly severe and the loss on both sides unusually large.

[20] Wellman, *op. cit.,* 400.

He added, significantly, "There is no great trouble in dealing with them when found. The difficulty is to find them."[21]

Just how many Mescaleros were mixed up in this business is hard to determine. Agent Llewellyn declared that none of his Indians were absent, but General Pope was just as sure that "a considerable number" of them were with Nana.[22]

Nana and his men did not come back to settle any such arguments. They were still in Mexico in 1883 when General Crook persuaded many of the Indian exiles to come in to San Carlos and settle down. Nana rode in with the peace seekers. He continued to exercise some authority, usually trying to hold the rebellious ones in line,[23] but he went out with Geronimo in the big break of 1885 and made his last surrender in January, 1886, when he gave up to Lieutenant Maus down in Mexico.

Meanwhile, the survivors of Victorio's "army" were hunted down and wiped out wherever they could be found. The last Indian fight in Texas disposed of a remnant of them.

It seems that the night before Victorio began his last engagement, twelve of his braves, with their women and children, stole away through the darkness and started a small war on their own. They made their headquarters in the fastnesses of the Davis Mountains and preyed for several months on soldiers, sheepherders, and travelers, without ever being called to account. At last, in January, 1881, they held up the San Antonio stage in Quitman Canyon and made off with the driver and one passenger—a gambler named Crenshaw. This put a detachment of George W. Baylor's Rangers on their trail. Another Ranger detachment under Lieutenant Nevill joined Baylor near Eagle

[21] *Report of the Secretary of War for 1881*, 117–18 (Report of Gen. John Pope).

[22] *Ibid.*, 118.

[23] Lieutenant Britton Davis, *The Truth About Geronimo*, 126.

Springs, and they followed the sign into the Diablo Mountains south of Guadalupe Peak.

They were on a high plateau in the most rugged sort of terrain, and the weather was so cold that the men's canteens froze solid and burst. On the morning of January 29, just before daylight, the Ranger force crept to the top of a crest and saw the sleeping encampment below them. There were two tipis, and the women were just beginning to stir about, getting breakfast. Baylor fired the first shot, and the Indians ran in confusion. All the Mescaleros were wrapped in blankets, which made it hard to tell a man from a woman, but this gave the Rangers no concern. Baylor remarked later that the "law under which the Frontier Battalion was organized don't require it."[24]

Four warriors, three women, and two children were killed, and others died of wounds after escaping from the battle. Sixteen horses and mules were captured. The Rangers seem to have enjoyed their victory thoroughly and fell with good appetites on the Apaches' abandoned breakfast, while admiring the magnificent desert scenery.

> Some of the men found horse meat pretty good and whilst others found venison and roasted Mescal good enough we had almost a boundless view from our breakfast table towards the North the Grand Old Cathedral Peak of the Guadaloupe Mountains, further west the San Antonio Mountains, the Cornudas Las Alamas, Sierra Alto, at the Hueco Tanks only 24 miles from Headquarters [at Ysleta] to the east El Muerto, and south the Eagle Mountains, the beauty of the scenery only marred by man's inhumanity to man, the ghostly forms of the dead lying around.[25]

[24] John L. Waller, "Colonel George Wythe Baylor," *The Southwestern Social Science Quarterly*, Vol. XXIV (June, 1943), 32.
[25] *Ibid.*, 32–33.

That disposed of most of the rebellious blood left in the Mescaleros, but Victorio's and Nana's campaigns will be discussed as long as people remember our Indian-fighting days. Bloody as they were, those campaigns were still fantastically effective.

Victorio's band consisted at top strength of not more than three hundred fighting men; yet those ferocious warriors massacred about two hundred Americans and at least an equal number of Mexicans.[26] Two armies could not catch them. There is no telling how long Victorio could have held out if he had cared to. But he grew tired, and the troops were persistent. His men had already begun to disperse by his orders when he and his little remnant finally turned at bay.

Tacticians compare his campaigns to the most skillful military movements of all time. How did he do it? The answer lies in the desert which bred those indestructible warriors. A hundred miles in the saddle was just a good long ride for them. A couple of days without water was merely part of the task. A meal of mesquite beans would keep them going until something better turned up.

The whole difference between them and their pursuers is summed up in one detail. When Colonel Buell went into Mexico on Victorio's track, he cast proud glances at a four-hundred-gallon water wagon which he had invented himself. The Indians, if they carried anything to drink at all, transported it in a thirty-foot length of horse intestines, casually cleaned out, filled with drinkable (by their standards) fluid, and wrapped around the neck and body of a pack horse. They did not have much, but they used what they had with incomparable efficiency.

---

[26] Twitchell, *op. cit.*, II, 439–40. Acting Governor W. G. Ritch, writing to S. J. Kirkwood, secretary of the interior, on August 22, 1881, estimated the casualties as "over 300 lives" (Ritch Collection, No. 1940).

Chapter XII

PRISONERS OF WAR

The Apaches in Exile

THE INDIAN WARS came to their climax in Arizona in 1886 as five thousand soldiers organized to run down Geronimo and Naiche and their little band of murderous renegades. The chapter ended with the transportation to Florida of all the Chiricahua and Warm Springs Apaches. A more disgraceful display of callousness and bad faith cannot be found in our annals, and white Americans still remember it with shame and regret.

Only a few Mescaleros were directly involved, but when the remnants of the exiled bands made their final move to New Mexico almost thirty years after their betrayal, the whole tragic episode became a part of the Mescalero story.

On March 27, 1886, Geronimo surrendered to General Crook in Mexico. He changed his mind after a big drunk, however, and returned to the warpath next day. Not all his followers wanted to go back with him to a fugitive and fearful life. Seventy-seven of them preferred to accept Crook's offer—to ship them out of the country and bring them back after two years. Crook said Nana would not have to go since he was "seventy years of age and superannuated."[1]

[1] *Letter from the Secretary of War . . . Correspondence between Lt. Gen. P. H. Sheridan and Brig. Gen. George H. Crook,* 2; Crook, *op. cit.,* 263–65.

When Crook reported the details of the bargain he had made, General Sheridan telegraphed from Washington that the agreement would not do—that the President would grant no terms to the Indians but unconditional surrender. More telegrams flashed back and forth, many of them from Arizona citizens who clamored so loudly for the removal of all the Apaches that Sheridan thought he had to listen. He ordered that the warriors who had refused to go out again with Geronimo should be sent off to Florida for good, no matter what Crook had promised them.

Crook had built up a tremendous reputation with the Indians as a man of his word, and he was highly embarrassed by this development. He informed Sheridan that he could not tell the Indians of their fate for fear Geronimo would hear of it and refuse to negotiate, and asked to be relieved of his command.[2] Within twenty-four hours he had been replaced by General Nelson A. Miles. On April 7, the seventy-seven former hostiles were shipped off under escort to Fort Marion, Florida. They never came back.

Still General Miles was not satisfied. Nearly four hundred Apaches had been living in peace and poverty at or near Fort Apache. They had conscientiously kept out of trouble, coming in voluntarily to be counted every time there was a raid so that the soldiers would know they were not involved. A number of them enlisted as scouts and actually fought on the side of the government. To Miles, however, they were "a turbulent, desperate, disreputable band," and he determined (following Sheridan's suggestion)[3] to get them out of the country also.

His first idea was to transfer them to the Indian Territory,

---

[2] *Ibid.*, 9.

[3] *Letter from the Secretary of War . . . Reports Relative to the Treatment of Certain Apache Indians*, 5.

but Washington informed him that there was no legal basis for such a procedure. His second thought was that if he could get some of the Indian leaders to approve such a transfer and persuade their people to go voluntarily, the rest would be easy. Chato (Spanish for "Flat Nose") was the Apache he picked to work with him.

Chato, a Chiricahua, had been a very efficient hostile until 1883, but in the campaigns against Geronimo he was just as efficient on the white man's side. Lieutenant Britton Davis, who had much to do with managing the scouting, trusted him as he trusted no other Indian and felt that he richly deserved his sergeancy in the Indian auxiliary force. After going on his good behavior, Chato built himself a house at San Carlos with his own hands and accumulated horses, mules, and fourteen acres of land. He even saved General Crook's life once. Chato was an Indian to be reckoned with, and General Miles knew it. That was why he put him at the head of a delegation of fourteen Apaches, all of whom had been serviceable to the government, and sent him to Washington. There they were accorded all honors—they had an interview with the President and received medals from the Secretary of War. But when it was suggested to them that they should take the lead in promoting a removal of their people from Arizona, their reaction was vigorously negative.[4]

Since they would not agree to the plan for removal, the government decided to force a settlement. When the Indians got on the train for the return journey, they confidently expected to step off in Arizona at the point nearest their homes. Instead they were halted at Fort Leavenworth and held there while the officials debated what to do with them. The longer the Apaches

[4] Edward Everett Dale, *The Indians of the Southwest*, 110; Wellman, *op. cit.*, 448; Lockwood, *op. cit.*, 313–16; Ogle, *op. cit.*, 239.

marked time in Kansas, the more uneasy they became; and their increasing restiveness made the men in charge more and more unwilling to send them back to their reservation. Finally, on September 12, 1886, the order came to ship them to Fort Marion, Florida, "by the most direct and expeditious route."[5]

By now, Geronimo had come in for the second time and was, likewise, on his way to Florida with the last of the holdouts. Determined to make a clean sweep of the whole troublesome group, Miles had secured permission to round up the rest of the Warm Springs and Chiricahua bands and get rid of them, too. Stories differ about how the Indians were maneuvered into a position where resistance was impossible,[6] but the thing was done. The entire group, 397 persons, was marched one hundred miles to Holbrook and put on the train for Florida, never to see Arizona again.

Among them were men who had done invaluable service for the government and had risked their lives doing it. Gout-Klil, Toklanni, and Izilgan were trusted scouts under Crook. Dutchy was at Captain Emmett Crawford's side when he was treacherously shot in Mexico, and was the man who killed the murderer. Noche was Crawford's chief of scouts. Martine and Ka-e-ta risked their lives by going to Geronimo's camp in the wilds of the Sierra Madre and persuading him to think about giving up.[7] Instead of the reward which they insisted they had been promised, they were shipped off to a living death in an

[5] *Letter from the Secretary of War . . . Reports Relative to the Treatment of Certain Apache Indians,* 24.

[6] Wellman, *op. cit.,* 449, says that a false report of a raid was circulated so that the Indians would come in to be counted. Opler, "A Chiricahua Apache's Account," *N.M.H.R.,* Vol. XII (October, 1938), 360–86, quotes Sam Kenoi to the effect that the group was rounded up during a big social dance. "The shadow of the shameful way they treated these faithful Indians and the United States scouts still lies over us."

[7] Herbert Welsh, *The Apache Prisoners of War at Fort Marion,* 11.

alien land and thrown in with the renegades they had helped to subdue.[8]

Some of the army officers justified this outrageous act as best they could by minimizing the service of the Apache scouts and hinting that they were plotting a rebellion of their own at the time of the surrender, but the bulk of testimony indicates that the exiles were completely undeserving of the treatment meted out to them.[9]

General Crook himself went to see Chato in his captivity, and reported that his Indian friend showed him the medal President Cleveland had given him. "Why was I given that to wear in the guard house?" he asked. "I thought that something good would come to me when they gave it to me, but I have been in confinement ever since I have had it."

"By far the greater part of the tribe remained true to the Government in the outbreak of 1885," Crook added. "For their allegiance all have been rewarded alike—by captivity in a strange land."[10]

It is possible that the whole tragedy was brought on by the absent-mindedness of the President of the United States. Cleveland telegraphed from his summer place in the Adirondacks to General Drum, the acting secretary of war, in 1886: "All the hostiles should be very safely kept as prisoners of war until they can be tried for their crimes or otherwise disposed of."[11] That telegram kept them in captivity for almost thirty years. Captain John G. Bourke attended a cabinet meeting at which these mat-

[8] *Ibid.*, 7–9; John M. Oskison, "An Apache Problem," *Quarterly Journal of the Society of American Indians*, Vol. I (April, 1913), 25–29; Tom Charles, "Old Scouts," *New Mexico*, Vol. IX (August, 1931), 17–19.

[9] Welsh, *op. cit.*, Appendix, 39–40, answers the charges against the Apache scouts.

[10] *Letter from the Secretary of War . . . Reports Relative to the Treatment of Certain Apache Indians*, 30–33.

[11] O. K. Davis, "Our Prisoners of War," *North American Review*, Vol. XCV (March, 1912), 356.

ters were discussed and noted that the President "seemed to confound the two bands of Geronimo and Chato."[12] What seems to have been needed was not more punishment for the Indians, but more perception in Washington.

Most of the prisoners were confined in the old Spanish fort at St. Augustine (Geronimo and sixteen men were at Fort Pickens, on the west Florida coast). They camped in tents on the ramparts and cooked on open fires in corners. Drainage and sanitation were pitifully inadequate. Clothing was scarce. They visited the town occasionally under surveillance, and some of the townspeople took pity on their distress when the cold weather left them shivering. Three generous ladies set up an English class for children. The Sisters of St. Joseph started a school. But the men and women of the tribe had nothing to do but eat their meager rations (meat, bread, sugar, coffee, and beans) and rust in idleness.[13] The confinement and the damp climate were hard for those desert hawks to bear. To some came death—the only real solution to their problems. In 1886, they numbered 502; in 1887, there were 447.[14] Of the 82 men left, "not more than thirty were guilty of any recent wrongdoing."

Something needed to be done, but everything proposed proved to be unworkable for one reason or another. The citizens of Arizona raised a mighty clamor when it was suggested that the Indians should be brought back to their native deserts.[15] The whole sad business caused a violent controvery in the press and within the Indian Bureau itself. The result was the transfer of the entire establishment to Mount Vernon Barracks, Alabama,

[12] *Letter from the Secretary of War . . . Reports Relative to the Treatment of Certain Apache Prisoners,* 51–53.

[13] Welsh, *op. cit.,* 12–16, describes conditions at the fort in 1887.

[14] At Fort Marion six women, one man, and fifteen children died. ("The Apache Prisoners," Indian Rights Association, *Fifth Annual Report,* 1888, 27–37.)

[15] M. K. Sniffen, "The Record of Thirty Years," Indian Rights Association, *Publications,* Ser. II, No. 90 (April, 1913), 5.

in 1887, and the removal of some of the children to Carlisle Indian School, where thirty of them died.

The only prisoners to escape from their confinement were a small group of Mescaleros—five families headed by "Alabama Charlie"—who were allowed to return to New Mexico in the spring of 1889. They left fourteen of their fellow tribesmen behind. Why one group was allowed to go and the other was detained remains a mystery. Agent Joseph Bennett reminded his superiors that the fourteen wanted to return. "They are not charged with any crimes," he stated, "and I think it would be wise, humane, and economical to allow them to come back."[16]

In spite of their natural resentment and profound unhappiness, the captive Apaches made some effort to build a home in the South. Consequently, they were thrown into dejection once more when, in 1894, they received sudden and unexpected orders to move to Fort Sill in Oklahoma. Although they did not know the order was coming, other people did, apparently, and as early as 1890 the President was receiving calls from citizens of New Mexico protesting the removal.[17] At Fort Sill the Indians would be too close to their old haunts, said these citizens. New Mexico, only six hundred miles away, would be once again in danger.

Nevertheless, in the fall of 1894, with winter just around the corner, the 407 Indians who were left alive were "dumped unprotected" on the military reservation at Fort Sill. The army had turned over to them a quantity of abandoned material from Camp Supply, fifty miles distant, including harness and wagons, and they went to work building picket houses while camping

[16] *Report of the Commissioner of Indian Affairs for 1889* (Report of Joseph F. Bennett). The record does not say how these Mescaleros came to be with the Chiricahuas.

[17] *Río Grande Republican*, Feb. 8, 1890: "W. L. Rynerson, Brewster Cameron, W. H. H. Llewellyn and George Crist have called on the President."

temporarily in brush and canvas shelters. Some of them actually saw a bright side and figured that at last they could look forward to having homes of their own. At least they were back in open country, much more like the old haunts they longed for than anything they had seen since 1886.[18]

It was true also that for the first time in history some real steps were being taken to make the captives independent. Captain Hugh L. Scott, who came with them from Mount Vernon Barracks, was a "very enthusiastic and ardent believer in the possibilities of Indian civilization; a man of unlimited energy and good sense."[19] Under his supervision the first step was taken toward making the Indians comfortable and self-sufficient. Nearly 30,000 acres were released to the government by the Comanches and Kiowas, with the understanding that the Apaches would be given a share. Fort Sill was to be abandoned and its area added to the Indian lands. This additional 23,000 acres would have given every Indian 160 acres which he could call his own, and the surplus was to be sold for the benefit of the tribesmen.[20] The exiles hoped and worked, but hope and work were not enough. The outbreak of the Spanish-American War led to a reactivation of all things military. The allotments were not made.

Time went on, but there was still no allotment. Even the most optimistic Apaches gradually lost hope again.[21]

In 1911, a bill was actually introduced in Congress to eject them from the reservation they occupied and leave them homeless once more. Fort Sill needed more land, and who should give

[18] "The Apache Prisoners," Indian Rights Association, *Twelfth Annual Report*, 1895 (*Publications*, Ser. II, No. 20), 57.

[19] *Ibid.*

[20] "Appeal on Behalf of the Apaches, Kiowas, and Comanches," Indian Rights Association, *Publications*, Ser. II, No. 51 (Feb. 15, 1889), 1-8.

[21] "Prisoners of War for Thirty Years," *The Outlook*, Vol. XCIX (November 4, 1911), 555-56.

it up but the Indian prisoners of war?[22] It looked as if the old game of Fleece-the-Red Man was starting again; but this time the Apaches made up their minds that they would have something to say about it, and they began an active campaign to find some place where they could establish themselves and be free from the fear of removal.

For once the government listened to them. In October, 1911, a number of the tribesmen went back to New Mexico to look for a permanent home.[23] After some confusion and disagreement, they decided that Mescalero was the place.

Not all of the Oklahoma Apaches wanted to go there, however. The younger and more progressive men, who had been educated and had accumulated some property, were unwilling to start over. When the chips were down, less than one hundred of them stayed. The rest, 187 in all, were moved in boxcars to New Mexico in April, 1913.[24]

The Mescaleros on the reservation were glad to have them, although only a few of the immigrants belonged to the tribe, and agreed to make them full sharers in what they had. This generosity was not strictly disinterested, for, as usual, white men were nibbling at the Indians' land, and it was thought that greater numbers on the reservation would mean greater security.[25]

In 1912, and again in 1916, Senator Albert B. Fall of New Mexico, who owned the Three Rivers Ranch at the western edge of the reservation, introduced a bill to make a public park out of the Mescalero holdings. The proposal never came close to success, but Fall persisted in it for years; his bill did not finally die

[22] *Ibid.*

[23] Oskison, *loc. cit.*, 27–29.

[24] S. M. Brosius, "The Apache Prisoners of War," Indian Rights Association, *Thirtieth Annual Report*, 1912 (*Publications*, Ser. II, No. 68), 77–79.

[25] Indian Rights Association, *Thirty-sixth Annual Report*, 1918 (*Publications*, Ser. II, No. 115), 19 (M. K. Sniffen).

until 1922.[26] During all those years, the Apaches lived in fear and were glad to have the weight of the Chiricahuas on their side.

That explains why the Mescalero tribe today is a mixture of Mescaleros and Chiricahuas, with some Lipans in the background and a few relics of Comanche and Mexican blood. The imports from Oklahoma settled mostly in the White Tail community. Now they live in many places—on and off the reservation. You never know when you see a present-day Mescalero whether you are looking at a descendant of Santana's White Mountain group or a near relative of the fierce fighters of 1886.

Geronimo and Nana died in Oklahoma, but Naiche, who was the real chief and actually gave orders to Geronimo, lived out his old age at Mescalero, trying hard to be a good Christian. His children and grandchildren are still there. Robert Geronimo, a capable and intelligent Indian stock raiser, is Geronimo's son. Asa Daklugie, who died in 1955, was a son of Juh; his wife is a daughter of Chihuahua.[27]

The old scouts, whose betrayal had aroused so much fruitless protest, passed their last years in peace at Mescalero and are resting now under the junipers. Chato and Noche went first—in 1914. Ka-e-ta died in 1934. Martine and Toklanni lasted a few years longer, still asking *why*.

[26] Lockwood, *op. cit.*, 333; *Quarterly Journal of the Society of American Indians*, Vol. II (January–March, 1914), 51–55; John Collier, *The Indians of the Americas*, 246–57. Collier gives an account of Fall's persistent attempts to loot the Indian holdings.

[27] Lockwood, *op. cit.*, 324–28.

Chapter XIII

IN SLOW MOTION
Fifty Years of Difficulty

AFTER 1880, the Mescaleros moved out of the shadow of sudden death and wanton destruction but not into the sunlight of progress and prosperity. For the next fifty years they inched forward, but so slowly that one had to look back over a great lapse of time to see any change at all.

This lethargy was at least partly due to the fact that only a small handful of white men thought they had a chance. "It is idle," declared General Pope in 1881, "to talk of civilizing the Mescalero Apaches. They are savages, pure and simple, and in the country they occupy, with the inducements to raid and the present management of the tribe, it is worse than childish to believe that they are being, or ever will be reclaimed."[1]

It was assumed by all that the red man was a fourth-rate specimen of humanity. "The Indians as a race are, of course, far inferior to white men in intellectual capacity"[2]—so the argument always ran. No white man could foresee a time when Indians would be going to college, entering professions, and taking their part in the world's work. The most that was ever prophesied was

---

[1] *Report of the Secretary of War for 1881,* 118 (Report of Gen. John Pope).
[2] Harrison, *The Latest Studies on Indian Reservations,* 168.

a day when they would be able to support themselves by farming and so cut down what they were costing the government.

"White Americans of the 1880's were serenely convinced that their way of doing, thinking, eating, dressing, worshipping, was the best, the only way," Oliver La Farge sums it up. "Doubting that the Indians were quite capable of that highest human achievement of becoming exactly the same as white men, yet they were sure that the best thing they could do for them was to make them over into the closest possible imitations."[3]

Apparently, the way to make fourth-rate citizens out of the Indians was to send fourth-class white men to manage them. This was another reason for the slow and spasmodic progress of the Indian communities. Political hacks, crypto-crooks, and tarnished relatives of influential people continued to be sent to the reservations. Salaries continued to be insignificant; working conditions were impossible.

Thoughtful observers noted with amazement how much the government was willing to spend to kill an Indian, and how little to keep him alive. Vincent Colyer estimated in 1872 that Indian warfare in the last ten years had cost "a thousand lives and over forty millions of dollars."[4] The astronomical total to which that sum would have mounted by the end of the Apache wars of the eighties can be imagined. And yet the pittances doled out to the people who were expected to lead the tribesmen in the paths of peace were too small to attract anybody who could find something better to do.

It was fortunate for the Mescaleros that one of the few really efficient agents assigned to them in those days arrived on June 16, 1881. This was W. H. H. Llewellyn, a frontier adven-

[3] La Farge, *As Long as the Grass Shall Grow*, 12.
[4] Colyer, *Peace with the Apaches of New Mexico and Arizona. Report of . . . 1871*, 1.

209

turer, who had come to the Southwest from Nebraska not long before. People learned to discount his stories of his own exploits, but his ideas about Indian management were definitely constructive. He had a suave and quietly polite manner. He considered the welfare of his charges, went hunting with them, subjected them to discipline, and won their respect. They called him "Tata Crooked Nose."

The night he arrived there was a witch-burning. The next month Nana began his raids in the Tularosa country. Mrs. Llewellyn just missed him as she was coming to the agency to join her husband. Near the White Sands she passed a covered wagon with a man's hand dangling out beneath the canvas. An entire Mexican family was piled up inside—dead.[5]

One of the first decisions Llewellyn had to make was forced upon him when an Indian family brought him a pair of newborn twins. It was customary to kill one of the babies. They wanted "Tata Crooked Nose" to decide which one. Both children lived, and Llewellyn had no more such problems to solve.

As soon as might be after his arrival, he organized an Indian police force of fifteen men under Captain Thomas Branigan of Las Cruces—a measure which did more to stabilize conditions than anything conceived up to that time.[6] He detailed some of the Apaches as herders to watch the stock and put others to work with spades, hoes, and axes. He got ready to add fifty acres of farmland to the sixty-six under cultivation.

"Furnishing them with employment of various kinds, and humane and careful management will, in my opinion, soon bring them within the pale of civilization, and they will in a few years become self-sustaining," prophesied Llewellyn.[7]

[5] Mrs. Katherine D. Stoes, MS, biographical sketch of Ida May Llewellyn.
[6] Agent S. A. Russell had proposed to organize a force in 1879 and had received approval from the commissioner (E. A. Hayt to S. A. Russell, April 7, 1879; Russell to Hayt, May 5, 1879, in the Mescalero Agency files).

Optimistic as he was, the new agent did not minimize the bad side of the situation. School had been kept for five months during the preceding winter, he noted, "with indifferent success." Inefficient teachers were to blame. No progress was being made in religious instruction, he said, "because no missionary has ever visited this agency." To cap it all, there was a feud raging among the tribesmen—the result of a drunken brawl the preceding fall which had cost the lives of José Manzanita and his three sons. Llewellyn took care of that by "inviting" Colonel Hatch to send an officer to help keep order on the reservation.

A year later he was still confident and still reporting progress: seventy more acres under cultivation, a doctor added to the agency staff, school in session for a full term, the first Mescalero children ever to leave the reservation sent to school at Albuquerque, and two log houses built as a start toward better housing.[8]

To remain hopeful through 1882 took some strength of character, for it was a year of great changes and much potential and actual trouble. Squatters continued to be a headache to the agent, and they were joined by frenzied prospectors who overran the reservation hoping to find gold. The story was told then, as it is told today, that the Apaches knew where fabulous deposits were to be found but refused to tell. If one of their number showed signs of getting ready to talk, he was apt to disappear without trace. The prospectors kept on searching anyhow, and at last struck pay dirt in the Nogal Mountain country inside the northern boundary of the reservation.

Indian ownership was no barrier to the hard-rock men. They appealed to the army for help, and recommendations went

[7] *Report of the Commissioner of Indian Affairs for 1881*, 194 (Report of W. H. H. Llewellyn).

[8] *Ibid., 1882*, 124 (Report of W. H. H. Llewellyn).

to Washington that the reservation line should be changed so as to throw the gold claims into the public domain. The Commissioner of Indian Affairs picked his way delicately among the drawbacks as he stated the outcome: "Upon proper presentation of the facts by their agent, the Indians appeared to appreciate the situation, and finally became convinced that it would be to their interest to yield to the fair demands of the miners . . . with the understanding, however, that a strip of country should be added to the reservation on the east, which would afford them additional grazing ground."[9]

The Mescaleros understood well enough that the reservation belonged to them until the white men wanted it, and that there was not much point in resisting those "fair demands." They made no objection when the boundaries were revised early in 1882. A strip nine miles wide by twenty-one miles long was added on the east, and the miners had their claims. Commissioner Price gravely pointed out that the change had removed from the reservation all but two of the tracts occupied by American squatters—obviously a constructive step.

Meanwhile, the rough element among the whites continued to prey on the Indians in one way or another. Horse-stealing was their favorite outdoor sport. They got six animals from Nautzile on June 15, 1882, and came back "time and again" for more.

What trouble the whites did not concoct for them, the Mescaleros stirred up for themselves. A wild Apache named appropriately Give-Me-a-Horse escaped from confinement at Fort Union in the early winter of 1882 and headed for home. Going over to the Peñasco valley, he picked up six horses belonging to somebody else. The Indian police, whose numbers had just been increased to twenty, took him in tow and saw that the horses were returned to their owners. This did not promote tranquillity

[9] *Ibid., lxvii* (Report of Commissioner H. Price).

212

Peaker

1882

in the breast of Give-Me-a-Horse, however, and he joined forces with a small band of renegades who invaded the reservation about the middle of June. They took refuge in the camp of Nautzile, who was the mightiest man of the Mescaleros in those days, and was regarded as the head chief. According to newspaper accounts of the time, Llewellyn had already taken it upon himself to replace Nautzile, with the consent of the authorities in Washington, because he was "protecting outlaws."[10] There was undoubtedly more to this than can now be learned, but at any rate Give-Me-a-Horse and his allies were in Nautzile's camp when Llewellyn and his policemen sallied forth to give them battle. Three of the outlaws, including Give-Me-a-Horse, were killed. Llewellyn was shot twice through the arm. He gave his police credit for saving the lives of himself, Dr. Jackson, and agency clerk Easton.[11]

Two months later, on August 12, trouble turned up again in the person of Ho-nes-co, a former fighter under Victorio and Nana. He came in a mood of nostalgia for the old vigorous days and tried to interest some of the young men in organizing a raid. Again the police moved in, disarmed him, brought him to Llewellyn, and approved when the agent turned the man over to the military authorities.[12]

After a year's residence, Llewellyn was beginning to penetrate a little into the Indian mind. He noted that his charges carried out their secret religious rites "with great solemnity" and seemed to feel that "their religion bears as good fruit as that of others, basing their opinions on the conduct of the American element." He saw that it would be good to have a boarding school on the reservation in which some of the Indian mothers

[10] *Río Grande Republican*, Sept. 16, 1882.
[11] *Ibid.*, Nov. 25, 1882.
[12] *Report of the Commissioner of Indian Affairs for 1882*, 123–25.

213

could be employed. It was hard to detach an Indian child from its home, "owing to their peculiar ideas in regard to females, and their custom of having all female children under the exclusive control of their mothers or other female relatives—this appears to be a fixed and rigid law among this people, and doubtless arises from their strict customs regarding female chastity."

A boarding school large enough to accommodate thirty pupils was actually set up in the following year, and there were other indications of progress. More land was put under plow. The Indian police continued to catch their erring brothers and almost drove the *tiswin* makers out of business—descending on the manufacturers as soon as a wisp of smoke appeared in the loneliest canyon. Padre Sambrano, the first missionary to visit the Mescaleros, baptized 173 Apaches into the Roman Catholic faith. The agency buildings were renovated and enlarged, the Indians doing much of the heavy work.

There was never an end to the complications, however. In the fall of 1883, the Jicarillas came to Mescalero, following an edict issued the year before.[13] Llewellyn himself supervised the transfer, which began at Amargo on August 20. It took forty-seven days to cover the 502 miles between the two agencies. Smallpox broke out on the road and six people died. The Jicarillas were in no rosy mood when they arrived and settled in three camps—on the Tularosa, at Three Rivers, and on Carrizo Creek.[14] As time went on, they grew more and more discontented.

Llewellyn now had 462 Mescaleros and 721 Jicarillas to look out for—all "blanket Indians." He did his best for all of them. When the boarding school at Mescalero was full, he

---

[13] *Ibid.,* 123. It was first proposed that the Mescaleros should be sent to join the Jicarillas, but when an inspector came from Washington to look into the matter, the order was changed.

[14] *Ibid., 1884,* 130–33 (Report of W. H. H. Llewellyn).

214

started another one at Three Rivers. From that he turned to a stock-raising project. He bought five hundred head of cattle to be divided between the Mescaleros and the Jicarillas, took out a membership for them in the Lincoln County Cattle Growers Association, and sat back to watch the herds increase. Then he ran into disappointment. He found that to an Apache a horse was valuable property (the Jicarillas had about one thousand— the Mescaleros five hundred), but a cow was just food on the hoof. He complained that some of them gambled away their cattle at the first opportunity, and the winner led his prize off for immediate conversion into beef.

At the end of 1884—Llewellyn's last year at the agency—he was still finding something to be cheerful about, however. He reported that a telephone line had been run to Fort Stanton and that Chief San Juan had been taking instructions from the wife of the Apaches' lawyer friend, Colonel A. J. Fountain of Mesilla, with the object of being baptized into the Roman Catholic church.

On November 18, 1885, Fletcher J. Cowart arrived at Mescalero to take over the agent's duties. And now a very different note began to be heard. Where Llewellyn had seen rays of hope, Cowart perceived nothing but darkness and discouragement. The Indians, he said, would not work their fields until he cut off their rations. Every Apache father was "bitterly opposed" to the idea of sending his children to school and would hide them or send them to the mountains when the police came after them. They all gambled—even the school boys, who played monte for buttons cut from their clothes. Little girls were sold into polygamous marriages. Middle-aged women were thrust out into the cold by husbands who preferred younger blood.

A major difficulty was the fear of witches, which kept the Apaches constantly stirred up. Cowart had to use firm measures

215

when two medicine men who attended Chief San Juan in his last illness accused two Lipans of finishing their patient by witchcraft. He threatened to put the accusers in irons if there was any more talk. "I make it a rule to ridicule and reprimand their foolish beliefs," he said with really sublime smugness. His ridicule did not stop the activities of the medicine men, however, and they continued to scatter pollen and knead the stomachs of the sick as before. "The result, especially in children, is almost certain death," Cowart declared.[15]

His disillusion reached its peak when he contemplated the Court of Indian Offenses, organized in the winter of 1886 to supplement the work of the Indian police. It was composed of three of the most "sensible and influential" Indians and should have done effective work. Unfortunately, it got off to a bad start. A typical case involved "a brace of policemen, who came to the agency one night very happy and very boisterous, with a bottle of whiskey in their possession. They were arrested and duly arraigned. The accustomed sentence of a week in the calaboose was imposed. The sight of the full bottle of liquor, which had been put in evidence, had greatly unsettled the judge, however, and hastening to adjourn court he took the chief of police aside and asked for the bottle as a present. When this was refused he offered to go to jail with the prisoners and stay there the whole week if allowed to drink the liquor. This affords a fair idea of the importance, impartiality, and dignity of a court of Indian offenses."

Concluding his catalog of sins and abuses, Cowart remarked that "the greatest of their crimes are abortion and infanticide. There is reason to believe that these two horrible practices are carried on to quite an extent, especially among unmarried women."[16]

[15] *Ibid.*, 1886, 198–202 (Report of Fletcher J. Cowart).

Cowart's troubles were complicated by the removal of the Jicarillas in 1887. Restless from the beginning, they finally left the Mescaleros for good.[17] Their withdrawal left only 438 Apaches on the reservation and cut the school population in half. The agent had to send out the police to collect enough recruits to keep his school full, and this time the policemen showed that they sympathized in their hearts with the outraged parents. Three of them were discharged when they would not co-operate. Some of the fathers tried to bribe Cowart to leave their children alone. Others paid poor members of the tribe to send their own children as substitutes.[18]

How Cowart lasted for three years at Mescalero is hard to understand; but he did, and he actually discovered some signs of progress before he left. Three-quarters of the eligible children were in school in 1889. Regular monthly services were being held in the boarding school by a Methodist minister. The Indians were doing their own freighting, some families were settling away from the agency, and a few Apaches were actually milking cows—"a thing never known until recently."[19]

As the years went on, the progress of the Mescaleros had to be measured by signs as small as these. Improvement came slowly; every advance seemed temporary and costly. The Llewellyns who had faith were always outnumbered by the Cowarts who had none.

Joseph F. Bennett, who accepted a temporary appointment in 1889, inched things forward a little. He noticed that all the neighboring ranchers were pasturing their herds on reservation

---

[16] *Ibid., 1887*, 169 (Report of Fletcher J. Cowart).

[17] *Ibid., lxxii* (Report of J. D. C. Adkins). Two hundred Jicarillas left in the fall of 1886, camped near Santa Fé, and refused to come back. A new reservation was laid out for them (the one they now occupy), and in May, 1887, the rest of the tribe was removed from Mescalero and transferred there.

[18] *Ibid.*, 169 (Report of Fletcher J. Cowart).

[19] *Ibid., 1888*, 186 (Report of Fletcher J. Cowart).

grass at no expense whatever. He estimated that eight thousand head were involved and got out circulars to the owners, advising them that they were breaking the law. It is true that three years later, in 1891, the agent was still complaining that when he drove bovine poachers off the reservation at one point, they always returned at another,[20] but at least the problem had been recognized.

By August, 1889, according to the agent's report, fourteen houses were being occupied by Indian families, and a new school building was almost completed. A Sunday school was functioning regularly. Six Indians had cookstoves in their kitchens. A cemetery had been laid out near the agency, and two school children who died of smallpox during the year had the honor of being the first to occupy a corner of it. Finally, the Court of Indian Offenses, with Nautzile and José Torres as judges, had begun to function—mostly by arbitrating disputes.

Bennett's reports, unfortunately, were not completely reliable, probably because of his natural desire to make himself and his work look good. This was an occupational disease among agents, whose jobs depended on convincing their superiors that all was well on the reservation. But Bennett was certainly overplaying his hand when he assured his chief in Washington that "the Apaches uniformly treat their wives and families with kindness"; that there "are but few cases of plural marriages in this tribe"; that "drunkenness is of rare occurrence"; and that every one of his employees was "sober, zealous, conscientious and efficient."[21] No man ever showed that much faith in Indian and human nature unless he was either stupid or a liar.

Bennett seems to have been a creature of the notorious "Santa Fé Ring," which was running New Mexico for its own

[20] *Ibid.*, *1891*, 306 (Report of Hinman Rhodes).
[21] *Ibid.*, *1890*, 155–57 (Report of Joseph F. Bennett).

benefit at this time, but his character and record were such that even powerful friends could not keep him in office, and he was out at the end of 1890.

Colonel Hinman Rhodes, father of the important Western writer Eugene Manlove Rhodes, succeeded him. Colonel Rhodes's first report showed how brazenly Bennett had misrepresented the truth. There had been a quarrel between Bennett and M. A. Crouse, superintendent of the school. They had come to blows. Bennett had suspended Crouse, then found that he could not appoint a successor under the law, and had let the school go completely to pieces. Not an Indian child was in school when Rhodes took charge.[22]

Crouse did not last much longer than Bennett. His place had to be refilled twice during the year. Andrew Atchison took charge on February 1, 1892, and Rhodes thought the school picked up a little as a result. Atchison's first account of his work showed that there had been some forward motion in spite of the difficulties. In 1883, he said, only five Mescaleros could read. In 1892, thirty-five could read and write "fairly well." Thirty-one boys and eleven girls had gone away to school.

Atchison put his finger on one sore spot when he commented that "both boys and girls are employed too many hours at labor—have too little time for play." The little Indians had to make their own clothes, take care of the school buildings, and work the school farm. Sometimes there were few hours left for education after they had performed these necessary tasks.[23]

A bitter truth about the young Apaches who went away to school was pointed out by Richard Hudson, a political appointee

[22] *Report of the Commissioner of Indian Affairs for 1891*, 308 (Report of M. A. Crouse). See W. H. Hutchinson, *A Bar Cross Man*, 37–43, for an account of Bennett's attempts to keep Rhodes out, Rhodes' successful effort to get in, and his unexplained dismissal.

[23] *Ibid., 1892*, 330 (Report of Andrew Atchison).

from the Silver City area, who succeeded Rhodes in the summer of 1892. At least twenty young men and women had returned from schools in Colorado and New Mexico, according to him, and "in less than ten days after their return to this reservation they are wearing the breechcloth and other apparel of agency Indians, and will not speak English to any one, unless almost compelled to do so."[24]

The agents came and went, and each one found more to regret than to approve. Captain Levi Burnett arrived in 1893, the first fruit of the new policy of appointing army officers to Indian agency posts as they fell vacant. Burnett noted that widows and orphans had a difficult time getting enough to eat; that it was hard to keep children in school; that *tiswin* brawls were still occurring;[25] that the 250 cattle provided for the Mescaleros by Llewellyn had dwindled to 124. Nobody wanted to work, he said, and at the school there was great lack of "promptness and diligence" in keeping up with extracurricular chores. He saw hope for the future, however, in the fact that "the newly appointed matron wears on her countenance an expression of determined force, and is undoubtedly the woman for her position."

Divorce and remarriage were treated so casually that many of the men and women had three or four former mates still living. Burnett took a special interest in the Mescalero family situation and recorded some interesting facts about it:

Sometimes the husband illtreats his wife and she runs away to her parents. They often make up and live together again. Several

[24] *Ibid.*, 1893, 216 (Report of Richard Hudson).
[25] Fletcher Cowart reported a big battle in 1888 in which Zacate and his son Tomás were shot, along with a policeman, two women, and a child. Later the mother-in-law of one of the dead men was fatally stabbed by the mother of another. There was another famous brawl in 1892 at Trias Springs, in which Charley Wyeth and Patos Chiquito were killed. Rhodes' report for 1892 (p. 329) tells about it. See also Meadows, "Tribal Fight between Mescalero and Lipan Indians," in the Alamogordo *News*, February 20, 1936.

cases have occurred during the past year where parents have induced a man to marry their girl, aged, perhaps, not over 13 or 14 years, for the sole purpose of keeping her out of school. It usually happens that the parties soon separate, the girl returning to her parents, often against the wishes of her husband. . . . Polygamy is practiced to some extent. Twelve Indians have each two wives, and one has three wives. I advise against this on all occasions, but they do not like any person to interfere with such things.[26]

What the Indians liked or did not like mattered not at all to the man who followed Captain Burnett. Lieutenant V. E. Stottler moved in on December 11, 1895, and things were never quite the same around Mescalero again. Stottler was a man of considerable culture. He could write well, and loved to tell about his experiences. At the same time he had a streak of the Prussian officer in him. He never doubted that his judgment was correct, and was ruthless in carrying out his ideas. He honestly believed that the Mescaleros could be civilized by force.

As he looked over the situation which he had to face, he came to the conclusion that the old women of the tribe—the grandmothers and mothers-in-law—were making most of the trouble. It was they, he thought, who "strenuously objected to having the girls attend school, preferring to keep them to sell in marriage at the tender ages of 8 to 12 years."

The men suffered as much as the children, in his opinion. He wrote:

In spite of the easy divorce this tribe is about as badly henpecked as it were possible to imagine. The "old" woman, not the "new," reigns on this reservation. A simple superstition of these people creates a stumbling block that is made manifest very often. . . . Just why it is no Indian has been able to explain to me,

[26] *Report of the Commissioner of Indian Affairs for 1894*, 205–207 (Report of Capt. Levi F. Burnett).

but an Indian can not look at his mother-in-law. If she enters his tepee he leaves. If he enters and she is within he flies at once. He can not stay in her august presence. If his wife and he quarrel, his mother-in-law puts in an appearance and manages his domestic affairs during his enforced absence so long as she pleases. Perhaps she takes his wife to her tepee, where he dare not follow. He comes to terms or the situation constitutes a divorce. Does the agent wish a child brought to school, or a head of a family to take land and try to farm it, the mother-in-law, if hostile—and she usually is—appears on the scene and the head of the family hunts the woods. The sight of several stalwart bucks hiding behind doors, barrels, and steps because a dried-up, wizened squaw heaves in sight is a spectacle that would be ludicrous were it not for its far-reaching results. A man with polygamist practices should be entitled to some sympathy when one considers that the incubus increases with his added wives. . . . The inevitable result is that if the agent encounters the ill will of these women his trouble will begin. Even a threat of a visit from his wife's mother will deter an Indian from doing the agent's bidding. If she should come and sit on his earthly possessions she could reduce him in one instant from affluence to beggary. . . .

It will be seen that the agent practically has innumerable mothers-in-law doing his duty.[27]

Stottler thought he had arrived at the solution for this problem. When the children dodged school, he put the grandmothers in jail and cut off supplies to the parents.

One cannot help feeling a little sympathy for those Indian grandmothers when one considers their situation now. Everything they held dear was being rooted out and destroyed. When they had the strength and courage to resist, they got no credit for heroic firmness of mind—they were rebellious and must be punished. "No attention was paid to the prejudices or whims of

[27] *Ibid.*, *1895*, *217* (Report of V. E. Stottler).

their old relations," Stottler said. "The latter have been made to understand that the United States has for years footed the bills that maintained them in idleness, filth, immorality, and barbarism, and that where a policy for their good has been adopted, they will not be consulted."[28]

Since Stottler's job did not depend on political considerations, he was able to carry his policy of "repression and force" (as he called it) as far as he liked. In the three and one-half years he was in charge, he accomplished a great deal, but whether his methods were good from a long-range point of view is another question. "As a relief from a certain class of political Agents who used to be the curse of the service," wrote former Commissioner Francis E. Leupp in 1910, "a military man was a godsend, but his best influence upon the Indians themselves was found among tribes still in a very backward state."[29] Perhaps Leupp had Stottler in mind when he made this statement.

Stottler's first drastic order eliminated long hair among the males on the reservation:

> As with Samson of old, the Indians' wildness lay in their long hair, which the returned educated Indians wore because, as they boasted, "it made them wild." All energies were bent to compel the adult males to cut their hair and adopt civilized attire in vain. Even the police would not wear their uniforms. A proposition to cut their hair from a former Agent, resulted in a mutiny. . . . Rations were considerably increased to the police to make it worth their while to think twice before leaving the force. . . . Two members who had been to school were discharged for wearing long hair. One old fellow, as a special favor, cut his hair, but it cost me five dollars. His wife made his life a burden, and he in turn appealed to me to hasten with the rest. By using rations and

[28] Stottler, "Pressure as a Civilizer of Wild Indians," *The Outlook*, Vol. LVI (January 12, 1897), 398.

[29] Leupp, *The Indian and His Problem*, 105.

other supplies as a lever, I induced a few more to cut, and then
I directed the police to cut theirs or leave the force. They re-
luctantly complied, but once accomplished they were only too
eager to compel the rest, and they cheerfully, under orders, arrested and brought to me every educated Indian on the Reservation. There were twenty of these, gorgeous in paint, feathers,
long hair, breech-clouts and blankets. . . . The Indian Office, at
my request, issued a peremptory order for all to cut their hair[30]
and adopt civilized attire; and in six weeks from the start every
male Indian had been changed into the semblance of a decent
man, with the warning that confinement at hard labor awaited
any backsliders. There have been none; and the task of moving
them upwards has been perceptibly easier from the time scissors
clipped off their wildness.[31]

With the Indians thus far along the road to "civilization,"
Stottler applied another galvanizer—"No Work, No Rations!"
Every man had to labor on a two-mile-long ditch intended to
bring water to the school farm. Those who did not work did not
eat. The project seemed crazy to the Apaches, and hunger was
all that kept them on the job. "It was not until the running water
in the ditch actually demonstrated that the transit really 'made
the water run up hill,' " Stottler said, "that they commenced to
have any confidence in me."

Next, he went to work on tribal government. The head men
of the four main bands had been filling the posts of judge, chief
of police, and agency farmer, with pay and presents. They spoke
for their people and apparently had kept former agents in a
nervous condition trying to secure their co-operation. Stottler
discarded all that and let it be known that from now on every
Indian must speak for himself. Pull would get him nowhere; he
must cast his own vote.

[30] Dale, *op. cit.*, 150, says that in 1896 "an order went out from Washington that all male Indians should be required to wear their hair short."
[31] Stottler, *loc. cit.*, 398.

The next order said that every male Indian must select a piece of land and fence it. There would be no rations until the fencing was completed. Six months later fourteen miles of oak posts had been set—the holes dug with knives and scooped out by hand—and the new land was being broken.

Even the women came in for some of Stottler's prodding. He brought in a number of Navajos in December, 1895, to teach the Apaches how to weave blankets. "Already a number of them are as expert as their Navajo instructors," he declared a few months later.

To a man like Stottler, of course, the Indian ceremonials were barbarous rites which ought to be suppressed, and he suppressed them. "These dances had been used principally to advertise the grown girls for sale to the highest bidder," he said in his ignorance. Along with paint, feathers, and long hair, the Mountain Gods had to go.

So did the making of *tiswin*. In the past, the police, under supervision of a white employee, had broken up *tiswin* camps whenever they could find them, but they went no farther than that. Stottler was the man to put teeth in the anti-tiswin program. "In six months the last tiswin camp was broken up, but it took a free use of the guard-house, and necessitated making a bonfire of everything in sight, and incarcerating the offenders at hard labor for several months. . . . Opposition was met with from the start, but the guard-house yawned for recalcitrants, and open defiance was not attempted."[32]

Now that the Mescaleros were shorn, laborious, sober, and subdued, the order went forth that they were all to live in houses. Every man had to cut logs and transport them to the sawmill. When the houses were finished, Stottler saw to it that a cook-stove and cooking utensils were supplied. He saw to it also that

[32] *Ibid.*

chimneys with fireplaces were not installed "as this invited a continuance of the camp cooking."[33]

When Stottler retired in June, 1898, he could boast that there were eighty-six houses occupied by Indians on the reservation, that their general health was good, although the tribe was "slowly on the decrease," that all the school children took "a full bath with plenty of soap and warm water once a week,"[34] that the Apaches had "completely abandoned" their medicine men (undoubtedly an illusion on the part of Dr. Luttrell, the agency physician), and that all of the children five years old and over were in school.

Citizens and government officials shared Stottler's feeling of triumph in his accomplishments when he left. There was the new 30,000-gallon water tank that everybody could see, the school full of children, the men with short hair, the new log cabins, and all the people at work, driven to labor by Stottler's policy of gradually "pinching off" rations. The top men in the Interior Department back in Washington considered it a "marvelous transformation," and believed that instead of "lazy, filthy savages in red paint and breech clouts" the Apaches were now "reasonable working human beings with a care for to-morrow and a desire to become useful citizens."[35]

It never occurred to those officials to ask whether the resentments built up in the harried tribesmen might outweigh the value of a 30,000-gallon water tank and 500 acres of farm land. But the history of the tribe during the next thirty years showed how these things operate. As soon as Stottler and his iron fist

[33] *Ibid.*

[34] *Report of the Commissioner of Indian Affairs for 1898*, 205 (Report of V. E. Stottler).

[35] *Annual Reports of the Department of the Interior for 1899, Miscellaneous Reports*, II, 436, "Mescalero Reservation."

went over the horizon, matters returned almost, if not quite, to their original status.

If there had been any intelligent effort to educate the Indian boys and girls, such relapses might not have occurred, but of all the departments which were intended to improve the lot of the Indian, the school system was the most benighted and tradition bound. It was still assumed that the red man was inferior and that his education must fit him to take his place in the lower order of society as a hewer of wood and a drawer of water. Industrial and agricultural training came first. What academic discipline he got was cut out for a child in New England or New York; it had no relation to what he was and what he might become. And if he was bewildered and homesick and backward, he could be locked up to teach him the error of his ways. School jails on the reservations were not abolished until 1927.[36]

A course of study, approved and issued by the Indian Office in 1901, shows very clearly what was wrong. In it there are photographs of big and little Indian children at work—the boys dressed in Civil War-type uniforms with forage caps, military blouses, and stripes down the trousers; the girls in horrible Mother Hubbard dresses. The program laid out is divided into "years," and subjects are listed alphabetically: Agriculture, Arithmetic, Bakery, Basketry, Blacksmithing—through Tailoring, Upholstering, and Writing.

The sort of thing the teachers were supposed to aim at comes out in a section called "Evening Hour":

> The superintendent must call upon all employees in the school to unite in making the evening sessions of the school pleasant as well as beneficial. This is a most excellent time for vocal music.

[36] Evelyn C. Adams, *American Indian Education,* 56.

A short time should be devoted every evening to note reading, the scales, part singing, and general chorus work. The patriotic songs must be taught in every school. . . .

One evening in the week should be a social hour, when the pupils may spend the evening in conversation, grand marches, etc., under the direction of the teachers, who are expected to see that pupils conduct themselves as the sons and daughters in a well-regulated home under the care of the mother. . . .

A short exercise in calisthenics must be given every evening, giving the pupils breathing exercises and proper positions in standing and exercise in using the various muscles, improved health and grace of movement being the ends sought in this work. Some of the exercises may be given with music, which adds to the interest.[37]

When one thinks of those bewildered Indian children struggling to learn the words of "The Star Spangled Banner" and taking breathing exercises, one can understand better the determination of their mothers and grandmothers to stave off as long as possible the day when all Mescaleros would have to submit to an "Evening Hour."

"At that time long ago, they lived poorly but the Indian women taught their children well," said the wise men of the Mescaleros. "My child, one does not curse. One hates no one. One behaves foolishly to no one. One laughs at no one."

What white man in the early days would have believed that an Indian could conceive or express such refined moral sentiments? Commissioner W. A. Jones could not and did not believe it when he wrote as follows in 1903:

It is probably true that the majority of our wild Indians have no inherited tendencies whatever toward morality and chastity, according to an enlightened standard. Chastity and morality among them must come from education and contact with the

[37] Estelle Reel, *Course of Study for the Indian Schools,* 109–10.

228

better element of the whites. An Indian girl who returns home to her parents does not have the same restraints thrown around her as does the white girl. Superintendents, teachers, and other employees in Indian schools therefore receive scant support from the wild Indian parents at home, who can not appreciate the anxiety of white mothers to guard their offspring. It must be taken into consideration, in dealing with this vital question of Indian civilization, that it is not an easy matter in one generation to engraft our standard of morality, evolved from centuries of Christianity, upon the children of the forest who have for generations followed the instincts of nature.[38]

Such determined ignorance of any possible Indian point of view, like Stottler's policy of "repression and force," could only alienate the Mescaleros and harden them in their determination to resist the white man's impositions. Superintendent James A. Carroll admitted this without realizing it, when he wrote in 1904:

The progress of these people, as a whole, is not sufficiently manifest to afford much encouragement . . . it is a fact that a great many members, notably the old women, have determined that they will never—no, never—abandon their nomadic habits. They were born savages, have relapsed into savagery, and will die savages. They cling tenaciously to savage customs, cultivate that hatred of the white man which is innate, exert every influence to prevent the young from adopting the pursuits of civilized life, and thus constitute a millstone around the neck of the tribe against which the younger element must constantly struggle.[39]

It took decades to work out the stalemate resulting from the white man's determination to rule and the red man's determination to resist, but the wheels of evolution were turning slowly all the time. By 1902, the Mescaleros were able to eke out a living for themselves, and rations were entirely cut off, except for

[38] *Report of the Commissioner of Indian Affairs for 1903*, 9.
[39] *Ibid.*, 1904, 250 (Report of James A. Carroll).

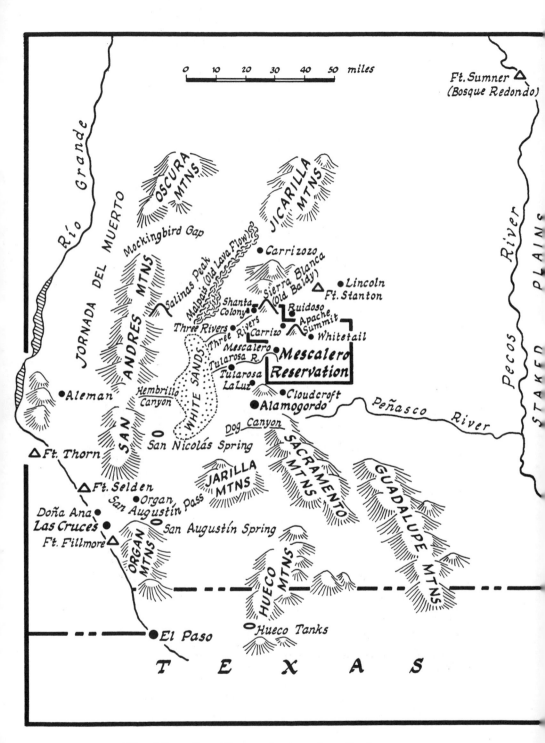

The Mescalero Range during the 1800's

aged and helpless people. The herd of sheep and goats which Lieutenant Stottler had thrust upon them in 1897 increased and added something to their income.[40] By 1902, the government was ready to give the Mescaleros a chance to work, and the edict went forth that a man would be paid $1.25 a day for his labor; a man with a team of horses would get $2.50.[41] In order to channel the money thus earned into the proper places, a system of coupon books was set up, whereby an Apache who had worked for a few days could buy necessary supplies without drawing any money.[42]

In 1903, five hundred of the ponies so dear to the Mescalero heart were sold, so that draft horses could be bought. It was a battle to get the Indians to give up their worthless beasts, but at last they gave in.[43]

By such small degrees conditions improved, but often it seemed that the tribe was actually going backward. In 1903, and again in 1904, the crops failed. The death rate remained high, especially from tuberculosis. Each year the head count of the Mescaleros dropped a little lower—464 in 1885; 453 in 1895. In 1905 thirty-seven Lipans, many of them intermarried with Mescalero families, were allowed to come to the reservation from Mexico, where they had been living for over twenty-five years. The head count would have dropped to 425 had they not arrived.[44]

And now, at this low ebb of Mescalero fortunes, was heard the slogan, first put forward in the sixties and revived more than once up to our own day: Terminate federal wardship! Turn the

[40] *Ibid., 1899,* 240 (Report of Walter M. Luttrell).
[41] *Ibid., 1903,* 27.
[42] *Report of the Secretary of the Interior for 1902,* 33.
[43] T. T. McCord, Jr., An Economic History of the Mescalero Apache Indians. Unpublished M. A. thesis, University of New Mexico, 1946, 53.
[44] *Report of the Commissioner of Indian Affairs for 1904,* 464 (Report of James A. Carroll).

Indian loose to make his own way! Commissioner Francis E. Leupp phrased it thus: ". . . all my work is guided by the general aim of preparing the whole Indian establishment for going out of business at no very distant date."[45] He even went so far as to set up an employment agency—a forerunner of today's Relocation Program—intended to get the tribesmen off the reservation and promote what is known in our time as "integration."[46]

The Commissioner's dream was certainly premature for the Mescaleros. The tribe was still in a state of stagnation—hanging between the old ways which were dying and the new ones which could not be born. Superintendent James A. Carroll, a good man, tried from 1902 until 1912 to get something done, but even he could do little to speed up the evolutionary process.

How strongly tradition still operated in the Apache mind appeared in 1908 when Kadinschin lost his life because of an excessive appetite for somebody else's beef. Kadinschin was a middle-aged Mescalero of no particular note, except that he was stone deaf and had only one eye. Minnie, his wife, did much of his seeing and all of his hearing for him. Just before things began to happen, he was working on a road crew some distance down the Tularosa Canyon from the agency and apparently behaving himself.

At that time the Flying H cattle outfit was leasing a big pasture on the reservation, with Roy McLane as foreman. One chilly January day as he was riding fence, Roy saw cattle tracks leading off into the reservation through a gate which somebody had left open. He had no time to follow and round up the stock,

---

[45] *Ibid., 1908,* 9.

[46] *Ibid., 1906,* 12; *1907,* 15. An educated Peoria Indian named Charles E. Dagenett was placed in charge. Only the humblest kind of day labor was available—mostly on railroad, irrigation, and construction projects. The program was less than successful, since the Indians hated to be away from home and could not adjust to whistle-and-time-clock routine.

but next day—it was Sunday, January 12, 1908—he sent his eighteen-year-old brother Don to do the job.

Don rode from Elk to Mescalero that morning, stopped briefly at the store, and came down the highway toward Tularosa. Paul Blazer was out in his yard and talked to him. Yes, Paul had seen four or five big Flying H steers on the ridge across the valley. He showed Don the place, and the boy rode off to hunt the trail.

He did not come home that night. The next day (Monday) his brother Roy came to Mescalero looking for him. On Tuesday, Roy called in a couple of Indian trackers. On Wednesday, Don's horse was found wandering along the trail to Three Rivers, and the trackers went on from there. On a mountain ridge six miles west of the agency, a few hundred yards off the trail, they found a partially butchered beef—one of the Flying H steers. Near by was Don's frozen body. He had been shot through the head. The Indians read the sign and said that Don had ridden up on the man who was doing the butchering—had probably surprised him. With no time to think, the thief had fired the fatal shot, tied the boy's horse in the bushes where he would not be noticed, and made a hasty retreat. When the horse got hungry and thirsty enough, he slipped his bridle and gave the show away.

Superintendent Carroll took the next step. He called in his three head men, Peso, Magoosh, and Sans Peur, and with their help proceeded to find out where every member of the tribe had spent his time on the preceding Sunday. Two Apaches were missing—Kadinschin and Minnie. They had left the reservation.

The murder now became more understandable. Don must have ridden up on Kadinschin's blind side. Confronted so suddenly and unexpectedly, the more so because of his deafness, the Indian had seized his rifle and shot fast. He had spent the following day at his job in the road camp; then he slipped away with Minnie to the wild mountain country where only another Indian could follow him.

The Mescaleros were accustomed to handling their own lawbreakers, including murderers, and they knew what they had to do. Twenty of them formed a posse. Sans Peur and his brother Crookneck were in it, with Sam Chino, Elmer Wilson, Willie Comanche, Antonio Joseph, Caje, and Muchacho Negro. A white deputy sheriff and a state policeman went along. Roy McLane undertook to keep everybody supplied with food.

For four days they trailed the fugitives through the rough, precipitous canyons on the west side of the Sacramentos. They found the place where Kadinschin had killed his horse, eaten some of the meat, and made moccasins out of the green hide. All day each day the Indian trailers followed the tracks. At night they bedded down in nests of pine needles, while the white men looked for a house or shivered by a carefully hidden fire.

The trail began to get warm at last. And just at that time the Apaches seemed to lose interest in the chase. They poked around casually, made no progress, and finally just sat down and did nothing. The white men asked why and got no answer. Finally, the band divided. One half struck off down the mountain slopes toward the Tularosa Valley; the rest stayed where they were. The two white officers and McLane, eager for action, followed the first party to the foot of the mountain before they realized that they had been decoyed away from the field of operations. The next day Roy McLane climbed back to the heights and found, as he had suspected he would, that Kadinschin was already dead. His old friends had taken care of him in their own way somewhere in Grapevine Canyon. They wanted no white man there when it happened.

McLane took them all to Alamogordo and fed them. They slept that night on the floor of the courthouse, and in the morning E. S. Ward, owner of the Flying H, gave every Indian a twenty-dollar gold piece—$400 for twenty men.[47]

That was more money than most of them were likely to see for a long time. In 1908, the Mescaleros were still living in abject poverty. With all their land and timber they had almost no income, although they were providing the means for a number of white men to profit. In 1904, their annual revenue from grazing permits was $8,000, of which about half was doled out in per capita allotments.[48] In 1914, the income was exactly the same.[49] At that time Superintendent C. R. Jefferis wanted to sell some timber in order to improve the reservation and stock it with more cattle and sheep so that profits could be diverted from the pockets of white lessees who had been collecting for more than a decade. But like most of his predecessors he was able to make very little headway. He did succeed in setting up a sawmill and starting a house-building program.[50] Then he, too, ran into the ancient barrier of indifference and delay.

When M. K. Sniffen, field man for the Indian Rights Association, came to the reservation in 1918, he found no sign of progress. The Apaches were living in "the most wretched condition" in brush shelters and tipis. An official explained to him that "there is no use of building houses for them; they will not live in them. Some cabins were put up for them years ago, but they would not live in them."[51]

"When I saw some of those cabins, later on, I did not blame

[47] Dr. Irving McNeil was the agency physician at this time and took pains to collect the details. He published his version of the story as "Indian Justice," *N.M.H.R.*, Vol. XIX (October, 1944), 261–70. Paul Blazer (Nov. 30, 1956) supplied further facts.

[48] *Report of the Commissioner of Indian Affairs for 1904*, 464 (Report of James A. Carroll).

[49] Indian Rights Association, *Publications*, Ser. II, No. 91 (1914), 31 (Report of Matthew K. Sniffen).

[50] *Ibid.*, 34.

[51] *Ibid.*, Ser. II, No. 115 (1918), 19 (M. K. Sniffen).

the Indians," Sniffen commented. "There seems to be some powerful influence at work to hold these Indians back," he added. By implication he pointed a finger at Senator A. B. Fall, whose perennial bill to make a national park out of the Mescaleros' homeland was pending in Congress.

Sniffen could think of only one progressive step which was taken in 1918—the organization of a Business Committee to manage the affairs of the tribe. Since that time the Business Committee has been the governing body. Its president is the closest thing the Mescaleros have to a principal chief.

For fifteen years after World War I, the tribe continued to mark time. Small gains were offset always by great discouragements. A step forward seemed always to be followed by a step back. What happened in 1920 was typical. A new superintendent, Captain Ernest Stecker, supported the Business Committee in a proposal to get Congressional authorization for the sale of timber over a period of ten years. One-half of the estimated revenue of half a million dollars was to be invested in Hereford cattle; the rest in the construction of "real homes." Congress was to advance the entire sum, and timber cuttings were to pay off the loan.

For a short time, hope was reborn at Mescalero. An influential Apache wrote to Mr. Sniffen describing his feelings about the proposed step. "This is the first time in our lives," he said, "that the future has really looked bright for us. Our plan is practical and reasonable. We will work and do our part."[52]

The idea was probably a good one, but like all other schemes that had been thought up for the betterment of the Mescaleros, it died on the vine. We do not know why. Lethargy in Washington—lack of follow-through on the reservation—

[52] *Ibid.*, Ser. II, No. 120 (1920), 8–10 (M. K. Sniffen).

236

whatever the cause, the Mescaleros made no headway with it and remained immovably fixed in poverty and misery.

Year by year there were small advances that nobody paid much attention to. In 1922—at last—Congress confirmed the title of the Mescaleros to their reservation. In 1923, they had six thousand head of cattle. By that time both the Reformed and Roman Catholic churches were maintaining missions and working energetically to save the souls of the Apaches. Although overcrowded, the school was functioning successfully.[53] In 1924, the Mescaleros became, at least on paper, citizens of the United States, and the economic prospects of the tribe improved when a five-year program allotted ten sheep or twenty goats to each individual who would sign up, thereby putting ready cash in their pockets "for the first time in many years."[54]

Still the people were unhappy and discouraged, unable or unwilling to make any real effort to help themselves. A member of the Board of Indian Commissioners, who came to Mescalero to make an inspection in 1932, blamed it all on the Apaches. He looked at filthy hovels near the agency, cast his eye over their beautiful, unoccupied reservation, and pronounced judgment: "Social life and the joys of sitting on the fence between the agency office and the trader's store appeal to the adult Apache far more than considerations of health and economics. . . . He has imbibed the state of mind which wardship seems to create— a combination of arrogance and importunity which is pitiful in itself and an obstacle to advancement."[55]

[53] G. E. Lindquist, *The Red Man in the United States,* 255–60. The Reformed church came in 1907; the Roman Catholics in 1911. Between 450 and 500 Mescaleros were nominal Christians in the early twenties, and 113 children were attending school. There was one primary teacher who cared for 70 small children in one inadequate room.

[54] M. K. Sniffen in *Indian Truth* (August–September, 1924).

[55] Department of the Interior, *Report of the Board of Indian Commissioners for 1932,* 26–27, "Mescalero Agency, New Mexico."

Commissioner Seymour might have mentioned the fact that 1932 was a tough year for everybody, and got tougher as the weeks went by. Drought, crop failure, and hard times were followed by great storms in late fall and early winter. Deep snow lay everywhere, and relief measures were necessary in the Southwest. Indians who had been working away from the reservations had to come back because there was no place else to go, adding to the burdens of the old folks at home.[56]

Like the rest of the country, Mescalero benefited by such stop-gap measures as the creation of the Civilian Conservation Corps in 1933, but life was difficult on the eve of the new day which dawned in 1934. Debt and disease, poverty and discouragement sat with the Apaches in their poor houses and primitive shelters. They were almost completely dependent, unable to find any road out of their difficulties, more and more given to hanging around the agency (as one observer described them) "like hungry sparrows hoping for a crust of bread."[57]

With the passage of the Wheeler-Howard bill, or Indian Reorganization Act, in 1934, all this could have, should have, and partially did come to an end.

[56] *Report of the Commissioner of Indian Affairs for 1932,* 3.
[57] Alden Stevens, "Whither the American Indian," Survey-Graphic, Vol. XXIX (March, 1940), 168–74.

Chapter XIV

BETTER DAYS

The Indians Get a New Deal

THE GREAT REFORM of 1934 seemed to be an explosively sudden improvement—a real revolution. It was nothing of the kind. It was the product of a long series of misguided efforts.

Off and on, for three-quarters of a century, the government had been trying to get out of the Indian business—perhaps because of a real concern for the welfare of the red man, or perhaps because of a cosmic boredom with a seemingly hopeless task. Year after year good people, including some of the Indian commissioners, hammered on the idea that the only way was to give the Indian his own land "in severalty," force him to learn agriculture, and turn him out to succeed or fail according to his ability and industry.

"Let the laws that govern a white man govern the Indian," said one commissioner; "if he expects to live and prosper in this country, he must learn the English language, and learn to *work*."[1] "We only need to treat the Indians like men, treat them as we do ourselves," another early commentator said.[2]

---

[1] *Report of the Commissioner of Indian Affairs for 1881,* v.

[2] "What Shall We Do with the Indians?" *The Nation,* Vol. V (October 31, 1867), 356.

The Mescalero Apaches

In 1887, these people got what they thought they wanted, when the Dawes Act was passed. By this "Allotment Act" the President was authorized to break up any Indian reservation and parcel it out to the tribesmen. No allotment was to exceed 160 acres; none could be sold for a period of twenty-five years; each carried with it the promise of citizenship. It was supposed that the Indian who accepted an allotment would at once become civilized and responsible and stop being troublesome to white people.

The results were disappointing. In the first place, the allotments were too small for ranching and many of them were unfit for farming—even supposing the Indian owner had the equipment and technical knowledge to cultivate his acres. About all he could do was to lease his land to white operators. They had already bought up the surplus reservation land for $2.50 an acre and were willing to rent the rest. Eventually, with hunger pinching him, the Indian would sell out.

He was not asked to approve the act before it was passed, though the "consent of the governed" principle was certainly involved.

From 1890 to 1900, about one-third of the tribal lands in the United States were lost.[3] Even the dullest congressman realized that this was bad, and in order to slow down the rate of loss, the Burke Act was passed in 1906. It postponed the Indian's full ownership of his land and entrance into citizenship until such time as he could prove his competence to manage his own affairs.

The rape went on anyway. By 1934, two-thirds of the Indian land holdings, as they had existed in 1887, had gone with the wind[4]—ninety million acres in all.

[3] Adams, *op. cit.*, 58.
[4] *Report of the Secretary of the Interior for 1934*, 78. The estimate is Commissioner John Collier's.

The raiding came from all sides and from many interests. In 1891, for instance, an act was passed permitting white men to lease Indian grazing lands. It took the Mescaleros over forty years to put a stop to that, and meanwhile they went hungry while white ranchers made money off their resources.

Albert Bacon Fall, during his days as United States senator and secretary of the interior, never stopped trying to euchre the aborigine out of his property. He ruled against Navajo ownership when oil was struck on the Navajo Reservation. He was behind the Bursum Bill, which attempted to remove the Pueblo Indians from federal supervision and place them under control of the district courts—a death sentence for them. He was the father also of the "Indian Omnibus Bill," empowering the government to pay each reservation Indian for his stake in the tribal holdings, thereby washing its hands of him.[5] These attempts failed, but they showed the danger in which the First Americans continued to exist.

The Mescaleros were fortunate in never having been under pressure to individualize their land. It was not suitable for breaking up into allotments, since so much of it was rugged mountain and forest country. There were other ways of separating an Indian from his property, however, and they had learned not to be surprised when one or another of these methods was tried. Ever since the days when General Pope and his successors demanded that the Apaches be moved to the Indian Territory or some other remote and undesirable place, they had distrusted the stability of any arrangements made for them by either military or civilian officials. Hopeless of the future, they went on in the old shiftless way, not much concerned about the efforts which were made to help them.

During the twenties and thirties, however, these efforts be-

[5] Collier, *The Indians of the Americas*, 246–57.

came increasingly strenuous and effective, while criticism of the Indian Service and its program grew louder. Secretary of the Interior Hubert Work finally made up his mind that he would have to do something, and as a preliminary step he had a survey made of conditions among Indians throughout the United States. The report of the survey board, completed by supervisor Lewis Meriam and known as the *Meriam Report,* was published in 1928. It provided the groundwork for the cellar-to-attic house cleaning which Indian management underwent during the next decade.

The *Report* recommended establishing a Division of Planning and Development, more money for medical service, higher salaries for workers in the Indian Service, more profitable employment for the impoverished tribesmen, and more participation by the Indians in the management of their own affairs.

The United States Senate took the cue from Secretary Work and sent a number of its members on a tour of their own to gather information for the Senate Committee on Indian Affairs. Between 1928 and 1933, the senators and their assistants held hearings and conducted investigations from one end of the Indian country to the other. On May 4, 1931, they came to Mescalero, and learned that affairs on that reservation were in a terrible mess. All the failures and resentments that had been festering in the unhappy community now came boiling to the surface.

Some of the Indians who were called as witnesses objected to everything that was being done, or not being done, for them. Nothing was right—no individual cattle brands—an incompetent field matron—too many white men using tribal grass and water—not enough individually owned sheep to pay the shepherds for "running themselves ragged." Sam Kenoi and some of his friends had drawn up a petition asking for the removal of Agent P. W. Danielson and most of the agency staff.

Senator Burton K. Wheeler, chief of the investigators, listened and asked questions and finally got hold of the basic fact that the Mescaleros were doing very little to improve their own condition. They hired Mexicans to take care of their sheep and cattle, for one thing.

"What do they do themselves?" Senator Wheeler wanted to know.

"Sit around up on the fence at the agency there," Danielson told him.

"It seems to me," Wheeler said, "this is about the richest reservation that we have visited here in New Mexico. They have the best opportunities for grazing and the best timber and they have got more per capita than any of the Indians we have visited."

Solon Sombrero, a wise Apache from Elk Springs, showed him why the Mescaleros had stopped struggling. "We are always in debt," he explained. "The total goes beyond $250,000. $190,000 is for roads. We owe $26,000 on the tribal herd. And then there is the debt to the trader. We do all our business on credit."

He went on to show that the timber money, which was to pay for their cattle, was used for support of the agency, depriving the Apaches of about $100 per person. All the income, except from the sale of wool and mohair, garden stuff, individually owned lambs and cattle, and the like, went into the United States Treasury and was appropriated back to run the agency and build up tribal holdings. Per capita payments were made to the Indians twice a year, and Mr. Prude, the trader, carried them for the rest of the time. (Prude testified that most of the

Mescaleros were honest and paid their debts when they had any cash.) It seemed wrong to Solon, as to other Indians, that their money was put into the treasury and that they had to earn it a second time by working on the roads and other projects. As the picture was filled in, it became obvious that the tribe was hopelessly in debt and had no way of paying off.

"How do you expect these Indians ever to pay this money back to the Government?" Senator Thomas demanded of the agent. Danielson admitted that there was $103,000 in the tribal fund which he had hoped to use to get the Indians back on their feet, but he had not done anything constructive about it at that time.

"The whole tribe is hungry right now," Sam Chino testified. "The old people need houses."[6]

The Senate investigation revealed quite clearly, for those who were interested enough to listen, that the Mescaleros had touched bottom. They had just enough vitality left to blame somebody—anybody—for their plight. The Indians' great friend John Collier summed it up in language more poetic than one usually hears from government administrators: "Death-doomed, robbed of their war-way, the Mescaleros had regressed, and then silently immured themselves in their despondency."[7]

When Collier became commissioner in 1933, he set going the first successful effort to get the Mescaleros on their feet. He was assisted by the Great Depression, which proved to be something of a blessing for the Indians. Relief measures took care of the destitution of the moment. Debts which could never be repaid were cancelled. The Civilian Conservation Corps was born, with a separate branch for the Indians. These measures helped

[6] *Survey of Conditions*, 71 Cong., 2 sess., *Senate Report* (1932), Part 19, p. 10513.
[7] Collier, "Indians Come Alive," *The Atlantic*, Vol. CLXX (September, 1942), 78.

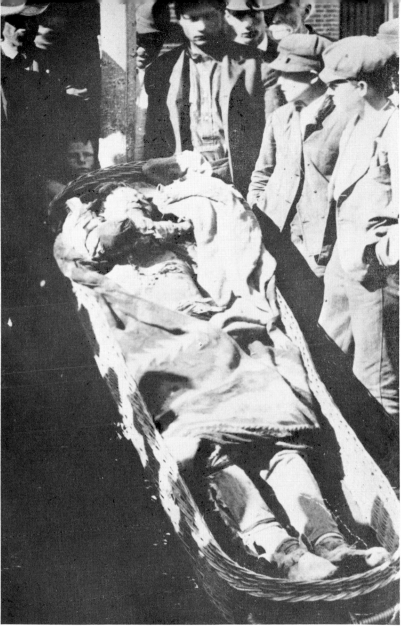

Kadinschin after execution.

Art Blazer, cattle foreman, and two of his cowboys.

OFFICIAL PHOTOGRAPHS OF THE INDIAN SERVICE
BOTH COURTESY MESCALERO AGENCY FILES

Alton Peso handles heavy machinery.

break the deadlock which had paralyzed the Apaches for so long. But it was the Indian Reorganization Act of 1934, an outgrowth of almost a decade of planning and probing, which reversed the trend of the last half-century.

First of all, it stopped the breaking up of Indian landholdings and actually set up provisions for buying back the lost acreage. Even more fundamental was the reorientation of official attitudes toward Indian life and culture. The Service now became enthusiastically pro-Indian. No longer was the red man a barbarian, whose life pattern must be rooted out and replaced by a white model. He was now a human being with an interesting heritage which must be fostered and preserved. His religion was not to be interfered with; his language was to be considered an asset; his arts and crafts were to be cultivated and restored. For the first time in history, anthropologists were called in to examine the cultural heritage of the Indian and help in the effort to preserve it.

This was a revolution indeed—one which Southwesterners in the days of Victorio and Nana would never have believed possible. But there was more to come. Good hard cash was at last set aside to pay for an Indian New Deal. A "revolving fund" was set up and made available to any tribe which wanted to get some money-making project going. Competent government men were ready to show the tribesmen how to conserve their resources and rebuild their soil and timber.

The Indians were not obliged to accept this help. Well-meant assistance was not to be crammed down their throats. If they wanted it, well and good. As a matter of fact, seventy-three tribes, including the Navajos, voted to reject the Act. Collier thought the rejection was due to "energetic campaigns of misrepresentation carried on by special interests which feared that

245

they would lose positions of advantage and . . . spread extreme and bizarre falsehoods concerning the effects of the act."[8]

A Mescalero delegation came to the meeting at Santo Domingo Pueblo in 1934 to hear the program discussed. "Incredulous, they went home," Collier said, "thinking, 'This is our own old-time way' "—hardly able to believe that the new day had actually arrived.[9] When the time came, the tribe voted to go along with the program, formulated a constitution and a charter, and borrowed $163,000[10] to build homes, buy stock and implements, and improve the reservation. They were in business for themselves at last, and the government was willing that they should learn by making and correcting their own mistakes.

The Business Committee became the governing force on the reservation, with power to allot and withdraw houses and lands, negotiate contracts, and settle tribal disputes. The tribal court followed along in second place, handling all cases not under the jurisdiction of federal authorities. Finally, the Cattle Growers Association, headed by an executive committee, stepped in to manage the reservation stock-raising program. Self-government was the ideal, and the superintendent was an adviser—not, as of old, a dictator.

In education, also, Commissioner Collier made his ideas felt. The obsolete boarding school, set up to keep children from adverse home influences, had to go. Community day schools under specially trained teachers took their place, and a strong effort was made to open white public schools to Indian children. On the reservations, the educational program was reorganized

---

[8] *Report of the Secretary of the Interior for 1935* (Office of Indian Affairs), 128.

[9] Collier, "Indians Come Alive," *loc. cit.*, 78.

[10] *Report of the Secretary of the Interior for 1935* (Office of Indian Affairs), 128. By 1944, the Mescalero loan had been increased to $328,000 (Dale, *op. cit.*, 247).

to include adult training and to make the school buildings, for all practical purposes, community centers.[11]

Next, the Indian Service stepped up its health program, paying special attention to tuberculosis and trachoma,[12] and took the first step toward the final settlement of Indian grievances against the government by setting up an Indian Claims Commission and inviting each of the tribes to have its day in court.[13]

Of all the tribes in the Southwest, or even in the nation, the Mescaleros profited most by the New Deal. Such enormous advances were made that one commentator declared, "It almost seems that the Indian Service sought to use this little agency as a 'proving ground,' or experiment station, to show what it was possible to accomplish under the New Regime."[14]

In the rosy glow of first enthusiasm, Collier and his men certainly painted a fine picture of changed conditions:

> The Mescaleros abandoned their slum camp and resettled themselves out where farming and cattle-running could supplement each other. Their net income from cattle jumped from $18,000 to $101,000 in three years. They closed out all leases to whites and they now use their entire range and have built up its herbage and soil while using it. Their farm crops multiplied eight fold in value in three years. These figures are indices merely. Long-range economic planning has become a matter of course with the Mescaleros. Their energies surge. They have their war-way once more, their chance for combat, for leadership, the endless universal war-way wherein nature is antagonist and collaborator in one.[15]

[11] *Ibid.*, 225.

[12] *Ibid.*, 227.

[13] See *Reports of the Commissioner of Indian Affairs for 1945,* 245; 1949, 363; and 1950, 354, for establishment and procedures of the Claims Commission.

[14] Dale, *op. cit.,* 247.

[15] *Report of the Commissioner of Indian Affairs for 1943,* 286. John Collier quotes from his article, "Indians Come Alive," *loc. cit.*

Anyone in close contact with Indians was apt to be skeptical of Collier's lyric flights. The energies of the Mescaleros, as their friends very well knew, did not "surge." For too many decades they had listened apathetically to plans which did not materialize and had accepted handouts for which no repayment was planned or expected. Still skeptical, still slow to act, they needed someone who could throw the switch and get the wheels to turn. The right man came along in the person of E. R. McCray, superintendent from 1935 to 1938.

They still remember McCray at Mescalero as a man who never gave up or slowed down. He implemented the provisions of the Wheeler-Howard bill of 1934 and gave the tribesmen a strong shove toward better conditions. His method was a combination of the iron fist and the open hand. It was he who saw to it that timber was cut and houses built, and that the Indians actually moved into them and went to work on the land.[16]

The Chiricahua Apaches, who came from Oklahoma in 1913, were settled at White Tail, and a few other families were living here and there on the reservation, but McCray wanted no half-measures. Everybody who had no actual business at Mescalero was prodded into setting up for himself somewhere else. Neat, four-room houses with galvanized-iron roofs were put up for them wherever a patch of land in the bottom of a tree-lined canyon could be turned into a farm. By 1937, this "Community Project" had got most of the Apaches out of their tipis and brush shelters. By 1942, every family had a house.[17]

There was one big difficulty: too many Apaches were settled where there was too little arable land. Twenty-seven families located close to the schoolhouse at Carrizo, where

[16] John O. Crow, Nov. 22, 1946.
[17] McCord, *op. cit.*, 39.

248

realistically minded land-management officials today can find adequate resources for only two.[18]

So matters stood when Pearl Harbor was bombed, and then came another revolution. Many Apaches enlisted and went off to fight. Many others were drawn into industry and various types of war work. There was an exodus from the Mescalero Reservation, as from all others. Income for the *émigrés* went up. They had a long look at the outside world. New desires and new awarenesses were born. When the war ended, they all came back to the reservation and found it too small to hold them. They had never made much more than a bare living, even under the Collier regime. Now there were more of them, and the reservation was no bigger than before. Consequently, there was less for each. It became obvious that the Indian Reorganization Act, tremendous as its effects had been, was not going to be enough.

William A. Brophy, who succeeded Collier in 1945, stated the problem clearly: "Even with the most efficient use, Indian resources in some areas are far from sufficient to provide a decent livelihood for all Indians. . . . Since Indian resources cannot be sufficiently augmented to support the population, which is increasing rapidly, many thousands of Indians must be helped to find economic opportunity and acceptance in the general national economy."[19]

In 1946, Brophy pointed out that reservation Indians were poorer than ever—one-third of them averaging less than $500 per family per year, the other two-thirds averaging less than $1,000. Such observations led directly to the Relocation Program, which began to move in 1952 and is the subject of a hot controversy today.

18 Pat Wehling, Sept. 30, 1956.
19 *Report of the Commissioner of Indian Affairs for 1945*, 233.

The Mescalero Apaches

With the rebirth of the theory that Indians must learn to get along off the reservations, another venerable notion came back to life: the conviction that the government should get out of the Indian business as soon as possible. Collier himself, in his appropriations request for 1944, asked for more money so that progress could be made in the "liquidation of the Indian Bureau,"[20] and Brophy and Nichols, his successors, stated officially that the aim of the administration was to "remove itself as trustee" and turn over its functions to "a trained and responsible people."[21]

To show that he meant business, Commissioner Nichols ordered the termination of Indian Bureau control over "certain tribal affairs" of the Saginaw Chippewas and the Stockbridge-Munsee Indians.[22] The Bureau went on, in the years which followed, to attempt virtual nullification of the Reorganization Act of 1934—the "Magna Charta of the Indians."

First came the slowing down of credit. After lending more than $12,000,000 from the revolving fund to Indian corporations, with an unusually good record of repayment, the Department of the Interior, in 1952, stopped making loans out of the $6,000,000 remaining. The next year the Eighty-third Congress passed a resolution (known as *H. Con. Res. 108*) announcing its desire and intention that governmental supervision over the tribes should "terminate" as quickly as possible, at the same time directing the Department of the Interior to suggest legislation which would bring about such termination.

In 1953, Congress followed this up by passing Public Law 280, which authorized any state to set up civil and criminal juris-

[20] *Survey of Conditions among Indians of the United States, Partial Report by Mr. Thomas of Oklahoma,* 78 Cong., 1 sess., *Senate Report 310.* The report is extremely critical of Mr. Collier.
[21] *Report of the Commissioner of Indian Affairs for 1947,* 345; 1949, 338.
[22] *Ibid.,* 1949, 338.

250

*Mescaleros, as other Inds were heavily
dependent upon Federal AID.*

diction over any reservation within its borders without even asking the consent of the tribe. This might seem like a justifiable and even praiseworthy withdrawal of the government from what should be the state's business until one remembers that pressure groups can and do take advantage of a state government much more easily than they can manipulate federal matters.[23] President Eisenhower realized this and registered a protest when he signed the bill—but he signed it.

Immediately there was violent public reaction. John Collier, who saw his years of work and progress tottering on the edge of the precipice, begged the President to think about what he was doing—to drop Commissioner Myer and appoint somebody with "sophisticated understanding of the basic American concept of due process of law, with respect for human differences, and with sympathetic knowledge of the facts of Indian life."[24] Following Collier's lead, dozens of influential men and women raised their voices in determined protest.

The outcry reached the ears of Congress. In 1954, only six out of almost a dozen termination bills were passed, indicating that the legislators were taking careful note of what was going on. Nevertheless, the Commissioner, on May 26, 1955, issued a directive that "allotted" Indian lands should be patented and made available for sale.

This directive was, of course, a complete reversal of the spirit of the Reorganization Act, and brought fierce condemnation and indignant resolutions from interested groups all over the nation, white and Indian alike. Even the Southwestern

[23] Dorothy Van de Mark, "The Raid on the Reservations," *Harper's*, Vol. CCXII (March, 1956), 51.

[24] Collier, "Letter to General Eisenhower," *The Nation*, Vol. CLXXVI (January 10, 1953), 20–30. See also Collier's article, "Back to Dishonor," in the *Christian Century*, Vol. LXXI (May 12, 1954), 578–80. For an argument on the other side, see "Do the Indians want to be Free?" in the *Saturday Evening Post*, Vol. CCXXVII (July 31, 1954), 10–12.

tribes, whose land was not much affected by allotment questions, raised their voices, for they knew what would come next.[25]

And it did come. The Klamaths in Oregon and the Menominees in Wisconsin, possessors of rich timber lands which the white man wanted, faced ruin and tribal disintegration through the breaking up of their holdings. The Nevada Indians were removed from federal trusteeship and placed under control of the state, through the operation of Public Law 280. They were not consulted and had no chance to express their wishes in the matter.[26] Half a dozen bills were introduced in Congress, such as the Competency Bill and the Butler-Malone Bill, which would have wiped out for good the tribal ownership of lands. The whole thing was so obviously a setup for another grab that everybody interested in Indian welfare was soon on his feet shouting for justice.

Only ten days after the Commissioner's directive concerning allotted lands, the four most important organizations working for Indian welfare—the Association on American Indian Affairs, the Indian Rights Association, the Friends Committee on Legislation, and the National Congress of American Indians —descended on Commissioner Emmons like a swarm of angry bees. He softened the terms of the original directive somewhat but staged no real retreat.[27]

At this moment, Oliver La Farge, president of the Association on American Indian Affairs, decided that the moment for attack had come. He wrote an open letter to President Eisenhower asking that the Point 4 Program for the upbuilding of depressed areas throughout the world be extended to our own Indians. It was the opinion of President Eisenhower, according

[25] *Indian Affairs*, New Series, No. 12 (October–November, 1955), 3.
[26] *Ibid.*, New Series, No. 10 (June, 1955), 1–3; *Indian Truth*, Vol. XXXII (April–July, 1955), 3–5.
[27] "Late Bulletin," *Indian Affairs*, New Series, No. 13 (December, 1955).

to his own words, that the depressed areas of the United States had as much right to this sort of help as those of any foreign land. It seemed to Mr. La Farge that the program could hardly bypass the poor people on the reservations, "as chronically depressed a group as any in the country."[28]

In general, the press of the nation approved of La Farge's proposal, but the Indian Bureau itself continued to try to liquidate the Indians by "denying them home rule in their communities, by cutting off credit to Indian business enterprises, by preparing legislation to 'terminate' tribes, by encouraging the passing of Indian land out of Indian ownership."[29] It all seemed to the friends of the Indians to be a renewal of the ancient warfare of extermination, once conducted hand to hand, now "disguised as a program to give them equal rights."[30]

Hope was revived when the Point 4 proposal went before the Senate, but hope had to be deferred when Senator Murray's bill failed of enactment. The record of the Eighty-fourth Congress seemed to indicate, nevertheless, that the movement to abolish the Indian by dividing up his land was slowing down. Three termination bills were passed, but they were requested by tribesmen who had reason to think themselves ready for independence. In addition, a number of beneficial measures were enacted, including a provision of $3,500,000 annually for adult Indian education. For a whole year, there seemed to be no great cause for alarm about the future of Indian landholdings. By early 1958, however, the Cheyennes of Montana and the Omahas of Nebraska were being separated from their real estate and the protectors of the red man were in full cry again.[31]

[28] *Ibid.*, New Series, No. 13 (December, 1955), 1–4.
[29] Oliver La Farge to C. L. Sonnichsen, Dec. 14, 1955.
[30] LaVerne Madigan, "Books," *The American Indian* (Spring, 1955), 62.
[31] "Indian Legislation in the 84th Congress," *Indian Affairs*, New Series (Supplement), No. 18 (September–October, 1956); No. 26 (May, 1958), "Annual Report of Oliver La Farge, president of the Association on American Indian Affairs, April 22, 1958," 1–4.

The Mescalero Apaches

Meanwhile, the Indian Bureau was setting up another scheme for reducing the population of the reservations. It started with the idea that if the tribesmen could not make a living at home, they would have to make it somewhere else.[32] Industries in the big cities offered the best market for unskilled labor. Why not set up a bureau to find jobs for those who could "integrate" in a white community?

The idea itself was good. Even the Friends of the Indian, in their various organizations, agreed that it could and should succeed. In practice, however, relocation did not work out according to plan. Some Indians were ready to invade the white man's world; others—many others—were not. Those who went forth had troubles and often came back defeated. It seemed to the Friends of the Indian that oftentimes those who were relocated were victims of misrepresentation; that they were inadequately cared for and advised after their arrival; that—in short—the whole thing was just an extension of the conspiracy to get rid of the Indian.

Those who believe in the program have been just as earnest in defending it. Mrs. Mary Nan Gamble of the Indian Field Relocation Office in Los Angeles, the largest center for relocation, thinks the program is turning out very well. She works closely with the California Employment Office and has a list of several hundred firms that are willing to employ Indians. One garment factory is so pleased with them that it now employs ninety per cent Indians. "Nobody who has ever come to us and really wanted work has ever failed to find more than one opening," she says.[33]

At the Los Angeles Indian Center, Mrs. Stevie Standing-

[32] *The Relocation Program,* issued by the Los Angeles Field Office, 1031 South Broadway, Los Angeles, California.

[33] August 4, 1955.

254

bear, an extremely competent Ponca Indian woman, will tell you that the Relocation Program produces many difficulties and disappointments:

> Too many Indians are being sent. They see pictures of relocated Indians in fine houses and think that is what they are getting into. They come without money and with inadequate household goods. Their children have to go to school and do not have proper clothing. Then they find they are not prepared for their jobs. They have no conception of budgeting and can't catch onto the idea of paying rent. They have to live in slum districts. Pretty soon they get lonesome and go down to the Torch Bar at Third and Main, hoping to see somebody they know. Then it happens. We go through the jails every week end to see if there are any Indians who need help. Sad cases come to light.[34]

When people in close touch with the program hold views so completely opposite, the rest of us can only wonder where the truth about relocation lies. And a flurry of magazine articles taking contrary points of view increases our wonder.[35] Time alone can tell who is right.

At Mescalero, there was considerable hope at first that the Relocation Program would be of help. A number of families signed up and headed for San Francisco and Los Angeles. All of them are back now. Anthony Treas went out in the summer of 1955 and got a job in a Los Angeles sheet-metal plant. He and his wife speak good English and were better prepared than most to "integrate," but they were uneasy the whole time they stayed. Mrs. Treas hated the stream of door-to-door salesmen who pes-

---

[34] August 24, 1955.

[35] For a favorable reaction to relocation, see O. K. and Marjorie Armstrong, "Indians Are Going to Town," *Reader's Digest*, Vol. LXVI (January, 1955). For the opposition are Dorothy Van de Mark, "The Raid on the Reservations," *loc. cit.*, and Ruth Mulvey Harmer, "Uprooting the Indians," *The Atlantic*, Vol. CXCVII (March, 1956). A middle ground is taken by LaVerne Madigan, *The American Indian Relocation Program*.

tered her. She hated paying seventy dollars a month rent. Anthony felt that he was in competition at the plant with men who had many more years of experience and came from a white background. Both of them suffered from inability to fill their spare time. "There is nothing to do," Anthony said to me. "I wish I had some tools to make belt buckles. I know how to do that. Television? I thought of that, but my wife persuaded me to get a washing machine."[36]

The Treases returned to the reservation for visits every time they had a chance and finally came back to stay. It has been the same with all the rest who tried the new system. Whether any more of them will try is doubtful.

In view of all these earnest efforts to push the Indian into the main stream of American life, there is one question that needs to be answered: What would happen if the government actually did go out of the Indian business—if the Bureau of Indian Affairs should divide up the reservation and leave the Mescaleros to work out their own salvation? While Walter O. Olson was superintendent, he estimated that if everything were sold off at current prices, there would be about $8,000 for every Indian.[37] Some of them might sell their birthright for such a sum, set themselves up in business somewhere, and get along very well. But what of the old people who speak no English—the men and women who have never been off the reservation—the widows and orphans—the sick and the blind? It is doubtful that they would last very long, with cash in hand and nothing to protect them. Most of them would probably soon be back where their ancestors started.

No one wants that to happen. The reservation is all the

[36] August 14, 1955.
[37] July 4, 1956.

security the Mescaleros have, and the race which owes them guidance and protection should see that they keep it until they are ready to make their own decisions. The better day which has dawned at Mescalero must not be allowed to close.

Chapter XV

TODAY AND TOMORROW

The Mescaleros Face the Future

It is now eighty-five years since the Mescaleros were given their reservation and a chance to make something of it and of themselves. They have accomplished much in that brief interval. It is time now to ask what their chances are for the future. What do they have to work with? How fast are they going ahead?

Their raw material includes only two things: their reservation and themselves. The land comprises just under 500,000 acres. It is mostly timber and range, but there is enough farm acreage to support the present population—about one thousand people—and perhaps a few more. Approximately 4,000 acres can be brought under cultivation; 200,000 are classified as grazing land, 250,000 as forest.

These figures are impressive and important, but they convey nothing of one important aspect of the reservation—its sheer beauty. Symbols on paper can give no idea of the loveliness and peace of those green mountain slopes, those quiet, lonesome valleys, those clear, cold streams—all dominated by the majesty of Sierra Blanca soaring into the serene blue heavens. It is no wonder that every Mescalero who leaves his homeland wants to come back and wants to keep this Indian heaven intact for his children.

Hub of the reservation—the capital of Mescalero—is Mescalero town, a three-tiered village which straggles a little way up the hill on the north side of the Tularosa Valley twenty miles from the railroad. U. S. Highway 70 flows around it in a sweeping curve, giving tourists and truck drivers a brief glimpse of the little Indian metropolis dreaming on its mountain slope.

The main street runs past the store, the post office, the old school building, and the community center. Here the Indians come to do their household business and to sun themselves and talk to their friends. Most mornings there will be from one to twenty relaxed tribesmen leaning against the east wall of the store, soaking up sun and looking at the beautiful world. A white man wonders why they waste their time this way. The Indians undoubtedly wonder why the white man has to work so furiously without ever stopping to look around him.

On two levels above the main street, the agency employees and some Indian families live. Even in this small world, society is stratified; the top level is the place to be if you belong to the aristocracy. The houses are well-kept frame buildings with good lawns. At the west end is the superintendent's house. Then comes the Mescalero Club for official and unofficial visitors; then the hospital, which was once the Mescalero Boarding School; then half a dozen dwellings; and finally, at the end of the row, the brick agency building in a shady bower of trees. Behind the town the green mountain slope soars up and away, and across the Valley to the south rises another green bastion, hemming in this Indian oasis and keeping out most of the clamor and hurry of the white man's world.

Picked out against the southern slope and standing high on

its own special hill is Father Albert Braun's magnificent Catholic church, built by the Reverend Father himself, with the help of his parishioners, out of native stone and mortar and finished after nearly thirty years of labor.

The agency is the nerve center of Mescalero. There the superintendent carries on as the *da-go-tai* ("father") of the tribe in a big office with good Navajo rugs on the floor and Indian paintings on the walls. The president of the Business Committee has an office across the lobby. In the rear, the affairs of the tribe are attended to by the men in charge of roads, forestry, cattle, and land management. The agency is run like any efficiently managed American business office—complete with files, calculating machines, and telephones.

On the mesa one-half mile to the east, the camp ground offers complete contrast—the old ways surviving in the shadow of the new. The puberty ceremony takes place there in July, and many tents and brush shelters house Apaches visiting from outlying communities. A good many tribesmen live there the year round, however, their huts and tipis dotting the steeply rising slope above the feast grounds. The whole primitive community looks much like the ones we see in pictures taken back in the eighties, except that horses are few and many trucks and automobiles are scattered about.

This is the Mescalero slum, and it is no credit to the tribe. Every agent who has had the welfare of the Mescaleros at heart and every progressive tribal leader has tried to find some way to eliminate this malodorous area. None has succeeded. Superintendent E. R. McCray came close when he pushed through his "Community Project" twenty years ago, persuading most of the Indian families to settle in outlying communities. They did not stay away long. The White Tail, Carrizo, Three Rivers, and Elk-Silver schools were discontinued in 1949 because most of the

302-53.32

OFFICIAL PHOTOGRAPH OF THE INDIAN SERVICE
COURTESY MESCALERO AGENCY FILES

The Red Hats at work.

The Summit Enterprise.

children were gone. Those who remained began riding daily to Mescalero, Tularosa, and Ruidoso by bus.

Most of those who left came back to Mescalero town and some of them settled in the brush and canvas slum. It is hard to tell whether they have gone back to their primitive life because they had to or because they wanted to.

From Mescalero, the roads and trails strike out through timbered slopes and hidden valleys to the cow camps and bottom lands, from which the Indians derive the greatest part of their living. Farming, stock-raising, and timber-cutting keep them in clothes and food.

Of the three, farming is the least important. For years the government has tried its best to make the Indians till the soil as a means of making them independent. For just as many years, the Indians have put up a successful resistance. At the present time, only a handful of Mescaleros depend on the fields for their support, and in many places the little patches of bottom land have gone back to weeds and grass.

There are two reasons for the decline of agriculture among the Apaches. One is their traditional dislike of plowing and reaping. The other is the increase in the number of desirable jobs on and off the reservation. Some have found work at the Holloman Air Development Center near Alamogordo. A few have gone off to California and made a place for themselves without any help from the Relocation Program. For most of them, however, the best opportunities are at home, where various tribal enterprises absorb much of the tribal man power. Crews are at work all year round caring for dams, corrals, ditches, and roads.[1] Maintenance men keep up buildings and machinery. Wood has to be cut and hauled for reservation use

[1] Melvin Fairbanks, Mescalero road engineer, November 30, 1956, says that road work adds $60,000 to $70,000 annually to the tribal income.

261

and for sale. Policemen and fire fighters have to be recruited from Indian ranks.

The few Mescaleros who work full time on the land are good farmers. They take care of their soil and keep their places neat. If one of them, through indolence or drunkenness, lets his farm run down, the tribe has one effective tool for changing his habits. The Business Committee can re-allocate the land.[2]

For one farmer there are several dozen cattle raisers among these people. Practically every family has a few cows, and many run sizable herds. Altogether, the stock population of the reservation consists of about 6,000 head of cattle, 1,000 horses, and a few sheep and goats. Besides the individually owned animals, there is the tribal herd and another herd belonging to the Cattle Growers Association. In good years the range will carry 10,500 head, producing an income as high as $340,000.[3] A long series of dry years has made it necessary to reduce the size of the herds, but even drastic cutting has not been able to save the pasture land from serious deterioration. Poor management has resulted in further loss, and declining cattle prices have completed the damage. In 1956, the tribe lost $13,000 on its investment and the Cattle Growers' Association has begun a program of reorganization which it will take some years to complete.[4]

Timber is an even more important resource than cattle. Under the supervision of a forester and his staff, the crop is scientifically harvested by lumber companies who bid for the contracts. Here again, however, prosperity is not automatic. A few years ago a variety of dwarf mistletoe began attacking the ponderosa pine and Douglas fir stands, and timber-cutting is proceeding at twice the normal rate of speed in order to make sure

[2] Solon Sombrero, June 8, 1955.
[3] "Mescalero Reservation Cattle Sales Bring Record Prices," El Paso *Times,* Sept. 21, 1946; Pat Wehling, Mescalero land management head, Sept. 30, 1956.
[4] Mescalero Agency *Monthly Progress Report* (Sept. 27, Dec. 18, 1956).

the trees are used before they can be destroyed by the parasite. Plans are under way to convert the saplings into charcoal, and perhaps to start a pulpwood industry.[5]

The fact that big cuts will double the timber revenue for a few years, after which there will be twenty or thirty years of little or no revenue, is causing no small concern to the Mescaleros. Shortsighted members of the tribe want to use the extra timber money to supplement their declining incomes. The Business Committee wants to put the extra cash into enterprises that will produce something later on.[6] The resulting argument has called attention to the increasingly difficult economic situation of the Apaches.

Ever since rations were cut off in 1902, the reservation has provided a living—sometimes a poor one—for most of them. Cattle money, timber money, and income from various jobs brought in cash for daily needs. During the forties and early fifties the tribe got along well enough. The Branch of Land Operations at the agency estimates that the average per capita income for adults from 1946 to 1956 was $1,800.[7] Add to this the amount saved for each individual by government health and educational services, and the sum would be higher. Compared with the rest of the Indians in the United States, the Mescaleros up to the present time have been fortunate. But now the good times seem to be over. In November, 1956, the superintendent issued a warning that Cattle Association funds would not take care of fences, wells, corrals, and salt, and that as a result per capita payments, if there were any, would be too small to buy many necessities.[8] Since then, as matters have grown more serious, articles in Southwestern newspapers have painted

[5] Barton Wetzel, forest administrator, Nov. 30, 1956.
[6] W. O. Olson, Sept. 7, 1955.
[7] W. O. Olson and Mrs. E. Breuninger to C. L. Sonnichsen, Oct. 15, 1956.
[8] W. O. Olson, undated "Notice" to all Mescalero Apaches.

exaggerated pictures of starvation and destitution among the Mescaleros.[9]

Times are indeed hard for the Apaches, but this time the Indians have not given up the struggle. They have canvassed every possibility for putting their reservation to profitable use and have got hold of a number of promising ideas. Future generations may decide that the crisis of 1956 and 1957 provided just the stimulus needed at exactly the right moment.

It was this emergency which put the Mescaleros in the tourist business. For ten years the tribe had been talking about the "Summit Enterprise"—a scheme for setting up a tourist center at the top of the eight thousand-foot pass between Mescalero and the summer-resort town of Ruidoso. After much debate and delay, they finally drew $200,000 from their funds in the U. S. Treasury, cleared the grounds, and put down a well. Construction was slow until they hired Wallace Hiatt, a former dude-ranch operator, teacher, engineer, and newspaperman, to run the Summit and all the other money-making enterprises which the tribe sponsors. The program picked up speed under his direction. Tribal leaders Wendell Chino and Fred Pellman worked long and hard to bring their dream to realization. In September, 1956, Apache Summit was opened to the public with a barbecue, tours of the reservation, and band concerts by the Albuquerque Indian School band.[10]

Other tribal projects are getting under way. Those who can paint pictures, make baskets, or manufacture cradle boards and moccasins are turning out products for the curio shop. A big crew gets in Christmas trees just before the holidays. Another crew sells firewood in neighboring towns. A number of women

[9] Bill Montgomery, "Drought-Stricken Mescaleros Get No Aid from Government," El Paso *Times*, July 18, 1957. See also July 17, 19, 20, 21, 22.

[10] Marshal Hail, El Paso *Herald-Post*, Oct. 1, 1956.

are making squaw dresses. Dave Belen has developed a talent for turning out metal fireplace furniture.[11]

The biggest enterprise of all is a suit against the United States asking compensation for loss of the original homelands of the tribe. The Indian Claims Commission Act of August 13, 1946, opened the way for final settlement of all Indian claims by permitting every tribe with a grievance to have its day in court. The "Apache Nation"[12] (which includes the Mescaleros) now has a suit pending before the Commission, with separate hearings in prospect for each tribe.

The petition filed alleges, among other things, that the treaty of July 1, 1852, made with the Apache Nation—the said treaty having been duly ratified by the Senate on March 23, 1853 —undertook to "designate, settle, and adjust" the territorial boundaries of the Apache lands. Instead of carrying out this promise, the United States assumed "exclusive proprietary ownership of all the lands of the plaintiffs . . . to the great damage of the plaintiffs."[13]

The Eastern Apaches (Jicarillas and Mescaleros) are claiming an enormous section of the Southwest—roughly the territory from the Río Grande eastward to the Pecos and from the Colorado line southward to the Big Bend of Texas. They were at home in every part of this region. Whether they "owned" it or not is the question which must be decided. The United States has settled with the Utes for $32,000,000—a fact which gives the Mescaleros hope. Specialists from the University of New Mexico are doing research on their claim, and they have hired a good

---

[11] Mrs. Alice Hiatt, Wallace Hiatt, Nov. 29, 1956.

[12] I. S. Weissbrodt to C. L. Sonnichsen, Sept. 5, 1956: "The petition was filed in this 'joint' manner for technical reasons arising primarily out of the treaty of July 1, 1852, which the United States purported to make with the 'Apache Nation.' It is likely, however, that there will be separate trials of the claims of each of the 'tribes.'"

[13] Petition before the Indian Claims Commission, Docket No. 22.

firm of Washington lawyers to represent them in court. Their suit may bring results.

As well as they have done in holding on to and developing their material resources, the Mescaleros still have much to contend with. The chasm between the old life and the new has not been completely bridged and may not be bridged for a long time. The evolutionary process can be speeded up, but it can not be eliminated entirely, and the transitional period has to be gone through.

English is still not their native language, and a few of the older tribesmen have no English at all. Shyness and lack of aggressiveness handicap others. Some of them still live in the 1880's as far as their time sense is concerned and have little conception of schedules and deadlines. The average Mescalero male is not yet convinced of the virtue of hard physical toil. These things must change before the Indian can stand on his own feet in a competitive society.

There are deeper and more serious indications that the Mescaleros are having growing pains. One is the frequency of trouble in the Indian home. Psychologists, anthropologists, and medical men who have worked with the tribe since 1955 are studying this situation and trying to account for it.[14]

Another sign that the gap has not been bridged is the decay of the Apache's religious faith. His ancestral beliefs had beauty and dignity. The concept of a universal power in nature which a man could tap and use, the belief in a friendly deity who slew

[14] Recent observers at Mescalero include Professor and Mrs. W. T. Ross of Michigan State University—one an anthropologist, the other a psychologist—who spent the summers of 1955 and 1956 at Mescalero setting up a vocational guidance program and doing individual counseling with the Apaches. Mrs. Ross returned in the summer of 1957. Professor David M. Schneider of the University of California and Professor Peter Kunstadter of the University of Arizona worked on anthropological projects in the summer of 1957. When these scientists publish their findings, we shall know more about what goes on inside the Mescalero community.

266

a variety of monsters so that men could live on the earth and be happy, the presence of the Mountain Spirits who could and sometimes did help the children of men, the ceremonials full of poetry and faith—such beliefs once gave the Apache a firm foundation on which he could build his life. Then came the missionaries, with the word that this was all superstition and that the Christian way was the best—the only—way. Quite naturally there were doubts and questionings, and even today many Mescaleros are not firm in either faith.

Several hundred of them are nominal Roman Catholics, but the resident priests struggle against lukewarmness and indifference.[15] The Reformed church has a steady group of Indian worshipers, but not a large one. In 1954, the Mormons and the Assembly of God established missions and attracted small congregations which are not growing very fast.

In one final way, the Apaches show themselves to be in the grip of transition. This is the persistence of the liquor problem. Drinking is as much of a curse today as it was fifty years ago—perhaps more so, since dealers can now legally sell intoxicants to Indians anywhere off the reservation. A kindly tavern keeper has set up a bar just across the reservation line to save time and trouble for everybody, and he gets plenty of business.

There is no simple explanation for excessive drinking, whether the drinker be Indian or white, but some fundamental dissatisfaction must be at work. "A people frustrated, discouraged, and made to feel that they are second-rate citizens," says one commentator, "are more likely to seek solace or escape than those with steady jobs and cash wages sufficient for their families' needs."[16]

[15] Brother Randall, July 28, 1956, estimates that there are seven hundred nominal Roman Catholics. Agency officials think this figure is too high.

[16] "The Liquor Problem among the Indians of the Southwest," condensed from the July, 1956, *Newsletter* of the New Mexico Association on Indian Affairs, in *Indian Affairs*, No. 18 (September–October, 1956), 3.

267

Hope

The hope of the Mescaleros is in their children. New leadership must come from them, and education alone will make them fit to lead. Training is still not easy for them to get, and some of them are still suspicious of it, but things look better every year.

In the fall of 1956, the old school became a thing of the past, and a new county school went into operation about a mile from Mescalero town—a fine building of glass and steel and concrete, as modern as a jet plane. The abandonment of the government school is part of a plan to fit all New Mexico's Indian children into the state public-school system. It will take fifteen years to complete the project, according to New Mexico school authorities, but the result should be a lowering of the barriers that make the Indian a stranger in his own country.[17]

The tradition of vocational training is still carried on in a painless way. The older girls in the home economics classes take an important part in the preparing and serving of meals. The school has all the latest kitchen facilities, where they can learn cooking and canning. There are classes in sewing and other domestic matters. The mothers and fathers are encouraged to use the school as a community center. More and more of the little ones can speak some English when they enter Mrs. Fleta Baldonado's beginning class.[18]

When one thinks of the schools of other days—crowded, dirty, understaffed, and unorganized—one realizes the progress that has been made at Mescalero.

Of course a grade school, or even a high school, cannot do all that needs to be done for the boys and girls who will lead the tribe tomorrow, and earnest attempts are being made to get some higher education for the ones who want it and can profit

[17] "New Mexico Indians Gradually Moving into Public Schools," El Paso *Times,* July 22, 1956.
[18] Mrs. Fleta Baldonado, Sept. 15, 1948, Nov. 29, 1956.

268

by it. The Business Committee has set up a scholarship fund, and several foundations have been appealed to for special assistance. Five young men and women were in college in 1956–57, and more will go as time goes by.

The Apache leaders know that education is the only solution for their difficulties. If they are to become self-sufficient, they must give their young people the training that will enable them to step into the shoes of the white men who are now managing reservation affairs. "Total replacement" is their aim—total replacement of every white man by an Indian. When this occurs, the government will indeed be out of the Indian business, but the Indians will be ready.

It is encouraging to their friends to note how constantly they hack away at the barriers that isolate them from the rest of the world. Anything that takes them off the reservation is a step in the right direction. Baseball teams and Four-H clubs help. The two world wars opened up a new universe to many of the young men. The Relocation Program has had its influence, even on the ones who could not stand the strain and came back defeated.

The boys who get out the most are the famous Red Hats—a group of volunteer fire fighters who wear a distinctive red-striped steel helmet and are in demand all over the West. When the siren blows the signal, they turn out on the run and depart, by bus or airplane, for far places where their courage and skill can be put to good use.

They came into existence in 1948 when Forest Ranger and Fire Chief A. B. Shields, now retired after more than thirty years' service, called for volunteers. Nineteen men, mostly veterans of World War II, responded and began training. The "Shields System" eventually included over two hundred men organized into twenty-four-man squads. Each man has his job to do, and by teamwork and fast action a squad can construct a fire trail as fast as a man can walk.

Their conspicuous success in fighting fires in New Mexico earned them a call to California in 1951, and in 1952 they were back, fighting the big blazes in California and the Pacific Northwest. They have been out time and again ever since, bringing back good money and much useful experience. They have a slogan, "Join the Red Hats and See the World."[19]

It is a far cry from Victorio's raiders to Mr. Shields' Red Hats and the young Apaches' learning to meet people and handle public relations at Apache Summit. The Mescaleros have much to be proud of today and much to hope for in the future. If the government does not liquidate them too soon—if they can get themselves educated fast enough—if they can continue to be Indians but learn the white man's methods, there will be a better day for all of them.

[19] Mrs. Tom Charles, "Mescalero Apache 'Red Hats' Hold National Reputation for Forest Fire Control Ability," El Paso *Times,* Dec. 7, 1952; John Krill, "Red Hat of the Brave," *Nation's Business,* Vol. XLI (September, 1953), 46.

BIBLIOGRAPHY

1. INTERVIEWS

Baldonado, Mrs. Fleta. Interviews at Mescalero, September 15, 1948; November 29, 1956.

Bigmouth, Percy. Interviews at Mescalero, October 2, 1954; September 8, 1955; July 28, 1956.

Blazer, A. N. Interview at Mescalero, December 30, 1946.

Blazer, Paul. Interviews at Mescalero, October 2, 1954; September 7, 8, 1955; July 28, November 30, 1956.

Chino, Wendell. Interview at Mescalero, October 3, 1954.

Cleve, Mr. and Mrs. Orris. Interview at Elk, New Mexico, November 27, 1954.

Crookneck. Interview at Mescalero, February 5, 1955.

Crow, John O. Interviews at Mescalero, November 22, December 30, 1946; July 5, 1948.

Fairbanks, Melvin. Interview at Mescalero, November 30, 1956.

Gamble, Mrs. Mary Nan. Interview at Los Angeles, California, August 4, 1955.

Hiatt, Mr. and Mrs. Wallace. Interview at Mescalero, November 29, 1956.

Magoosh, Mr. and Mrs. Willie. Interviews at Mescalero, February 5, 1955; July 28, 1956.

Olson, Walter O. Interviews at Mescalero, October 2, 1954; September 7, 1955; July 4, 27, November 30, 1956.

Randall, Brother. Interview at Mescalero, July 28, 1956.
Ross, Dr. and Mrs. W. T. Interviews at Mescalero, September 7, 1955; July 28, 1956.
Roastingear, Julius. Interview at Mescalero, November 29, 1956.
Sago, Rufus. Interview at Mescalero, September 9, 1955.
Sligh, George. Interview at El Paso, Texas, February 26, 1948.
Sombrero, Solon. Interview at Elk Springs, New Mexico, June 8, 1955.
Standingbear, Mrs. Stevie. Interview at Los Angeles, California, August 24, 1955.
Talley, Clinton. Interview at Mescalero, July 5, 1957.
Taylor, Claude. Interview at Mescalero, September 8, 1955.
Treas, Mr. and Mrs. Anthony. Interview at Hawthorne, California, August 14, 1955.
Trombley, Dr. Lauren. Interviews at Mescalero, July 28, November 30, 1956.
Wehling, Pat. Interviews at Mescalero, July 4, September 30, 1956.
Wetzel, Barton. Interview at Mescalero, November 30, 1956.

2. MANUSCRIPT MATERIALS

Andrews, Ferdinand. The Indians of New Mexico and Arizona. Manuscript in the Henry E. Huntington Library, San Marino, California.
Blazer, A. N. Santana, the Last Chief of the Mescaleros. Unpublished manuscript in the files of the Mescalero Indian Agency.
Clayton, Jane. Tularosa. Unpublished manuscript in the files of the Tularosa High School, Tularosa, New Mexico.
Correspondence Files, Mescalero Indian Agency.
Long, Grace. The Anglo-American Occupation of the El Paso District. M. A. thesis, University of Texas, 1931.
McCord, T. T., Jr. An Economic History of the Mescalero Apache Indians. Unpublished M. A. thesis, University of New Mexico, 1946.
Montes, Bertha. The Great Chieftains. Manuscript dated May, 1948, in possession of C. L. Sonnichsen.
Parish Records, St. Patrick's Church, El Paso, Texas.
Ritch, William Gillette. Papers in the Henry E. Huntington Library, San Marino, California.

Stoes, Mrs. Katherine D. Biographical Sketch of Ida May Llewellyn. Manuscript in the private collection of Mrs. Katherine D. Stoes.

Toulouse, Joseph H., Jr. History of the Salinas Province with a Classified Interpretative Bibliography. Manuscript in the Library of Gran Quivira National Monument.

3. GOVERNMENT DOCUMENTS AND PUBLICATIONS

Abel, Annie Heloise, ed. *The Official Correspondence of James S. Calhoun, while Indian Agent at Santa Fé and Superintendent of Indian Affairs in New Mexico.* Washington, Government Printing Office, 1915.

Annual Report of the Board of Indian Commissioners for 1932.

Annual Reports of the Commissioner of Indian Affairs, 1851–1955.

Annual Report of the Department of the Interior for 1899, Part II, "Mescalero Reservation." 56 Cong., 1 sess., *House Ex. Doc. 5.*

Annual Reports of the Secretary of War, 1849–81.

Boas, Franz. *Handbook of American Indian Languages,* Part I. Washington, Government Printing Office, 1911.

Bourke, John G. "The Medicine-Men of the Apache," *B. A. E. Ninth Annual Report,* 1887–88. Washington, Government Printing Office, 1892.

Colyer, Vincent. *Peace with the Apaches of New Mexico and Arizona. Report of Vincent Colyer, Member of Board of Indian Commissioners, 1871.* Washington, Government Printing Office, 1872.

Condition of the Indian Tribes. Report of the Joint Special Committee Appointed under Joint Resolution of March 3, 1865. Washington, Government Printing Office, 1867.

Hodge, Frederick Webb. *Handbook of Indians North of Mexico. B. A. E. Bulletin 30.* 2 vols. Washington, Government Printing Office, 1907, 1910.

Hrdlička, Ales. *Physiological and Medical Observations among the Indians of the Southwestern United States and Mexico. B. A. E. Bulletin 34.* Washington, Government Printing Office, 1908.

Kappler, Charles J. *Indian Affairs, Laws, and Treaties.* 2 vols. Washington, Government Printing Office, 1904.

Letter from the Secretary of War, transmitted in response to Senate resolution of January 28, 1890. Reports relative to the treatment of certain Apache Indians. 51 Cong., 1 sess., *Sen. Ex. Doc. 83.*

Letter from the Secretary of War, transmitted in response to Senate resolution of March 11, 1890. Correspondence between Lt. Gen. P. H. Sheridan and Brig. Gen. George H. Crook between March 26 and April 5, 1886. 51 Cong., 1 sess., *Sen. Ex. Doc. 88.*

Monthly Progress Reports, Mescalero Indian Agency, September 27, December 18, 1956.

Petition "Before the Indian Claims Commission," Docket No. 22.

Pope, Captain John. Report of Exploration of a Route for the Pacific Railroad near the Thirty-second Parallel of Latitude, from the Red River to the Río Grande. 33 Cong., 2 sess., *House Ex. Doc. 129* (1885).

Record of Engagements with Hostile Indians within the Military Division of the Missouri from 1868 to 1882, Lt. Gen. P. H. Sheridan Commanding. Compiled at Headquarters, Military Division of the Missouri, from Official Records. Washington, Government Printing Office, 1882.

Reel, Estelle. *Course of Study for the Indian Schools of the United States, Industrial and Literary.* Washington, Government Printing Office, 1901.

The Relocation Program, issued by the Los Angeles Field Office, 1031 South Broadway, Los Angeles, California.

Survey of Conditions among the Indians of the United States. Partial Report by Mr. Thomas of Oklahoma. 78 Cong., 1 sess., *Senate Report 310* (May 24, 1943).

Survey of Conditions among Indians of the United States. Hearings before a Subcommittee of the Committee on Indian Affairs. 71 Cong., 2 sess., *Senate Report* (1932), Part 19.

The War of the Rebellion: A Compilation of the Official Records of the Union and Confederate Armies. Series I, Vols. IV (1882), IX (1883), and XLVIII (1896).

4. NEWSPAPERS

Denver *Tribune,* May 4, 5, 1880.

El Paso *Times,* March 1, 1942; September 21, 1946; December 7, 1952; July 22, 1956.

El Paso *Herald-Post,* October 1, 1956; July 17, 19, 20, 21, 22, 1957.

Las Cruces *34,* January 1, 1879; June 23, 1880.

Mesilla *Miner,* June 9, 1860.

Mesilla *News,* October 17, 18, 1879.

Río Grande Republican, June 17, September 16, November 25, 1882; June 2, 1888; November 16, 1889; February 8, 1890.

Santa Fé *Era Southwestern,* April 15, June 1, 1880.

Santa Fé *New Mexican,* November 25, 1872, August 11, 1904.

5. BOOKS AND MONOGRAPHS

Adams, Evelyn C. *American Indian Education. Government Schools and Economic Progress.* New York, King's Crown Press, 1946.

Astrov, Margot. *The Winged Serpent.* New York, The John Day Company, 1946.

Bancroft, Hubert Howe. *History of the North-Mexican States and Texas.* (Vol. XV in *Works.*) The History Company, 1886.

Bandelier, Adolph F. A. *Final Report of Investigations among the Indians of the Southwestern United States, Carried on Mainly in the Years from 1880 to 1885. Papers* of the Archaeological Institute of America, No. 3. 2 vols. Cambridge, Massachusetts, John Wilson and Son, 1890.

——— and Fanny R. Bandelier. *Historical Documents Relating to New Mexico, Nueva Vizcaya, and Approaches Thereto to 1773,* ed. by Charles Wilson Hackett. 3 vols. Washington, The Carnegie Institution, 1923, 1926, 1937.

Barney, James M. *Tales of Apache Warfare. True Stories of Massacres, Fights, and Raids in Arizona and New Mexico.* Phoenix, 1933.

Bartlett, John R. *Personal Narrative of Explorations and Incidents in Texas, New Mexico, California, Sonora, and Chihuahua, Connected with the United States and Mexican Boundary during the Years 1850, '51, '52, and '53 . . . .* 2 vols. New York, D. Appleton and Co., 1854.

Bellah, Robert N. *Apache Kinship Systems.* Cambridge, Harvard University Press, 1942.

Benavides, Fray Alonso. *The Memorial of Fray Alonso de Benavides,*

1630, trans. by Mrs. Edward E. Ayer, annotated by F. W. Hodge and C. F. Lummis. Chicago, privately printed, 1916.

———. *Benavides Memorial of 1630*, trans. by Peter P. Forrestal, ed. and annotated by Cyprian J. Lynch. Washington, Academy of American Franciscan History, 1954.

Bennett, James A. *Forts and Forays. A Dragoon in New Mexico, 1850–56*, ed. by Clinton E. Brooks and Frank D. Reeve. Albuquerque, University of New Mexico Press, 1948.

Bolton, Herbert E., ed. and trans. *Athanase de Mézières and the Louisiana-Texas Frontier, 1768–80*. Cleveland, The Arthur H. Clark Company, 1914.

———, ed. *Spanish Exploration in the Southwest, 1542–1706*. New York, Charles Scribner's Sons, 1916.

Calvin, Ross. *Sky Determines*. New York, The Macmillan Company, 1934.

Carroll, H. Bailey and J. Villasana Haggard, eds. *Three New Mexico Chronicles*. Albuquerque, The Quivira Society, 1942.

Castetter, Edward F. and M. E. Opler. *The Ethnobotany of the Chiricahua and Mescalero Apaches. (Ethnobiological Studies in the American Southwest*, Vol. III.) Albuquerque, University of New Mexico Press, 1936.

———, Willis H. Bell, and Alvin R. Grove. *The Early Utilization and Distribution of Agave in the American Southwest*. (University of New Mexico *Ethnobiological Studies*, Vol. VI.) Albuquerque, University of New Mexico Press, 1938.

Cavo, Padre Andrés. *Supplemento a la Historia de los Tres Siglos de Mexico durante el Gobierno Español*. Tom. III, 1836.

Collier, John. *The Indians of the Americas*. New York, W. W. Norton, 1947.

Cremony, John C. *Life Among the Apaches*. San Francisco, A. Roman, 1868.

Crook, General George. *General George Crook, His Autobiography*, ed. by Martin Schmitt. Norman, University of Oklahoma Press, 1946.

Dale, Edward Everett. *The Indians of the Southwest*. Norman, University of Oklahoma Press, 1949.

Davis, Lieutenant Britton. *The Truth about Geronimo*, ed. by M. M. Quaife. New Haven, Yale University Press, 1929.

Dunn, J. P. *The Massacres of the Mountains*. New York, Harper & Brothers, 1886.

Ferguson, Philip Gooch. "Diary of Philip Gooch Ferguson," *Marching with the Army of the West*, ed. by Ralph P. Bieber. Glendale, California, The Arthur H. Clark Company, 1936.

Gálvez, Bernardo de. *Instructions for Governing the Interior Provinces of New Spain, 1786*, trans. and ed. by Donald E. Worcester. Berkeley (The Quivira Society, *Publication* XII), 1951.

Garrett, Pat F., *Authentic Life of Billy the Kid*, ed. by Maurice Garland Fulton. New York, The Macmillan Co., 1927.

Glass, Major E. N., compiler. *The History of the Tenth Cavalry*. Tucson, Acme Printing Company, 1901.

Hackett, Charles Wilson. *Revolt of the Pueblo Indians of New Mexico, and Otermin's Attempted Reconquest, 1680–82*. 2 vols. Albuquerque, University of New Mexico Press, 1942.

Harrington, John P. "Southern Peripheral Athapaskawan Origins, Divisions and Migrations," *Smithsonian Miscellaneous Collections*, Vol. C (Essays in Historical Anthropology of North America), May 25, 1940.

Harrison, J. B. *The Latest Studies on Indian Reservations*. Philadelphia, The Indian Rights Association, 1887.

Hoijer, Harry. *Chiricahua and Mescalero Texts*. Chicago, University of Chicago Press, 1938.

Hoopes, Alban W. *Indian Affairs and Their Administration, with Special Reference to the Far West, 1849–60*. Philadelphia, University of Pennsylvania Press, 1932.

Hughes, Annie E. *The Beginnings of Spanish Settlement in the El Paso District*. Berkeley, University of California Press, 1914.

Hunt, Aurora. *Major James Henry Carleton, 1814–73. Western Frontier Dragoon*. Glendale, California, The Arthur H. Clark Company, 1958.

Hutchinson, W. H. *A Bar Cross Man*. Norman, University of Oklahoma Press, 1956.

Keleher, William A. *Turmoil in New Mexico*. Santa Fé, The Rydal Press, 1952.

La Farge, Oliver. *As Long As the Grass Shall Grow*. New York, Longmans, Green, & Co., Inc., 1940.

Lane, Lydia Spencer. *I Married A Soldier*. Philadelphia, J. B. Lippincott Co., 1910.

Leupp, Francis E. *The Indian and His Problem*. New York, Charles Scribner's Sons, 1910.

Lindquist, G. E. *The Red Man in the United States*. New York, George H. Doran Co., 1923.

Lockwood, Frank P. *The Apache Indians*. New York, The Macmillan Co., 1938.

Lummis, Charles F. *The Land of Poco Tiempo*. Albuquerque, University of New Mexico Press, 1952, reprint.

Madigan, LaVerne. *The American Indian Relocation Program. A report undertaken with the assistance of the Field Foundation . . . .* New York, Association on American Indian Affairs, December, 1956.

Magoffin, Susan Shelby. *Down the Santa Fé Trail and into Mexico*, ed. by Stella M. Drumm. New Haven, Yale University Press, 1926.

Meriam, Lewis and others. *The Problem of Indian Administration. Report of a Survey Made at the Request of Hubert Work and Submitted to Him February 21, 1928*. Baltimore, Brookings Institution for Government Research, Studies in Administration, 1928.

Methuen, J. J. *Andele, or the Mexican Kiowa Captive*. Anadarko, Oklahoma, Plummer Printing Co., 1927.

Ogle, Ralph Hedrick. *Federal Control of the Western Apaches, 1848–86. New Mexico Historical Society Publications in History*, Vol. IX (July, 1940).

Opler, Morris Edward. "Three Types of Variation and Their Relation to Culture Change," *Language, Culture, and Personality*. Menasha, Wisconsin, n.d.

———. *An Apache Life Way*. Chicago, University of Chicago Press, 1941.

Pike, Zebulon M. *The Southwestern Expedition of . . .* , ed. by Milo M. Quaife. Chicago, R. R. Donnelley and Sons, 1925.

Raht, Carlysle Graham. *The Romance of the Davis Mountains and the Big Bend Country.* El Paso, Texas, Rahtbooks Co., 1919.

Reid, John C. *Reid's Tramp; or a Journal of the Incidents of Ten Months Travel through Texas, New Mexico, Arizona, Sonora, and California* . . . . Selma, Alabama, J. Hardy and Co., 1858. Reprint, Austin, Texas, The Steck Co., 1935.

Rister, Carl Coke. *The Southwestern Frontier.* Cleveland, The Arthur H. Clark Company, 1928.

———. *Fort Griffin on the Texas Frontier.* Norman, University of Oklahoma Press, 1956.

Rushmore, Elsie Mitchell. *The Indian Policy during Grant's Administration.* Jamaica, Queensborough, New York, The Marion Press, 1914.

Sabin, Edwin L. *Kit Carson Days.* 2 vols. New York, Pioneer Press, 1935.

Schmeckebier, Laurence F. *The Office of Indian Affairs, Its History, Activities, and Organization.* (Service monographs of the United States Government, No. 48.) Baltimore, The Johns Hopkins Press, 1927.

Scholes, France V. and H. P. Mera. "Some Aspects of the Jumano Problem." (Carnegie Institution of Washington, *Contributions to American Ethnology and History,* Vol. VI, No. 34, Publication No. 523.) Washington, 1940.

Thomas, Alfred Barnaby. "Antonio de Bonilla and Spanish Plans for the Defense of New Mexico, 1772–78," *New Spain and the Anglo-American West,* Vol. I. Lancaster, Pennsylvania, Lancaster Press, 1932.

———. *Forgotten Frontiers. A Study of the Spanish Indian Policy of Don Juan Bautista de Anza, Governor of New Mexico, 1777–87* . . . . Norman, University of Oklahoma Press, 1932.

———. *After Coronado.* Norman, University of Oklahoma Press, 1935.

———. *The Plains Indians and New Mexico, 1751–78. A Collection of Documents Illustrative of the History of the Eastern Frontier of New Mexico.* . . . Albuquerque, University of New Mexico Press, 1935.

———. *Teodoro de Croix and the Northern Frontier of New Spain, 1776–83.* Norman, University of Oklahoma Press, 1941.

Twitchell, Ralph Emerson. *The Leading Facts of New Mexican History.* 5 vols. Cedar Rapids, Iowa, The Torch Press, 1911–17.

Vestal, Stanley. *Bigfoot Wallace.* Boston, Houghton Mifflin Co., 1942.

Walker, Francis A. *The Indian Question.* Boston, James R. Osgood, 1874.

Wallace, Ernest and E. Adamson Hoebel. *The Comanches.* Norman, University of Oklahoma Press, 1952.

Wellman, Paul I. *The Indian Wars of the West.* Garden City, New York, Doubleday & Co., Inc., 1954.

Welsh, Herbert. *The Apache Prisoners of War at Fort Marion, St. Augustine, Florida.* Philadelphia, The Indian Rights Association, 1887.

Whiting, Lieutenant W. H. C. "Journal of William Henry Chase Whiting," in *Exploring Southwestern Trails,* ed. by Ralph P. Beiber. Glendale, California, The Arthur H. Clark Company, 1938.

Winship, George Parker, trans. *The Journey of Francisco Vázquez de Coronado, 1540–42, as Told by Pedro de Castaneda, Francisco Vázquez de Coronado, and Others.* San Francisco, The Grabhorn Press, 1933.

Wissler, Clark. *The American Indian.* New York, Oxford University Press, Inc., 1922.

6. ARTICLES

Abel, Annie Heloise, ed. "Indian Affairs in New Mexico under the Administration of William Carr Lane," from the Journal of John Ward, *New Mexico Historical Review,* Vol. XVI (April, 1941), 206–32, 328–58.

Amsden, Charles. "Navajo Origins," *New Mexico Historical Review,* Vol. VII (July, 1932), 193–209.

———. "The Navajo Exile at Bosque Redondo," *New Mexico Historical Review,* Vol. VIII (January, 1933), 31–50.

Anon. "Do the Indians Want to be Free?" *Saturday Evening Post,* Vol. CCXXVII (July 31, 1954), 10–12.

———. "The Liquor Problem among the Indians of the Southwest," condensed from the July, 1956, *Newsletter* of the New Mexico

Association on Indian Affairs, in *Indian Affairs,* No. XVIII (September–October, 1956), 3.

———. "Mescalero Reservation Cattle Sales Bring Record Prices," El Paso *Times,* September 21, 1946.

———. "Prisoners of War for Thirty Years," *The Outlook,* Vol. XCIX (November 4, 1911), 555–56.

———. "What Shall We Do with the Indians?" *The Nation,* Vol. V (October 31, 1867), 356.

Armstrong, O. K. "Let's Give the Indians Back to the Country," *Reader's Digest,* Vol. LII (April, 1948), 129.

———, and Marjorie Armstrong. "Indians Are Going to Town," *Reader's Digest,* Vol. LXVI (January, 1955), 39–43.

Baylor, Colonel George Wythe. *Historical Sketches of the Southwest, from the El Paso Herald.* (Typescript in the El Paso Public Library.)

Blazer, A. N. "Blazer's Mill," *New Mexico,* Vol. VI (January, 1938), 20, 48–49.

———. "Beginnings of an Indian War," *New Mexico,* Vol. XVI (February, 1938), 22 ff.

Bolton, Herbert E. "The Jumanos Indians in Texas," *Texas State Historical Association Quarterly,* Vol. XV (July, 1911), 66–84.

Bourke, John G. "Notes on Apache Mythology," *Journal of the American Folklore Society,* Vol. III (April–June, 1890), 209–12.

———. "The Folk Foods of the Río Grande and Northern Mexico," *Journal of American Folklore,* Vol. VIII (1895), 41–71.

Brosius, S. M. "The Apache Prisoners of War," Indian Rights Association, Thirtieth Annual Report, *Publications,* Series II, No. 68 (1912), 77–79.

Burton, Estelle Bennett. "Volunteer Soldiers of New Mexico and Their Conflicts with Indians in 1862 and 1863," *Old Santa Fé,* Vol. I (April, 1914), 386–419.

Charles, Tom. "Old Scouts of the Mescaleros," *New Mexico,* Vol. IX (August, 1931), 17–19.

Charles, Mrs. Tom. "Sam Chino Helped Direct Mescalero Apaches toward Peaceful Pursuits," El Paso *Times,* February 24, 1952.

———. "Mescalero Apache 'Red Hats' Hold National Reputation for Forest Fire Control Ability," El Paso *Times,* December 7, 1952.

Clendenin, Clarence C. "General James Henry Carleton," *New Mexico Historical Review,* Vol. XXX (January, 1955), 23–43.

Collier, John. "Indians Come Alive," *The Atlantic,* Vol. CLXX (September, 1942), 75–81.

———. "Letter to General Eisenhower," *The Nation,* Vol. CLXXVI (January 10, 1953), 20–30.

———. "Back to Dishonor," *The Christian Century,* Vol. LXXI (May 12, 1954), 578–80.

Cox, C. C. "From Texas to California in 1849" (Diary of C. C. Cox), ed. by Mabelle Eppard Martin, *Southwestern Historical Quarterly,* Vol. XXIX (July, 1925), 36–50, 128–46.

Cremony, John C. "The Apache Race," *Overland Monthly,* Vol. I (September, 1868), 201–209.

Crimmins, Colonel M. L. "The Mescalero Apaches," *Frontier Times,* Vol. VIII (September, 1931), 551–61.

———. "Colonel Buell's Expedition into Mexico in 1880," *New Mexico Historical Review,* Vol. X (April, 1935), 133–49.

Daklugie, Asa. "Coyote and the Flies," as told to Eve Ball, *New Mexico Folklore Record,* Vol. X (1955–56), 12–13.

Davis, Ann Pence. "Apache Debs," *New Mexico,* Vol. XV (April, 1937), 10–11.

Davis, O. K. "Our Prisoners of War," *North American Review,* Vol. XCV (March, 1912), 356–67.

Dunn, William Edward. "Apache Relations in Texas, 1718–90," *The Quarterly of the Texas State Historical Society,* Vol. XIV (January, 1911), 198–269.

Edgar, William. "One Wagon Train Boss of Texas," *Outing,* Vol. XXXIX (January, 1902), 381–83.

Fey, Harold E. "Most Indians Are Poor," *The Christian Century,* Vol. LXXII (May 18, 1955), 592–94.

Flannery, Regina. "The Position of Women among the Mescalero Apache," *Primitive Man,* Vol. V (April–July, 1932), 26–32.

Fuente, Pedro José de la. "Diary of Pedro José de la Fuente, Captain of the Presidio of El Paso del Norte, January–July, 1765," trans. and ed. by James M. Daniel, *Southwestern Historical Quarterly,* Vol. LX (October, 1956), 260–81.

Gatewood, Lieutenant C. B. "Campaigning Against Victorio in 1879," *The Great Divide,* Vol. XI, No. 4 (April, 1894), 102 ff.

Greiner, John. "The Journal of John Greiner," ed. by Annie Heloise Abel, *Old Santa Fé,* Vol. III (July, 1916), 220–43.

Gwyther, George, M.D. "An Indian Reservation," *The Overland Monthly,* Vol. X (February, 1873), 123–34.

Hail, Marshall. "Apache Indians 'Strike Gold' with Tourist Attraction," El Paso *Herald-Post,* October 1, 1956.

Hall, Edward Twitchell, Jr. "Recent Clues to Athapascan Pre-History in the Southwest," *American Anthropologist,* Vol. XLVI (January–March, 1944), 98–105.

Harmer, Ruth Mulvey. "Uprooting the Indians," *The Atlantic,* Vol. CXCVII (March, 1956), 54–57.

Harris, Francis. "Where Did the Plains Indians Get Their Horses?" *American Anthropologist,* Vol. XL (January–March, 1937), 112–17.

Hastings, James K. "A Boy's-Eye View of the Old Southwest," *New Mexico Historical Review,* Vol. XXVI (October, 1951), 287–301.

Hodge, Frederick Webb. "The Early Navajo and Apache," *American Anthropologist,* Vol. VIII (July, 1895), 232–40.

Indian Affairs, New Series, Nos. 10 (June, 1955); 12 (October–November, 1955); 13 (December, 1955); 13 (Supplement to Late Bulletin); 18 (September–October, 1956); 18 (Supplement).

Indian Rights Association. *Publications.* Series II, Nos. 20 (Twelfth Annual Report, 1895); 51 (Appeal on Behalf of the Apaches, Kiowas, and Comanches, February 15, 1899); 88 (Thirtieth Annual Report, 1912); 91 (Report of M. K. Sniffen, 1914); 115 (Report of M. K. Sniffen, 1918); 120 (M. K. Sniffen's Report on Field Work, 1920).

Indian Rights Association. *Indian Truth.* August–September, 1924; April–July, 1955.

Krill, John. "Red Hat of the Brave," *Nation's Business,* Vol. XLI (September, 1953), 46.

Kubler, George. "Gran Quivira and Jumanos," *New Mexico Historical Review,* Vol. XIV (October, 1939), 418–21.

La Farge, Oliver. "Assimilation—the Indian View," *New Mexico Quarterly,* Vol. XXVI (Spring, 1956), 5–13.

McNeil, Dr. Irving. "Indian Justice," *New Mexico Historical Review,* Vol. XIX (October, 1944), 261–70.

Madigan, LaVerne. "Books," *The American Indian,* Vol. VII (Spring, 1955), 62.

Marr, Colonel James. "In the Old Days," El Paso *Herald,* February 21, March 7, 1943. (Typescript in the El Paso Public Library.)

Matthews, Washington. "Ichthyophobia," *Journal of American Folklore,* Vol. XI (April–June, 1898), 105–12.

Meadows, John. "The Round Mountain Fight," Alamogordo *News,* January 30, 1936.

———. [Tom Keeney and Comesco], Alamogordo *News,* February 13, 1936.

———. "Tribal Fight between Mescalero and Lipan Indians," Alamogordo *News,* February 20, 1936.

Nelson, Al B. "Campaigning in the Big Bend of the Río Grande in 1787," *Southwestern Historical Quarterly,* Vol. XXXIX (January, 1936), 220–27.

———. "Juan de Ugalde and Picax-Ande Ins-Tinsle," *Southwestern Historical Quarterly,* Vol. XLIII (April, 1940), 438–64.

Nicholas, Dan. "Mescalero Puberty Ceremony," *El Palacio,* Vol. XLVI (September, 1939), 193–204.

Opler, Morris Edward. "The Concept of Supernatural Power among the Chiricahua and Mescalero Apaches," *American Anthropologist,* Vol. XXXVII (January–March, 1935), 65–70.

———. "The Sacred Clowns of the Chiricahua and Mescalero Indians," *El Palacio,* Vol. XLIV (March, 1938), 75–79.

———. "A Chiricahua Apache's Account of the Geronimo Campaign of 1886," *New Mexico Historical Review,* Vol. XII (October, 1938), 360–86.

——— and Hoijer, Harry. "The Raid and Warpath Language of the Chiricahua Apache," *American Anthropologist,* Vol. XLII (October–December, 1940), 617–34.

———. "The Role of Creative Shamanism in Mescalero Apache Mythology," *Journal of American Folklore,* Vol. LIX (July–September, 1946), 268–81.

———. "The Slaying of the Monsters," *El Palacio,* Vol. LIII (August, September, 1946), 215–25, 242–58.

————. "Reaction to Death among the Mescalero Apache," *Southwestern Journal of Anthropology*, Vol. II (Winter, 1946), 460–61.

————. "Notes on Chiricahua and Apache Culture. 1. Supernatural Power and the Shaman," *Primitive Man*, Vol. XX (January, April, 1947), 1–14.

————. "Mythology and Folk Belief in the Maintenance of Jicarilla Tribal Endogamy," *Journal of American Folklore*, Vol. LX (April–June, 1947), 126–29.

———— and Catherine H. Opler. "Mescalero Apache History in the Southwest, *New Mexico Historical Review*, Vol. XXV (January, 1950), 1–36.

Oskison, John M. "An Apache Problem," *Quarterly Journal of the Society of American Indians*, Vol. I (April, 1913), 25–29.

Quarterly Journal of the Society of American Indians, Vol. I (April 15, 1913), 25–29; Vol. II (January–March, 1914), 51–55.

Rafferty, Ken. "Mission at Mescalero," *New Mexico*, Vol. XVIII (October, 1940), 9, 30–31.

Reeve, Frank D. "The Federal Indian Policy in New Mexico, 1858–80," *New Mexico Historical Review*, Vol. XII (July, 1937), 218–69; Vol. XIII (January, 1938), 14–84; Vol. XIII (April, 1938), 146–91; Vol. XIII (July, 1938), 261–313.

Rippy, Fred J. "The Indians of the Southwest in the Diplomacy of the United States and Mexico, 1848–53," *Hispanic-American Review*, Vol. II (August, 1919), 363–66.

Scholes, France V. "Troublous Times in New Mexico," Ch. 3, *New Mexico Historical Review*, Vol. XII (October, 1937), 380–452.

Schwatka, Frederick. "Among the Apaches," *Century Magazine*, Vol. XXXIV (May, 1887), 41–53.

Sniffen, M. K. "The Record of Thirty Years," Indian Rights Association, *Publications*, Series II, No. 90, Revised edition (April, 1913).

Stevens, Alden. "Whither the American Indian," *Survey-Graphic*, Vol. XXIX (March, 1940), 168–74.

Stottler, V. E. "Pressure as a Civilizer of Wild Indians," *The Outlook*, Vol. LVI (January 12, 1897), 397–400.

Tassin, A. G. "Reminiscences of Indian Scouting," *Overland Monthly*, Series II, Vol. XIV (August, 1889), 155ff.

Van de Mark, Dorothy. "The Raid on the Reservations," *Harper's*, Vol. CCXII (March, 1956), 48–53.

Waller, John L. "Colonel George Wythe Baylor," *The Southwestern Social Science Quarterly*, Vol. XXIV (June, 1943), 23–25.

Worcester, Donald E. "The Beginning of the Apache Menace in the Southwest," *New Mexico Historical Review*, Vol. XVI (January, 1941), 1–14.

ACKNOWLEDGMENTS

THE MESCALEROS have always lived on the outer fringe of *Apachería* and have been less troublesome than the Arizona Apaches. Consequently, they have had only casual treatment from historians. Anthropologists have done considerably better by them. Important studies of their customs and language were made twenty-five years ago by M. E. Opler and Harry Hoijer, and other investigators have visited them from time to time in later years. The great books about the Apaches, however—Cremony, Goodwin, Lockwood, Cruse—have been concerned with the Western tribes. Opler's *Apache Life Way* deals with the Chiricahuas. Bourke and Britton Davis, General Crook and General Miles—all the chroniclers of the Apache campaigns—had little to say about the Mescaleros. This book attempts to tell their story in some detail.

Such a book has to be assembled from many sources, human and documentary, and the author has many debts to pay. The first bow should go to the Mescalero Business Committee, which authorized and encouraged the study, and to Wendell Chino, Fred Pellman, Percy Bigmouth, Solon Sombrero, and Rufus Sago, tribal leaders who helped in any way they could. Superintendents John Crow and Walter Olson talked frankly and gave friendship as well as information.

In the summer of 1955, a grant-in-aid from the Henry E. Huntington Library at San Marino, California, made it possible for me to complete ten years of work on the Mescaleros. I owe much to Director John E. Pomfret, Librarian Leslie Edgar Bliss, Godfrey Davies, Robert G. Cleland, Willard O. Waters, and the entire staff of the library.

I am deeply grateful, also, for the good will and assistance of the staff of the Southwest Museum in Los Angeles—especially to Director Carl S. Dentzell and Librarian Ella Robinson.

Other librarians and archivists to whom I am in debt include Mrs. Helen Kister, Miss Elizabeth Kelly, and Miss Erin Humphrey of the El Paso Public Library; Mr. Baxter Polk and Miss Frances Clayton of Texas Western College; Miss Gertrude Hill and Mrs. Elma Medearis of the Museum of New Mexico Library at Santa Fé; Miss J. Vivian Hedgcock and Mr. William S. Wallace of Highlands University, Las Vegas, New Mexico; Mrs. Marcelle Hamer, formerly librarian of the Texas Collection at the University of Texas.

On the reservation, the people who have helped, in addition to those already mentioned, include Mr. and Mrs. Willie Magoosh, Sampson Miller, Crookneck, Mr. and Mrs. Anthony Treas; staff members Pat Wehling (Land Management), Melvin E. Fairbanks (Roads), Barton Wetzel (Timber), Mr. and Mrs. Wallace Hiatt (Tribal Enterprises), Dr. and Mrs. W. T. Ross (Counseling and Testing Program), Dr. Lauren Trombley (Medical Service), Claude Taylor, Julius Roastingear, and Mrs. Fleta Baldonado (School); Dr. Blazer's descendants Paul Blazer, the late A. N. Blazer, and the late Emma B. Thompson; the Reverend Mr. Harvey Calsbeek of the Reformed church.

Off the reservation I have had indispensable assistance of

one kind or another from Mrs. Angie Cleve and Mr. and Mrs. Orris Cleve of Elk, New Mexico; Mrs. Irving McNeil and the late Dr. McNeil, Bob Hirsh, Mrs. Frank Barger, Mrs. Rose-marion Porter, and Mrs. George Brunner of El Paso; Mrs. Tom Charles of Alamogordo; the late Mrs. Katherine D. Stoes of Las Cruces; Mr. Thomas Fortune Ryan III of Three Rivers; Mrs. Katherine Kavanaugh of Santa Fé; E. H. Pubols, chief of the Federal Records Center in Denver. Miss Wanda Hill and Mrs. Eleanor Randolph typed the manuscript.

The first man to make a photographic record of the tribe was A. F. Randall of Willcox, Arizona, who came to the reservation about 1880. A number of his pictures are used here through the courtesy of the late Mrs. Emma Blazer Thompson. Tad Nichols of Tucson, Arizona, Vincent Mercaldo of New York, George Fitzpatrick of *New Mexico* Magazine, Mrs. Irving Mc-Neil and the late Dr. McNeil of El Paso, Texas, and Mrs. Elma Medearis of the Museum of New Mexico Library, have been especially helpful in locating photographs.

C. L. Sonnichsen

EL PASO, TEXAS
SEPTEMBER 10, 1958

of which *The Mescalero Apaches* is the fifty-first volume, was inaugurated in 1932 by the University of Oklahoma Press, and has as its purpose the reconstruction of American Indian civilization by presenting aboriginal, historical, and contemporary Indian life. The following list is complete as of the date of publication of this volume.

1. Alfred Barnaby Thomas (tr. and ed.). *Forgotten Frontiers:* A Study of the Spanish Indian Policy of Don Juan Bautista de Anza, Governor of New Mexico, 1777–1787. Out of print.
2. Grant Foreman. *Indian Removal:* The Emigration of the Five Civilized Tribes of Indians.
3. John Joseph Mathews. *Wah'Kon-Tah:* The Osage and the White Man's Road. Out of print.
4. Grant Foreman. *Advancing the Frontier, 1830–1860.* Out of print.
5. John H. Seger. *Early Days Among the Cheyenne and Arapahoe Indians.* Edited by Stanley Vestal.
6. Angie Debo. *The Rise and Fall of the Choctaw Republic.*
7. Stanley Vestal. *New Sources of Indian History, 1850–1891:* A Miscellany. Out of print.
8. Grant Foreman. *The Five Civilized Tribes.*
9. Alfred Barnaby Thomas (tr. and ed.). *After Coronado:* Spanish Exploration Northeast of New Mexico, 1696–1727.
10. Frank G. Speck. *Naskapi:* The Savage Hunters of the Labrador Peninsula. Out of print.
11. Elaine Goodale Eastman. *Pratt:* The Red Man's Moses. Out of print.
12. Althea Bass. *Cherokee Messenger:* A Life of Samuel Austin Worcester. Out of print.
13. Thomas Wildcat Alford. *Civilization.* As told to Florence Drake. Out of print.
14. Grant Foreman. *Indians and Pioneers:* The Story of the American Southwest Before 1830. Out of print.
15. George E. Hyde. *Red Cloud's Folk:* A History of the Oglala Sioux Indians.
16. Grant Foreman. *Sequoyah.*
17. Morris L. Wardell. *A Political History of the Cherokee Nation, 1838–1907.* Out of print.
18. John Walton Caughey. *McGillivray of the Creeks.*
19. Edward Everett Dale and Gaston Litton. *Cherokee Cavaliers:*

Forty Years of Cherokee History as Told in the Correspondence of the Ridge-Watie-Boudinot Family. Out of print.

20. Ralph Henry Gabriel. *Elias Boudinot, Cherokee, and His America.*
21. Karl N. Llewellyn and E. Adamson Hoebel. *The Cheyenne Way:* Conflict and Case Law in Primitive Jurisprudence.
22. Angie Debo. *The Road to Disappearance.* Out of print.
23. Oliver La Farge and others. *The Changing Indian.* Out of print.
24. Carolyn Thomas Foreman. *Indians Abroad.* Out of print.
25. John Adair. *The Navajo and Pueblo Silversmiths.*
26. Alice Marriott. *The Ten Grandmothers.*
27. Alice Marriott. *María:* The Potter of San Ildefonso.
28. Edward Everett Dale. *The Indians of the Southwest:* A Century of Development Under the United States. Out of print.
29. *Popol Vuh:* The Sacred Book of the Ancient Quiché Maya. English version by Delia Goetz and Sylvanus G. Morley from the translation of Adrián Recinos.
30. Walter Collins O'Kane. *Sun in the Sky.*
31. Stanley A. Stubbs. *Bird's-Eye View of the Pueblos.*
32. Katharine C. Turner. *Red Men Calling on the Great White Father.*
33. Muriel H. Wright. *A Guide to the Indian Tribes of Oklahoma.*
34. Ernest Wallace and E. Adamson Hoebel. *The Comanches:* Lords of the South Plains.
35. Walter Collins O'Kane. *The Hopis:* Portrait of a Desert People. Out of print.
36. Joseph Epes Brown (ed.). *The Sacred Pipe:* Black Elk's Account of the Seven Rites of the Oglala Sioux. Out of print.
37. *The Annals of the Cakchiquels,* translated from the Cakchiquel Maya by Adrián Recinos and Delia Goetz, with *Title of the Lords of Totonicapán,* translated from the Quiché text into Spanish by Dionisio José Chonay, English version by Delia Goetz.
38. R. S. Cotterill. *The Southern Indians:* The story of the Civilized Tribes Before Removal.
39. J. Eric S. Thompson. *The Rise and Fall of Maya Civilization.*
40. Robert Emmitt. *The Last War Trail:* The Utes and the Settlement of Colorado.
41. Frank Gilbert Roe. *The Indian and the Horse.*
42. Francis Haines. *The Nez Percés:* Tribesmen of the Columbia Plateau. Out of print.
43. Ruth M. Underhill. *The Navajos.*
44. George Bird Grinnell. *The Fighting Cheyennes.*
45. George E. Hyde. *A Sioux Chronicle.*

73. Franc Johnson Newcomb. *Hosteen Klah:* Navaho Medicine Man and Sand Painter.
74. Virginia Cole Trenholm and Maurine Carley. *The Shoshonis:* Sentinels of the Rockies.
75. Cohoe. *A Cheyenne Sketchbook.* Commentary by E. Adamson Hoebel and Karen Daniels Petersen.
76. Jack D. Forbes. *Warriors of the Colorado:* The Quechans and Their Neighbors.
77. Ralph L. Roys (tr. and ed.). *Ritual of the Bacabs.*
78. Lillian Estelle Fisher. *The Last Inca Revolt, 1780–1783.*
79. Lilly de Jongh Osborne. *Indian Crafts of Guatemala and El Salvador.*
80. Robert R. Ruby and John A. Brown. *Half-Sun on the Columbia:* A Biography of Chief Moses.
81. Jack Frederick and Anna Gritts Kilpatrick (tr. and ed.). *The Shadow of Sequoyah:* Social Documents of the Cherokees.

The Mescalero Apaches was set into type on the Linotype machine in eleven-point Caledonia with three points of space between the lines. Caledonia, an original design by W. A. Dwiggins, is a readable and very practical-looking typeface. The title page type is Neuland. The title page type, brown-toned frontispiece, and binding cloth have all been selected to further the feeling of the rugged country in which the Mescaleros lived.

University of Oklahoma Press : Norman